St. Paul, the Natural Law, and Contemporary Legal Theory

St. Paul, the Natural Law, and Contemporary Legal Theory

Edited by Jane Adolphe, Robert Fastiggi, and Michael Vacca

LEXINGTON BOOKS
Lanham • Boulder • New York • Toronto • Plymouth, UK

Published by Lexington Books
A wholly owned subsidiary of The Rowman & Littlefield Publishing Group, Inc.
4501 Forbes Boulevard, Suite 200, Lanham, Maryland 20706
www.rowman.com

10 Thornbury Road, Plymouth PL6 7PP, United Kingdom

British Library Cataloguing in Publication Information Available

Library of Congress Cataloging-in-Publication Data

CIP data available upon request.

™ The paper used in this publication meets the minimum requirements of American National Standard for Information Sciences—Permanence of Paper for Printed Library Materials, ANSI/NISO Z39.48-1992.

Printed in the United States of America

ISBN 978-0-7391-6857-8

Table of Contents

Acknowledgments

The editors wish to thank Professor Eugene Milhizer, the Dean and President of Ave Maria School of Law, and Monsignor Jeffrey Monforton, the Rector and President of Sacred Heart Major Seminary, for their encouragement and support of this project. They are truly grateful to Melissa Wilks of Lexington Books for her promotion of this volume's publication. Thanks must also be extended to Jacob Rhein, a graduate student at the University of St. Thomas, St. Paul, MN, for his careful copyediting of the volume; to Paula Murphy for her fine formatting of the volume for publication; and to Dr. Mary Healy of Sacred Heart Major Seminary for her help with the Greek citations. Finally, the editors express their gratitude to all who helped with the original 2008-2009 lecture series on which this volume is based, especially Professors W. Edward Afield and Kevin H. Govern of Ave Maria School of Law who served as moderators.

Preface

John J. Coughlin, O.F.M.,
Professor of Law and Concurrent Professor of Theology, University of Notre Dame

The general topic of this book, "Saint Paul and the Law," raises a host of specific questions as timeless as they are current, as broad in scope as deep in substance, and as theoretical as pastoral. The scholarship that attempts to respond to such questions is likely to yield results as almost enigmatic as rewarding. In this Preface, I shall touch upon only four such questions. First, I recall Paul's training in the Mosaic Law and his ambivalence about the Law in light of his Christian faith.[1] Second, I am also mindful of Paul's view that law is necessary to facilitate the order of the Christian community. Third, I acknowledge Paul's reference to a natural law and its interpretations in the Catholic and Reformed traditions. Finally, I mention Paul's insistence that the revelation of Christ is a public and not a private event.[2] In raising these four questions, I am obviously aware that my words barely scratch the surface of the deep oceans of meaning attributed to Saint Paul's thought over the course of two millennia of interpretation.[3] Some of the essays of this book treat these questions in greater detail, and other essays raise different but related questions. My humble hope is that this brief Introduction helps to afford some context from which the various essays of this book about Saint Paul and the law might be approached.

I.

The biblical scholar, John P. Meier, has remarked on the difficulty in trying to ascertain the relation between the historical Jesus and the Jewish or Mosaic Law. According to Meier, the task might be compared to aiming at "two distinct moving targets."[4] As in the case of the quest for the historical Jesus, attempts to define the Mosaic Law of first century Palestine remain elusive. Likewise, the scholar who is trying to grasp the stance of Saint Paul vis-à-vis the Law encounters to elusiveness of the historical person and his legal culture.

Paul belonged to a class of scholars for whom knowledge of the Jewish Law was paramount. As a young man, Paul had trained under the tutelage of the esteemed rabbinical scholar, Gamaliel. Paul has been described as an "Oriental lawyer."[5] Following his conversion to Christianity, Paul referred the Jewish Law as a "curse," and urged the early Christians to live as justified in the spirit.[6] In the Letter to the Romans, Paul contrasted "the law of the spirit" with "the law of sin and death."[7] The Jewish "Law" for Paul included the entire corpus of pentateuchal rules and regulations that consisted of approximately 248 positive commands and 365 prohibitions. Although various rabbinical schools calculated the exact number of precepts of the Law differently, they agreed that the Law pronounced a curse on those who did not keep it in its entirety. However, Paul called the Law a curse not so much because it gave rise to legalism, but because he believed that it was a hopeless business to seek justification by the Law. For Paul, the Law told people what to do, but it imparted no power to do it. In contrast to the Law, Paul preached that the Gospel imparts power to live a new life in Christ. In Paul's theology, it is through faith and not observance of the Law that one is justified. The "law of the spirit" imparts the blessing that God promised to Abraham, his offspring, and all nations. This "new law" removes the curse pronounced on the lawbreaker. According to Paul, the curse is lifted and the new law established not through strict observance of the Law but through Christ's enduring the Law in the manner of his passion and death.[8]

II.

Nonetheless, much of Paul's thought was expressed in legal language and metaphors. Describing Saint Paul's "career as an administrator," the biblical scholar John Knox observes:

> Among the issues Paul might be called upon to handle were Jew-Gentile relations, threats of schism, disorders in services of worship, irregularities in the observance of the Lord's Supper, a misunderstanding between two members of the local church, unhealthy excitement about the end of the world, litigation between Christians, occasional instances of serious immorality, the question of whether a Christian could eat food that had been consecrated by pagan rites, innumerable problems connected with marriage, the role of women in the church, various false teachings, the administration of charity by the churches, relations of Christians with their pagan neighbors and how Christian slaves and masters should treat each other.[9]

Paul understood that the Christian community could not be free from such issues and their legal aspects.

Perhaps, Paul's training in and concern for the law is nowhere more evident than in his first letter to the Corinthians, one of the earliest New Testament texts.[10] Chapter 6 of I Corinthians combines antinomian and legal elements.[11] The antinomian is evident in Paul's concern with the imminent return of Christ rendering all worldly concerns "trivial."[12] Verses 7-8 served to remind the

Corinthians that the ultimate court of appeal for Christian life is the teaching embodied on the cross of Christ.[13] Paul suggested that following Christ may sometimes require that one suffer some wrong or injustice for the sake of the community in the example of the Suffering Servant.[14] The eschatological perspective, however, did not prevent Paul from seeing the need for a juridic order in the early Church.[15] He admonished the Christian community to avoid lawsuits in the civil courts.[16] When there is a dispute among you, Paul queried the Corinthian community, why does one member of the community become a plaintiff and bring another Christian before the judgment of the civil magistrates?[17] Consistent with the rabbinical teaching that it was unlawful to plead a case before an idolatrous judge, Paul advocated the establishment of internal procedures to settle disputes among the members of the community.[18] Despite his admonition about avoiding the Roman courts, Paul resorted to the secular law to protect himself from his enemies. As a Roman citizen, Paul apparently utilized the imperial law and elected arrest and house custody in Rome.[19] Paul's travel to Rome served as the occasion of his second missionary journey that proved significant to the spread of Christianity particularly among the Gentiles. The mystical missionary of the kingdom to come appears also to have been a man of practical action, knowledgeable in the Jewish Law, and by borrowing from that Law, intent on establishing a just legal order for the Christian community in the here and now. The antinomian and legal elements of Paul's thought have continued to manifest themselves throughout the history of the Church.

III.

In his Letter to the Corinthians, Paul referred to Gentiles "who keep the law by instinct."[20] The idea of a natural law was not novel to Saint Paul. From the Greek Stoics to the Roman jurists, it was well accepted that there existed a common, transcendent body of fundamental human principles that could be known through the right use of human reason.[21] The extent to which the natural capacities of the human person were disordered by original sin has been the subject of considerable disagreement among Christian theologians. Although he recognized the disorder of the intellect and will as a result of original sin, Thomas Aquinas taught that human reason had the capacity to recognize the natural law.[22] More pessimistic than Thomas, the Reformer, John Calvin, thought that all natural faculties of the person (reason, will, conscience) were gravely corrupted, although not completely destroyed, by original sin.[23] Calvin drew an analogy to the person seeking natural knowledge without faith to "a traveler passing through a field at night who in a momentary lightening flash sees far and wide, but the sight vanishes so swiftly that he is plunged again into the darkness of the night before he can even take a step—let alone be directed on his way by its help."[24] He defined natural law as "that apprehension of the conscience which distinguishes sufficiently between just and unjust, and which deprives men of the excuse of ignorance, while it proves them guilty by their own testimony."[25] As a consequence of original sin, Calvin thought that the natural faculties could function without the help of grace, but only to the point of demonstrating a lack of justification.

In comparison to Calvin's assessment of the possibilities for the natural human faculties, the Catholic anthropological understanding based on Thomas Aquinas and twentieth century Catholic thought is more optimistic. From a theological perspective, Thomas did not hesitate to acknowledge that the soul's powers of reason and will have been disordered by original sin.[26] However, while Calvin depicts the human faculties as limited to convicting the human person of sin, Thomas believes that natural capacity of the human faculties to be more extensive. The natural capacity extends to the human person's knowledge of fundamental moral principles and goods as well as the ability to apply these to human situation. Based upon Thomas, twentieth century Catholic anthropology attempts to retrieve the understanding of the human person as endowed with reason and free will. The optimistic anthropology embraces the traditional Thomistic understanding of the human person as naturally good although disordered by original sin.

During the twentieth century, there has been considerable debate among theologians in the Reformed tradition about how to interpret Calvin. Denying the reality of natural law, Karl Barth emphasized the total corruption of human nature due to original sin. In Barth's theology, the accent is on the Protestant maxim of justification by faith alone, and that no human knowledge, effort, or good work can lead to righteousness.[27] In contrast, Emil Brunner interpreted Calvin to mean that the natural law, obscured by original sin, takes on a clearer focus as a result of reason's encounter with the grace of sacred scripture. For Brunner, the interior light of faith in the soul enables the believer to see more clearly the natural order and how original sin obfuscates it.[28] More recently, other Protestant theologians have interpreted Calvin's thought to contain ambiguity about the natural law. These theologians suggest that Calvin both affirms the natural law and holds that natural human reason possesses no knowledge of salvific significance.[29] This interpretation has allowed these theologians to conclude that there is no real discontinuity between Calvin and Thomas about the possibilities of natural knowledge and action based upon it.[30] Without trying to assess the historical accuracy of this interpretation of Calvin, it seems fair to surmise that Saint Paul's reference to a natural law distinct from divine revelation will continue to raise many interesting questions about the relation between faith and reason, nature and grace, and the creation and redemption.

IV.

The *Acts of the Apostles* records that Saint Paul disputed with Epicurean and Stoic philosophers at the Areopagus in Athens where his preaching the doctrine of the raising of the dead led some with a desire to hear more on the subject.[31] For Saint Paul, the revelation of Jesus Christ and its continuing proclamation in human history is decidedly a public, and not a private, event. Paul's view of the public nature of Christian revelation may not fully comport with the theory of the modern liberal state. John Rawls' liberal political theory tends to exclude appeals to revelation or other explicitly religious accounts of the human person.[32] Rawls admits at most a quite limited role for theological values and language in public discourse. Rawls considered the introduction of arguments based upon divine revelation to be too potentially divisive in a pluralistic society. In its original form, Rawls' so-called "legitimacy principle" framed the secular limits of reasoned public discourse.[33] The legitimacy principle means that religious language, values and ideas must be avoided in policy debates about the framing of law by the legislative, in the enforcement of the law by the executive, and in the interpretation of law by the judiciary.

Rawls' legitimacy principle coincided with secularism's invalidation of some of Western society's most deeply entrenched traditional values that were derived from revelation and other theological sources.[34] In its unmitigated form, the principle would presumably bar Catholic social thought's concept of the human being created in the *imago Dei.*[35] The principle would deprive public discourse of the strong theological foundation for values such as the sacredness of each human life, the social relationship of the human being and its corresponding values of participation and solidarity, and the common good and its requirements for a fair distribution of societal resources.[36] In my view, theological values such as these pose no threat to the public order, and have much to offer it.[37] In his later thought, Rawls himself acknowledged the limitation of his pristine theory.[38] Perhaps, Rawls' second thoughts about the legitimacy principle reflect in part an appreciation of the contribution that is offered by the derivative values of theological anthropology. In any event, Saint Paul's discourse among the Greek philosophers at the Areopagus suggests that from its origins Christianity has been a public faith, which is respectful of, but not limited to, matters of private individual conscience.

V.

The book constitutes a rich spiritual banquet that feeds the hunger and quenches the thirst for understanding of Saint Paul and the law. The various scholars who have contributed essays to this book offer theological, legal, historical, exegetical, philosophical, canonical, pastoral, sociological, and psychological insights. This splendid collection represents a contribution to the ongoing discussion about Saint Paul and the law. Penned at the beginning of the twenty-first century, the essays afford entry into the soul of the Jewish lawyer who became the great missionary of Christian faith.

Notes

1. By the Jewish or Mosaic "Law," I am referring to the Torah or Pentateuch, which is the divine revelation that includes a variety of literary forms such as narratives, commandments, prophecy, wisdom and religious codes. This sacred "Law" differs from the contemporary secular sense of "law" which refers to an individual rule, norm, or precept of conduct adopted through a legitimate political process and enforced through the power of the state.

2. The material is this Introduction is based upon some of my other published work. The first two parts of this Introduction are derived from *Canon Law: A Comparative Study with Anglo-American Legal Theory* (New York: Oxford University Press, 2010). The third part reflects *Law, Person, and Society* forthcoming Oxford University Press, 2011). Some of part four of this Introduction is from "The Human Being, Catholic Social Teaching and the Law," *Journal of Catholic Social Thought* 1 (2004) 313, 325-326.

3. For a classic study, *see* E. P. Sanders, *Saint Paul, the Law, and the Jewish people* (Minneapolis: Fortress Press, 1983).

4. See John P. Meir, *A Marginal Jew, Volume IV, Law and Love* (New Haven: Yale University Press, 2009), 10-11 & 28-29.

5. J. Duncan M. Derrett, *Law in the New Testament* (London: Darton, Longmann & Todd, 1970), 396-403.

6. See Gal. 3:13.

7. Rom. 8:2.

8. See F. F. Bruce, "The Curse of the Law," in *Paul and Paulinism: Essays in honour of C. K. Barrett* ed. M.D. Hooker and S.G. Wilson (Oxford: Alden Press, 1982), 27-35.

9. See John Knox, *Chapters in the Life of Paul*, ed. Douglas R. A. Hare (Macon, Georgia: Mercer University Press, 1987), 87

10. "Paul himself tells us that 1 Cor. was written in the spring from Ephesus (16:8), but the year is a matter of dispute. The suggested dates range from A.D. 52 to 57 with the majority opting for a date close to the middle of that span." *The New Jerome Biblical Commentary* ed. Raymond E. Brown, S.S., Joseph A. Fitzmyer, S.J. and Roland E. Murphy, O.Carm. (Englewood Cliffs, N.J.: Prentice Hall, 1990), 799.

11. For a general discussion of eschatology and ecclesiology in Pauline thought, *see* François Amiot, *Les Idées Maîtresses de Saint-Paul* (Paris: Les Éditions du Cerf, 1959), 151-258.

12. See F. W. Grosheide, "Commentary on the First Epistle to the Corinthians," in ed. Ned B. Stonehouse and F. F. Bruce *The New International Commentary of the New Testament* (Grand Rapids: Eerdmans Publishing, 1974), 132-142.

13. "To have lawsuits at all with one another is defeat for you. Why not rather suffer wrong? Why not rather be defrauded? But you yourselves wrong and defraud, and that even your own brethren." 1 Cor. 6: 7-8.

14. See Amiot, *Les Idées*, 209-213.

15. See Wilfred A. Knox, *Saint Paul and the Church of Jerusalem* (Cambridge: University Press, 1935), 23-35.

16. "When one of you has a grievance against a brother, does he dare to go to the law before the unrighteous instead of the saints? Do you not know that the saints will judge the world? And if the world is to be judged by you, are you incompetent to try trivial cases? Do you not know that we are to judge the angels? How much more, matters pertaining to this

life! If then you have such cases, why do you lay them before those who are least esteemed by the church? I say this to your shame. Can it be that there is no man among you wise enough to decide between members of the brotherhood, but brother goes to law against brother, and that before unbelievers?" 1 Cor. 6: 1-6.

17. The "judgment seat" or *bema* was publicly located in the heart of the market place where the Roman civil magistrates heard all types of petty grievances. See Acts 18: 12-17. For a general discussion of the role of magistrates and the exercise of executive power in Roman law, see Barry Nicholas, *An Introduction to Roman Law* (Oxford: Clarendon Press of Oxford University, 1962), 19-28.

18. See *The Interpreter's Bible* ed. George A. Buttricks (New York: Abingdon-Cokesbury, 1952), 69.

19. See ibid.

20. Rom. 2:14; translation from *New American Bible* (1970) (also translated as "the law written on the human heart.") See Ioannes Paulus Pp. II. Litterae Encyclicae, *Veritatis Splendor* (Die 6 m. aug. a. 1993), 46 (subtitle), in *Acta Apostolicae Sedis* 85 (1993), 1133-1228.

21. See Lloyd L. Weinreb, *Natural Law and Justice* (Cambridge, MA.: Harvard University Press, 1987), 15-49.

22. See Thomas Aquinas, *Summa Theologica*, I-II, 91, 2 trans. Fathers of the English Dominican Province 1948; hereinafter ST.

23. See John Calvin, *The Institutes of the Christian Religion*, 2, 2, 12, ed. John T. McNeill, trans. Ford Lewis Battles (Louisville & London: Westminster John Knox Press, 2006), vol. 1, 270-271.

24. Ibid. at 2, 2, 18, vol. 1, 277.

25. Ibid. at 2, 2, 22, vol. 1, 282.

26. ST, I-II, q. 109, art. 1.

27. See Karl Barth, "No! Answer to Emil Brunner" in *Natural Theology* ed. and trans. Peter Fraenkel (London: Centenary Press, 1946), 94-103.

28. See Emil Brunner, "Nature and Grace," in *Natural Theology* (London: Centenary Press, 1946), 39.

29. See e.g., Susan E. Schreiner, "Calvin's Use of Natural Theology" in *Protestants, Catholics, and Natural Law* ed. Michael Cromartie, ed (Grand Rapids, MI: Eerdmans Publishing, 1997), 51-76.

30. See e.g., Schreiner, "Calvin's Use of Natural Theology," 55; John T. McNeill "Natural Law in the Teaching of the Reformers," *Journal of Religion* 26 (1946), 162, 168.

31. Acts 17:16-34.

32. See John Rawls, *Political Liberalism* (New York: Columbia University Press, 1996), 147-149 (defining public reason as an "overlapping consensus," and arguing that political power may not be exercised on the basis of religious values).

33. See Robert Song, *Christianity and Liberal Society* (Oxford: Oxford University Press, 1997), 225-226 (suggesting that revelation offers a theological critique of liberalism).

34. See Gertrude Himmelfarb, *The Demoralization of Society* (New York: Random House Vintage Books, 1995), 257 (observing that the "ethos of a society, its moral and spiritual character, cannot be reduced to economic, material, political, or other factors, that values—or better yet, virtues are a determining factor in their own right.").

35. Cf. *Sacrosanctum Concilium Oecumenicum Vaticanum II. "Constitutio pastoralis de ecclesia in mundo huius temporis, Gaudium et Spes* (Die 7 m. decembris a. 1965)," 12,

in AAS 58 (1966),1025-1120.

36. See Rawls, *Political Liberalism*, at 243 ("What public reason asks is that citizens be able to explain their vote to one another in terms of a reasonable balance of public political values, it being understood by everyone of course the plurality of reasonable comprehensive doctrines held by citizens is thought by them to provide further and often transcendent backing for those values.").

37. See Michael J. Perry, "Why Political Reliance on Religiously Grounded Morality Does Not Violate the Establishment Clause," *William. & Mary Law Review* 42 (2001) 663 (arguing that reliance on religiously grounded moral values in public discourse is permitted and protected by the first amendment of the United States Constitution).

38. See e.g., John Rawls, "The Idea of Public Reason Revisited," *University of Chicago Law Review* 64 (1997), 765, 781 (asking whether it is even possible "for citizens of faith to be wholeheartedly members of democratic society who endorse society's intrinsic political ideas and values"). See also Patrick Neal, "Political Liberalism, Public Reason and the Citizen of Faith" in *Natural Law and Public Reason* ed. Robert P. George and Christopher Wolfe (Washington, D.C.: Georgetown University Press, 2000), 171, 177-78 (criticizing Rawls for not recognizing that persons with comprehensive religious worldviews may dissent from the doctrines of political liberalism, not on selfish grounds, but because they believe the liberal doctrine to be morally wrong); Paul Weithman, "Citizenship and Public Reason" in *Natural Law and Public Reason* ed. Robert P. George and Christopher Wolfe (Washington, D.C.: Georgetown University Press, 2000), 156-62 (rejecting John Rawl's position that citizens in the public forum ought not to make appeals to religious comprehensive world views).

Introduction

St. Paul, the Natural Law, and Contemporary Legal Theory

The present volume explores the relationship of St. Paul, the natural law and contemporary legal theory. It owes its initial inspiration to the special Jubilee Year celebrating the bi-millennium of the birth of the "Apostle to the Gentiles" proclaimed by Pope Benedict XVI on June 28, 2008, the eve of the Solemnity of St. Peter and Paul. The Pauline Year, which lasted from June 2008 through June 2009, was marked in numerous ways, including pilgrimages to Rome, special publications of Pauline texts and numerous lectures on the life and thought of the great saint.

The essays in this book are the fruit of the celebration of the Year of St. Paul undertaken by Ave Maria School of Law (then in Ann Arbor, Michigan) and Sacred Heart Major Seminary in Detroit. Between October 2008 and April 2009, a lecture series was held at the law school featuring speakers from the seminary and respondents from the law school. For centuries, the Catholic Church has stressed the relationship between civil law and the natural law, and this has been a special theme of the social doctrine of the Church since the pontificate of Leo XIII (1878-1903). More recently, Pope Benedict XVI has spoken of the dangers of "juridical positivism" in which the civil law reflects only "private interests" and "ideological manipulation" rather than the objective norms of morality reflected in the divine and natural law (cf. *Address of Pope Benedict XVI to the Participants in the International Congress on Natural Moral Law*, Feb. 12, 2007). The Pope has called upon Catholic lawyers in a special way to know and understand the natural law because "every juridical methodology, be it on the local or international level, ultimately draws is legitimacy from its rooting in the natural law, in the ethical message inscribed in the actual human being" (Address of Feb. 12, 2007).

The lecture series on "St. Paul and the Natural Law" co-sponsored by Ave Maria School of Law and Sacred Heart Major Seminary was, in many ways, a response to the wish of Pope Benedict XVI to have lawyers understand and apply the natural law in their professional activities. The goal was to put law professors in conversation with Catholic professors of Scripture, theology and philosophy in the Year of St. Paul to explore more deeply the Pauline roots of the natural law and the implications for contemporary legal theory.

In many respects, the lecture series reflects the special mission of the collaborating institutions. Ave Maria School of Law sees its mission as offering "a distinctive legal education" characterized by "the harmony of faith and reason" and "the natural law written on the heart of every human being." Sacred Heart Major Seminary has aligned its mission, in a particular way, with the "New Evangelization" envisioned by the Venerable John Paul II. St. Paul embodies both these visions. As the "Apostle to the Gentiles," he proclaimed the Gospel with untiring dedication until his death as a martyr. In his evangelization, however, he appealed not only to the order of faith but also to the order of reason (cf. Rom 1:19-20), an order manifested by the natural law written on the human heart (cf. Rom 2:14-15). In preaching to the Gentiles, St. Paul drew upon the "seeds of the Word" contained in the common human awareness of the God "who made the world and everything in it," the one God in whom "we live and move and have our being" (Acts 17: 24-28).

The Pauline Year coincided with another significant event. In the late spring of 2009, the International Theological Commission made public a document in French entitled, *À la recherché d'une éthique universelle: noveau regard sur la loi naturelle* (In search of a universal ethic: a new look at the natural law). This document provides a detailed scriptural, historical and philosophical exposition of the natural law and its importance for politics, international relations and the common good. The appearance of this document in the Pauline Year seems appropriate for, as mentioned above, St. Paul testifies to common moral law written in the human heart. In light of the significance of this recent contribution of the International Theological Commission [ITC], the present volume includes an essay by Fr. J. Michael McDermott, S.J., a member of the sub-committee of the ITC that drafted the natural law document.

The essays in this book were originally given as public lectures and public responses in a program that took place between October 2008 and May 2009. These public talks have since been revised and edited for publication. The contributors reflect their own interests and specializations, ranging from biblical studies, theology, and philosophy to legal education, family law, and international law. In this sense, the present volume is different from other works based on conferences and lecture series. This is not simply a collection of essays written by experts in one specialized field of study, but a fruitful exchange between scholars of legal theory and professors of Scripture, theology and philosophy. The responses of the lawyers, therefore, are not simply comments of fellow specialists, but spirited reactions of those engaged in public affairs to the scriptural, theological and philosophical insights presented. Pope Benedict XVI has called upon legal experts to know and incorporate the natural law into their professional activities, and this volume reflects an effort to pursue this wish of the Holy Father.

In the first chapter, Fr. Richard J. Cassidy, the author of *Paul in Chains* (2001) presents a vivid description of the concrete situation of the Apostle as a prisoner facing the court of Roman justice. Using Second Timothy as his focus, Fr. Cassidy shows that, for Paul, all human tribunals are ultimately answerable to the higher law of Christ. By way of response, Patrick Quirk uses Paul's own awareness of his rights as a Roman citizen as a point of departure, and he offers a brief but insightful discussion of the meaning of citizenship. While there is a rightful autonomy enjoyed by both Church and State, Christians can never abandon moral principles in deference to the demands of secular authorities. Some things belong to Caesar, but other things to Christ.

Chapter 2 by Robert Fastiggi provides an overview of how the Catholic tradition has used St. Paul in developing its concept of the natural law. Although different approaches have been taken (e.g., Augustine and Aquinas), a consistent Catholic appeal to St. Paul on the natural law emerged during the thirteenth century. It continued to develop in Baroque scholastics such as Vitoria (c. 1483-1546) and Suárez (1548-1617), who offered a philosophical foundation for international law based on the unity of the human race. Recent magisterial statements have drawn upon this natural law tradition, which is rooted in several key insights of St. Paul.

In his response to Fastiggi's essay, Brian Scarnecchia focuses on St. Paul's affirmation of the natural knowledge of God (cf. Rom 1:19-20) and the current "eclipse of the sense of God," noted by John Paul II and others. The 1948 *Universal Declaration of Human Rights* assumed a common moral order with a transcendent point of reference. The loss of this moral order has led unfortunately to a "relativistic logic" in many contemporary circles. All this shows how important it is to revive the sense of God and the natural law as a basis for human rights in international relations.

In chapter 3, Fr. Earl Muller, S.J. examines the contrast between the wisdom of the Greeks and the wisdom of Christ. By a careful study of the literary structure of 1 Cor 1:17 –1 Cor 3:3, he shows that St. Paul employs both philosophical logic and rhetorical persuasion in his appeal to the Greek mind. The Apostle does this, however, in order to highlight the truth revealed in the crucified and risen Christ, a truth that transcends the finite wisdom of the Greeks.

In his response to Fr. Muller, Patrick Gillen perceptively notes how St. Paul's confrontation with the wisdom of the Greeks provides a model for how Christians today can confront the relativism and skepticism of the secular culture. In the face of widespread attacks on human life and the family, Christians of today should draw upon both speculative philosophy and the wisdom of faith when seeking to uphold human dignity in law and society.

In chapter 4, "Nature, Sin and Grace in St. Paul's Moral Doctrine," Eduardo Echeverria begins with a consideration of 2 Cor 5:17, which speaks of the "new creation" in Christ. He then investigates several approaches to the relationship between nature and grace in light of fallen human nature. Ultimately, the Catholic faith sees grace penetrating, transforming and perfecting fallen nature. God's grace heals our nature, creating us anew and endowing us with authentic freedom as opposed to the false freedom expressed by secular views of radical autonomy.

In responding to Echeverria's essay, Charles Lugosi shows how fallen human nature has led to a "jurisprudence of legal positivism" in the United States of America, which betrays the rational and religious foundations of the Constitution. In particular, Lugosi argues that the denial of the right to life of the unborn undermines the very basis of legal justice. Such a state of affairs cries out for the healing grace that St. Paul so eloquently preaches.

Philip Blosser takes up the theme of "St. Paul and the Philosophy of Law" in chapter 5 of the volume. Making use of Harold Berman (1918-2007) and other sources, he documents how American legal education has gradually moved away from an early twentieth century system (which recognized transcendent norms of justice) to a current system dominated by legal positivism, devoid of any Judeo-Christian sources. A Pauline response to the contemporary crisis can be found in the Apostle's address to the Athenians at the Areopagus in Acts 17:16-32. Paul tries to connect with the Greek intellectuals by making use of the truths they already know implicitly. In the same way, believers must try to engage contemporary legal scholars by elucidating those moral principles that all people of good will instinctually acknowledge, those truths of the natural law we cannot not know.

Fr. Joseph Isanga responds to Blosser's essay by tracing the historical move away from a natural law perspective (found in Greco-Roman sources as well as St. Paul) to a contemporary legal culture dominated by pragmatism, utilitarianism and positivism (all antagonistic to the natural law). In the light of the atrocities of Word War II and the more recent horrors of Kosovo, Bosnia and Rwanda, there is a pressing need for renewed attention to the natural law as a foundation for human rights in an international setting.

In chapter 6, "St. Paul, Ephesians 5 and Christian Marriage," Mary Healy discusses the duties of husbands and wives in mutual subordination to Christ as presented in Eph 5:21-33. She shows how the call for husbands to love their wives "just as Christ loved the Church" has no precedent in either Greco-Roman or rabbinical literature. This Pauline text, rooted in the theology of the body, highlights the natural complementarity of men and women, called to communion and self-donation in spousal love. It helps to clarify and deepen the public defense of marriage, which has been challenged by recent efforts to grant legal status to homosexual unions.

In her response, Jane Adolphe argues that legalization of "same-sex marriage" introduces a new chaos into the world, which undermines the human person's call to love according to the plan of the Creator, and in turn, threatens the social order. She draws upon her experience as an international lawyer seeking to defend the rights of children and the integrity of marriage. An eclipse of reason and civility is evident in the anger and antagonism directed against those who defend the natural family, emphasize the complementarity of men and women, and promote the welfare of children. When family life declines, love and communion deteriorate, and the social order is threatened, since this order ultimately depends on adherence to the moral law of God. On the international level, one possible meeting point for dialogue is the inherent dignity of the human person with reference to the essential characteristics of a universal human nature, known by reason, illumined by faith and largely recognized in the first article of the 1948 Universal Declaration of Human Rights.

In chapter 7, Fr. J. Michael McDermott, S.J. examines some of the philosophical and theological principles behind the 2009 document on the natural law issued by the International Theological Commission. The document, as he explains, is intended to assist bishops and others in the current debates on moral issues. Tracing the history of the natural law in its classical, biblical, Patristic, and scholastic expressions, Fr. McDermott brings to light the critical issues posed by competing theories of nature, person and freedom following the rise of modern science and the subsequent Enlightenment. Efforts to overcome the challenges of modern skepticism and positivism have given way to various "conceptualist" and "transcendental" approaches. These competing schools strive to overcome the fundamental tension between the finite and the infinite, especially with regard to human freedom. Ultimately, however, this tension can only be reconciled by God's love, which is supremely expressed in the Logos Incarnate.

CHAPTER ONE

St. Paul: Between the Law of Caesar and the Justice of Christ in Second Timothy[1]

Rev. Richard J. Cassidy
Professor of Sacred Scripture,
Sacred Heart Major Seminary, Detroit, Michigan

Introduction

The topic of St. Paul and the natural law should consider the apostle's own experience as a chained prisoner of the Roman *imperium*. As one of the "prison letters," 2 Timothy holds a special place. In order to bring into clear focus several features pertaining to the authorship and character of 2 Timothy, the present essay will begin with a brief note discussing pseudepigraphy followed by a brief section locating 2 Timothy in terms of Paul's trajectory as a prisoner. Section three will then analyze the text of the letter to consider the multiple purposes intended by the author. Finally, sections four, five, and six will treat the circumstances of Paul's imprisonment and his undiminished faithfulness to Jesus within these circumstances.

An Additional Note Regarding Pseudepigraphy

In the estimation of a majority of New Testament scholars, Colossians, and especially Ephesians and 2 Timothy, are pseudepigraphical letters. Within the perspective of the present study, Colossians, Ephesians, and 2 Timothy are remarkably comparable in the way in which each initially affirms Paul's calling as Christ's apostle and then proceeds to emphasize his standing as a chained prisoner. They are also comparable as regards the manner in which each effectively utilizes Paul's situation as a prisoner as a leading theme within the overall message of the letter.

The impact of these latter considerations for the question of pseudepigraphy resides in the insight that, if associates or later disciples of Paul wrote in his name, they did not hesitate to adopt the most politically controversial aspect of Paul's identity. For, within these letters, Paul's persona as a Roman prisoner is indeed presented in high relief. In Colossians and 2 Timothy, the positioning of the figure of Timothy also has relevance for the question of pseudepigraphy. In Colossians, Timothy is a co-sender of the letter, located at the side of Paul as Paul reflects on his sufferings and his chains.[2] In 2 Timothy, Paul apprises Timothy of developments in his judicial and personal situation, even as he summons Timothy to his side.[3] As previously articulated, the central theses of this study are being argued independently of the material contained in Colossians, Ephesians, and 2 Timothy. In other words, a conclusion that Paul himself authored one, two, or all three of these letters is not a necessary condition for sustaining the principal arguments of this study.[4] If one or more of these letters is authored by Paul, the impact that Paul's chains had upon him is delineated with greater amplitude. Yet, even if all three letters are deutero-Pauline, these texts still indicate that the chains worn by Paul were deemed by his disciples and associates to have been a highly significant phenomenon.

Timothy and Paul's Trajectory as a Prisoner

In chapter 7, it was observed that the portrayal of Paul's prison situation in Colossians and Ephesians is roughly approximate to the prison situation indicated by Paul's various references in Philemon. In the present section, it is now suggested that 2 Timothy appears to depict a later stage in Paul's "journey" as a prisoner. There are several aspects of 2 Timothy that support such a conclusion. First, it should be noted that 2 Timothy portrays Paul facing condemnation and death, outcomes that were never alluded to in Philemon. According to 2 Timothy, Paul has already experienced one judicial proceeding in which he narrowly escaped a negative outcome (4:16-17). At the time of writing, he faces an interval in chains (2:9b). Nevertheless, his condemnation is on the horizon. That Paul considers himself perilously close to the end of his journey and anticipates that his imprisonment may end in death is signaled in memorable terms by the following passage in chapter 4:[5]

> For I am already at the point of being sacrificed; the time of my departure has come. I have fought the good fight, I have finished the race; I have kept the faith. (2 Tim 4:6-7)

Second, it is also possible to argue the *conceptual* temporal priority of Philemon on the grounds that 2 Tim 4:6-7 and 4:16-17 can plausibly be interpreted as following Phlm 22 while the reverse sequence is much less plausible. In this interpretation, Paul's expectation for using Philemon's guest room was dissolved as his case took a turn for the worse, leaving Paul in grave jeopardy.[6] Finally, the references made in both letters to Demas (reliable in Philemon, unreliable in 2 Timothy), to Luke, and to Timothy also support the interpretation that Paul is imaged at a later stage of imprisonment in 2 Timothy. According to 2 Timothy, Paul has the steadfast support of Luke and Timothy just as he did at the time of Philemon. Demas, faithful to Paul at the time of Philemon, (Phlm 24), has subsequently proved unreliable (2 Tim 4:10).[7]

The Purposes of 2 Timothy

For the most part, this letter contains instructions and counsel that pertain to Timothy personally. Since other Christians, including those named at the end of the letter (4:19-20), will undoubtedly read the letter or become apprised of its contents, the directives communicated regarding false teaching were undoubtedly intended for others beyond Timothy. Nevertheless, the letter on the whole concentrates upon Timothy and the steps that this young associate of Paul is now called to take in support of his mentor, who is in chains.

First and foremost, Paul intensely desires that Timothy come to his side. Paul makes this request three times within the letter. Initially, in 1:4, he states poignantly: "As I remember your tears, I long night and day to see you, that I may be filled with joy." In 4:9, near the letter's conclusion, Paul explicitly requests that Timothy hasten on his way: "Do your best to come soon *(tacheos).*" At 4:21a this summons is made even more specific: "Do your best to come *before winter.*" Paul's second purpose is to emphasize that his own chains are not a cause for shame before God. Accordingly, Timothy should not be influenced to turn away from the imprisoned Paul; rather he should strive to be associated with Paul in his suffering.[8] It is worth considering in some detail the words that Paul pens in 2 Tim 1:1-17, a passage in which the concepts of shamefulness and faithfulness are clearly of central importance. In 1: 8a Timothy is urged, "Do not be ashamed then *(me oun epaischynthēs)* of testifying to our Lord, nor of me his prisoner *(ton desmion* autou), but share in suffering for the gospel in the power of God."[9] 2 Tim 1:9-10 then reflect on the sovereignty of God and the way in which God's plan has reached its culmination in the decisive "appearing" *(epiphaneias)* of Christ Jesus who is "our Savior" *(tou sōtēros hēmōn).*[10] Paul then expressly affirms that it is this Jesus "who abolished death and brought life and immortality to light through the gospel" (1:l0b).

After emphasizing Jesus' ultimate sovereignty, Paul then refers to his own suffering for Jesus' gospel. In 1:11 he notes that he has been "a preacher and apostle and teacher" for this gospel, thereby indicating that he has been called to serve the gospel in a prominent and significant way. Now his call to serve the gospel has brought him into Roman custody. Despite being in circumstances that might well be considered shameful, however, Paul states resolutely and emphatically (1:12b), "But, I am not ashamed" *(all' ouk epaischynomai).*[11]

Two distinct yet related considerations are fundamental to any understanding of why Paul is not ashamed. Both of these points are touched upon as Paul continues in v. 12. The first consideration is embedded in the admonition with which he began this series of reflections at v. 8. Paul is a prisoner for the Lord's sake. He is in chains not for any other reason save for the testimony he has given regarding Christ Jesus.

Second, Paul is not ashamed because he is convinced of Jesus' capacity to vindicate faithfulness on the day of his triumph. In his heart Paul is fully convinced that Jesus will ultimately uphold his faithfulness and give him vindication. This second aspect will be taken up again in section six below.

As his reflections on shamefulness and faithfulness proceed, Paul cites two examples for Timothy to consider, one negative and one positive. The exact nature of the negative development that is referred to in 1:15 is difficult to determine: "You are aware that all who are in Asia turned away from me and among them Phygelus and Hermogenes" (2 Tim *1:15).* Probably the meaning here is that an extraordinary number of Christians (this number is so proportionately high that Paul writes "all" [*pantes*][12]) in the province of Asia have refused to support Paul, in effect, turning their backs on him.

Paul explicitly states that Timothy is aware of this discouraging development. The sense of Paul's wording is that Timothy has met Phygelus and Hermogenes, members of the group that has turned away from Paul. If 2 Timothy presumes that Timothy is somewhere in Asia,[13] then he may indeed, be well informed about the entire situation.

Why this group of Christians has proved disloyal to Paul is an intriguing question. Paul's circumstances as a Roman prisoner may well be the grounds on which this group has deserted him. In other words, this group may have turned away from Paul because they have become *ashamed* of his *chains.*

This hypothesis emerges from a consideration of the next verses, in which attention is directed to someone who is highly faithful to Paul, despite Paul's humiliating circumstances. In order to appreciate the full scope of Onesiphorus' fidelity, it is desirable to cite verses 1:16-18 in their entirety. Clearly, Onesiphorus' refusal to be ashamed of Paul in chains contrasts with the response of the group who turned from Paul. As will be explicated in the following section, these verses are also significant for the light that they shed on Paul's exact circumstances as a prisoner:

> May the Lord grant mercy to the household of Onesiphorus, for he often refreshed me; he was not ashamed of my chains, but when he arrived in Rome he searched for me eagerly and found me—may the Lord grant him to find mercy from the Lord on that Day—and you well know all the service that he rendered at Ephesus. (2 Tim 1:16-18)

In writing that Onesiphorus sought him out diligently and "refreshed" him,[14] Paul is seemingly providing new information to Timothy. Do his words also convey the meaning that Onesiphorus has since died? Paul's petition that the Lord grant mercy to the household of Onesiphorus could imply this meaning. So also could Paul's prayer that Onesiphorus himself receive mercy from the Lord on the Day of Christ's appearing?[15] If Onesiphorus were no longer providing support to Paul because he had recently died, there would be a further rationale for the urgency in Paul's request that Timothy join him in Rome.

Whether Onesiphorus had died in the meantime, is on his way to another destination, or remains in Rome, what is clear is that Timothy should take encouragement from Onesiphorus' refusal to be ashamed of Paul's chains. Onesiphorus has previously served Paul well at Ephesus. Now, in marked contrast with many others who were previously associated with Paul's ministry, he has explicitly gazed on Paul bound with chains and far from turning away, often refreshed him.

Besides having the objectives that Timothy not be ashamed of Paul's chains and that he proceed directly to Paul's side, the letter also has the purpose of providing admonitions regarding false teachers and pagan surroundings.[16] Further, Timothy himself is given extensive instructions concerning his own progress toward mature discipleship.[17] Because it dwells on these and related themes, the letter has sometimes been assessed as having the character of a final testament.[18] Several passages in which Paul himself retrospectively reflects on his journey in Christ's service also give the letter this character. These last mentioned passages will be considered in section five below.

Paul's Faithfulness as a Prisoner in Rome

2 Timothy provides a memorable portrait of Paul as a Roman prisoner suffering abandonment. If authored by another Christian in Paul's name, that author was not merely concerned to portray Paul's chains but also the apostle's experience of isolation and abandonment. In the paragraphs that follow it will emerge that Paul's prison circumstances and his response to them are, indeed, central to the meaning of 2 Timothy.

As regards Paul's circumstances, it bears emphasizing first that Rome is unmistakably the site of his imprisonment. Presumably aware that Paul was being held in Rome, Onesiphorus traveled to the imperial capital and it was there that he searched diligently for Paul and found him (1:17).[19] Second, Paul is very definitely in chains. To Onesiphorus' credit (1:16), he was not ashamed of Paul's chains *(tēn halysin mou)*. It will be elaborated below that Paul's chains affront him because they are the chains that befit a criminal (2:9). The fact that he is in chains does not signify that Paul is being held in an official public prison. Rather, his confinement is at a less prominent location. This conclusion is first suggested by Paul's mention that Onesiphorus searched for him eagerly before finally finding him. If Paul were situated in an official *carcer*, Onesiphorus presumably would not have needed to search for him so diligently. A second factor, already mentioned, is that Onesiphorus was able to "refresh" Paul on an ongoing basis once he found him. This would not be easily accomplished if Paul were under severe custody. Third, the very fact that this letter could be written at all argues for conditions of confinement more relaxed than those normally associated with confinement in a *carcer.*

If 2 Timothy portrays Paul as far from being "ashamed" of his chains, the letter does not portray him as acquiescing in them either. Indeed, the modifiers "resentful" and "resistant" can be utilized in describing Paul's attitudinal response toward his bonds. In 2 Timothy, Paul is not *ashamed* of his chains, but he does *resent* them.

What is the basis for Paul's resentment? The fundamental fact that he is not a criminal is what engenders his resentment. Since he is innocent of wrongdoing, Paul's sharp comment in 2:9a is that he should not be "wearing chains like a criminal" *(mechri desmōn hōs kakourgos)*

In effect, what Paul has been doing is proclaiming the word of God in Christ. That is why he has been put into chains, wrongfully so. In the next part of this verse, Paul's words suggest an attitude of resistance and defiance regarding the injustice of his chains: "But the word of God is not chained" (2 Tim 2:9b).

On one level, these words can be regarded as a kind of resistance slogan imparted to Timothy. Yet on another level they express Paul's defiance toward those who have chained him: it is impossible for them to imprison and circumscribe the message that Paul has been commissioned to deliver.

Upon a moment's reflection, it can be recognized that the Roman authorities themselves are the only possible referents for Paul's words of reproach. Who else is treating Paul like a criminal, chaining him in a demeaning fashion? It is the Roman authorities and no one else. And who is implicitly operating on the premise that they will contain Paul's message if they chain and execute Paul? Only the Roman authorities. That Paul anticipates his death at the hands of these authorities is also a key feature of the circumstances that 2 Timothy portrays. This aspect has already received attention in section two above. There is still time for Timothy to undertake the journey and still time for him to be of service to Paul once he arrives. Nevertheless, Paul's time is limited; he is convinced that the end of his life is at hand.

Because it also emphasizes his faithfulness, the passage in which Paul indicates his sense of impending death deserves to be cited again in its entirety. In 2 Tim 4:5 Paul counseled Timothy to fulfill his ministry with great steadfastness, regardless of the suffering that might come. Within this context, he then reflects that the end of his own service is at hand:

> For I am already on the point of being sacrificed; the time of my departure has come. I have fought the good fight, I have finished the race, I have kept the faith. (2 Tim 4:6-7)

Two nuances of temporal meaning contribute to the definiteness with which

Paul speaks about his death here. He is "already" *(hëdë)* at the point of being sacrificed.[20] The "time" *(kairos),* the decisive time, of his "departure" (*analyseōs*) is at hand. Paul will soon be leaving this life.[21] It is in this context that he evidences a certain satisfaction as regards his own steadfastness in Christ's service. It must be emphasized that, according to 2 Timothy, these memorable words are enunciated while Paul continues as a Roman prisoner. These circumstances add a particular poignancy to Paul's words. "I have fought the good fight." Paul has conducted himself well in various situations of hardship and has continued to do so despite his sense of being abandoned by many. "I have finished the race." For many, it is a cause for shame that Paul's "race" *(ton dromon)* has brought him first to Roman chains and now to the verge of Roman execution. Yet for Paul himself, his death represents the sealing of his course of discipleship, the achievement of his goal.

"I have kept the faith." As Paul looks backward, he knows unalterably that he has been faithful to Christ. Now he will not shrink from faithfulness unto death. The same faithfulness manifested in all that has transpired previously will be manifested anew when the verdict of his Roman judges propels him toward a martyr's death.

Reliable and Unreliable Christians

If 2 Timothy highlights Paul's faithfulness during the period before his condemnation, it also presents a wide spectrum of responses by other Christians to Paul in chains. Timothy himself is portrayed as steadfastly loyal, and Paul presumes Timothy's reliability throughout the letter. Others such as Luke are also faithful and reliable. To a noteworthy degree, however, 2 Timothy portrays the responses of a goodly number of Christians to Paul, Christ's prisoner, in severe terms.

In analyzing the distressful situation that Paul was facing, it is useful to begin with Hymanaeus and Philetus and the larger group to which they belong. From the character of Paul's instructions in 2:14-19, it can be deduced that Timothy knows these individuals, possibly they are located together in the same region. In this passage, nothing is mentioned explicitly regarding Hymenaeus' and Philetus' response to Paul's chains. Rather it is their false teaching and their generally ignoble conduct that is critiqued. For they "have swerved from the truth by holding that the resurrection is already past. They are upsetting the faith of some" (2:18).

Alexander the coppersmith, mentioned in 2 Tim 4:14, is another figure with whom Timothy has contact at his present location, or with whom he may well have contact as he journeys to Paul's side in Rome. Again, nothing in the text explicitly indicates that Alexander was ashamed of Paul's chains. But if the "harm" to which Paul refers is the harm of Paul's abandonment, then Alexander may somehow have had a role in contributing to this abandonment. Whatever the nature of Alexander's offense, even if it has nothing to do with Paul's imprisonment, it is evidently a grievous one since Paul adverts to the divine retribution that will come upon his opponent. His forceful words against Alexander are the following:

> Alexander the coppersmith did me great harm *(polla . . . kaka);* the Lord will requite him for his deeds. Beware of him yourself, for he strongly opposed our message. (2 Tim *4:14-15)*

In addition to the three parties just mentioned (Hymenaeus, Philetus, and Alexander), Phygelus, and Hermogenes and the group to which they themselves belong should also be mentioned in this context. As discussed in section three above, the explanation for this group's "turning away" probably should be attributed to their perception that Paul's chains and imprisonment discredited him. While there is tone of lament in Paul's comment regarding this group (1:15), he does not criticize them severely or suggest that they will have a harsh reckoning on the day of the Lord's judgment.

To complete this overview of unreliable Christians in 2 Timothy, the responses given to Paul at the time of his formal juridical proceedings must be considered. On this topic, one verse of the letter is as significant as it is problematic: "At my first defense no one took my part; all deserted me. May it not be charged against them" (2 Tim 4:16).

This verse poses two fundamental challenges for interpretation. Paul's reference, "at my first defense," represents the first challenge. These words hold the key for understanding Paul's legal and political situation in 2 Timothy. The second challenge arises from Paul's repeated assertions, "No one took my part; all deserted me." The task of the following paragraphs is to comment on both of these enigmatic references, proceeding sequentially.

Regarding Paul's first statement, the principal issue is whether the Greek term *apologia* ("defense") here refers to Paul's full Roman trial or only to the preliminary investigation used to establish the basis for a full trial. Since *apologia* can have either meaning, it is useful to consider the implications of Paul's situation if this term denotes a preliminary hearing or if it denotes a full trial.

If *apologia* does mean a full trial and if Paul was "rescued" at the end of it, as 4:17 states, then Paul conceivably may have been free for a time to be arrested and cast back into chains. On this interpretation, he is now facing a *second* trial and fully expects that he will be condemned at the end of it.

The principal consideration arguing against this interpretation is the fact that had such events—official acquittal, release from chains, and new arrest—actually transpired, Timothy could be expected to know something about these developments already.[22] Yet, the contents and tone of 2 Timothy do not support the view that Timothy is aware of Paul's situation. In fact, Paul seemingly writes to familiarize Timothy with what has occurred since the time that Timothy was last with him.

On the other hand, if *apologia* refers to a preliminary hearing, then Paul has remained continuously in chains.[23] At the first court session Paul had no one take his part. Nevertheless, he was "rescued" from a totally negative outcome. His prospects are not favorable, however. He has a measure of time until his full trial commences. Convinced that this trial will end in his condemnation, Paul is at peace with the martyr's death that is on the horizon.

It should be emphasized that, in either of the two scenarios just described, Paul remains in chains awaiting a verdict that will condemn him. According to either scenario, there is still an interval of time before the final verdict will be pronounced. It is for this reason that Paul urges Timothy to join him. He desires to make good use of the time interval that he has until the Roman legal processes resume.

The present discussion now turns to consider the identity of those who were associated with Paul, yet failed to take his part at his *apologia*. This issue is the second challenge for interpretation presented in 4:16. Precisely to whom is Paul referring? And what was it that Paul expected from these Christians? What should they have done to assist him?

What complicates the interpretation of this part of 4:16 is the fact that Paul elsewhere in the letter speaks of Luke as still with him ("Luke alone is with me" [2 Tim 4:11]). Paul also sends Timothy greetings from Eubulus, Pudens, Linus, Claudia, and "all the brethren" (4:21), other Christians who are presumably present. The statement that Luke *alone* is with him seems to imply that Paul (and Timothy) considers Luke to be in a ministerial category that is distinct from the category of the four persons mentioned at the end of the letter. Paul thus appears to have a degree of support from one esteemed associate, from four other named individuals, and from others besides them. How then can he speak so sweepingly in 4:16 when he states that *no one* took his part and that *all* deserted him?

At least three possibilities should be mentioned here.[24] The first is that Paul may mean that, apart from those few he mentions favorably, no one took his part. In other words, except for the small handful of Christians referred to in the letter, everyone else deserted him. The second, less likely, possibility is that those mentioned favorably in the letter may have temporarily abandoned Paul at the time of his defense.[25]

The third interpretation is that Paul is referring to those Christians at Rome who have legal expertise and/or political influence and is indicating that all of *these* Christians abandoned him. According to this interpretation, Luke and the others referred to favorably were loyal to Paul at the time of his defense. Their skills and competence, however, were not such as to enable them to enter into the judicial proceedings in any way. Other Christians at Rome did possess the requisite skills and influence. But none of these Christians afforded help to Paul. Shocked by the manifest absence of support from this group, Paul emphasized this point in writing to Timothy.

Precisely what kind of support had Paul expected to receive at the time of his *apologia?* It is possible that Paul was expecting some type of legal counsel or legal intervention. The Greek *parageneto,* translated here as "take my part" has the root meaning of "be present."[26] It may indicate, however, service as a legal advocate, and it can also have the meaning of testifying as a witness at a trial.[27] If either of these latter meanings is present in Paul's use of this verb, then his expectation was for some of the Christians around him to have participated actively in his trial. But *none* of them did so.

Instead, Paul experienced abandonment and a certain isolation when he was before his judges. All of those he had been relying on for juridical assistance chose to be elsewhere. To use Paul's word, they *deserted* him.[28]

On the other hand, if Paul's use of *parageneto* does not have technical, legal meaning here but rather its fundamental meaning, "be present," then, what he is lamenting is the failure of certain Christians to be present to him, to stand with him, to minister to him. Instead of identifying themselves with Paul's cause, they have acted in the manner of Demas (4:10). They have put distance between themselves and Paul. They have all, every one of this group, deserted him.

Whatever their exact nuances of meaning, Paul's words within this passage indicate that he was still smarting over what had occurred. In the specific situation that Paul had faced, the conduct of these Christians was clearly less than what Paul had expected from them. This sharp disappointment is what he laments to Timothy.

If Paul's first words reflect an edge of bitterness as well as hurt, it is significant that his next words reflect concern for those who turned from him. "May it not be charged against them."[29] These words indicate Paul's conviction that an offense has been committed. Perhaps he does so haltingly. Paul nevertheless expresses forgiveness. The benign character of these last words is still more apparent when they are compared with the malediction regarding Alexander the coppersmith in 4:14. In the present passage, nothing suggests that these Christians have turned away from Christ Jesus. But they have turned away from Paul, Christ's prisoner.

In section two of this essay, the striking departure of Demas from Paul's side was considered as a datum that shed light on Paul's trajectory as a Roman prisoner. This event can now be regarded as one more reason why Paul is desirous of having Timothy hurry to his side before the winter season.

Within 2 Timothy, Paul does not utilize any designation such as "co-worker" in referring to Demas. It has been noted above that the same is true as regards Luke. The same absence of any ministerial designation is also a characteristic of Paul's references to Crescens and Titus in 4:10 and Tychicus in 4:12. Yet presumably Demas, Luke, Crescens, Titus, and Tychicus are to be located in a ministerial category that is distinct from the more general standing of Eubulus, Pudens, Linus, Claudia, and "all the brethren" who send greetings to Timothy at the very end of the letter.

In 4:llb Paul urges Timothy, "Get Mark and bring him with you; for he is very useful in serving me." And regarding Tychicus, Paul states in 4:12: "Tychicus I have sent to Ephesus." The inference may thus be drawn that Paul holds some form of moral influence with Mark, Tychicus, and the others he mentions at this point. Perhaps the implication is that those mentioned have ministered or served with Paul, or under his auspices.

If, as seems likely, Demas has been ministering with Paul or ministering to him, then how significant is his decision to leave Paul's side *for no worthy reason.*[30] Paul has himself sent Tychicus to Ephesus. Crescens and Titus have departed, respectively, for Galatia and Dalmatia. They have seemingly done so with Paul's acquiescence—he voices no criticism regarding their departures. In contrast, Demas has left in a manner that Paul considers unwise and irresponsible. The sharpness in Paul's words describing Demas' motivation is to be emphasized (4:10): "For Demas, *in love with the present world,* has deserted me and gone to Thessalonica."

What is the core meaning of "in love with the present world" *(agapēsas ton nun aiōna)?* Seemingly disdain, and perhaps even scorn, is expressed through these words. Why does Paul deem it so reprehensible that Demas has deserted him out of love for the present world?

Two related reasons suggest themselves. The first explanation emerges from Paul's conviction that, at the second "appearing" of Jesus,[31] all of humankind will be judged by the standards of Jesus. Thus, it is manifestly foolish for Demas to follow any course of action that is not in conformity with the standards of Jesus.

The second explanation relates to the validity of Paul's witness to Jesus through his chains. Paul himself is fully convinced that his chains are not grounds for shame, but rather the concrete symbols of his faithfulness. It may thus be that Paul considers Demas to be guided by the code of honor and shame followed by the secular Roman world instead of being oriented to the truly unimpeachable status that Paul possesses as Christ's prisoner.

With Demas' desertion and the departure of Tychicus, Crescens, and Titus, Paul is now cut off from everyone with whom he has previously ministered, save for Luke. It is this new situation that motivates him to appeal directly and authoritatively to Timothy.[32] Paul even appends detailed assignments to his fundamental request. As previously noted, Timothy is to get Mark and bring him along with him (4:llb). Timothy is also to bring the cloak that Paul left with Carpus at Troas and Paul's books, especially his parchments (4:13).[33]

Timothy, in contrast with Demas, will be Paul's unfailingly reliable co-minister. Far from distancing himself from Paul, Timothy will continue to revere Christ's chained prisoner and will speed to Paul's side bringing all the resources Paul has requested.

God's Salvation and Paul's Vindication

Although 2 Timothy images Paul experiencing abandonment and isolation, he also holds two convictions regarding salvation and personal vindication that encourage him to be resolutely faithful as Christ's prisoner. There are two passages in which

2 Timothy portrays Paul's belief that God is using his imprisonment for the purposes of salvation. In four highly significant passages, Paul also expresses the conviction that he himself will *ultimately* be vindicated by Christ. These various aspects of Paul's perspective will now be considered.

What good purpose is being served through Paul's imprisonment? As previously observed, 2:9a indicates that Paul resented being kept in chains as though he were a criminal. Continuing in 2:9b, Paul adds the defiant reflection that the word of God cannot be chained. In the verse now cited, he then reflects on God's saving purpose in this imprisonment. Paul describes the good that is being accomplished in the following way:

> Therefore I endure everything for the sake of the elect, that they also may obtain salvation in Christ Jesus with its eternal glory. (2 Tim 2:10)

Paul's fundamental meaning here is that his faithfulness in his imprisonment is somehow a part of God's plan to bring Paul and others ("the elect") to *salvation* in Christ.[34] By means of a causality that is affirmed but not explained, God will effect a salvation that is characterized by "eternal glory." Because Paul's steadfastness in his chains somehow serves God's salvific purposes, it is important that Paul endure his imprisonment with faithfulness; Paul is indeed doing this.

If the insight that is given by Paul's words later in the letter can be integrated validly at this point, God's achievement of salvation through Paul's imprisonment also involves Paul's own proclamation of the gospel as a chained prisoner. In 4:17, when he reflects on what occurred after others deserted him at his defense, Paul states, "But the Lord stood by me and gave me strength to proclaim the message fully, that all the Gentiles might hear it" (2 Tim 4:1 7a).

Note that what Paul receives strength for is "to proclaim the message fully" *(to kērygma plērophorēthē).* This full proclamation is seemingly crucial in that, without it, the Gentiles of Paul's audience will not become familiar with the central truths about Christ. The reference to "all the Gentiles" seemingly has immediate reference to the Roman officials who were present at Paul's first defense, that is, the judge(s), court personnel, and soldiers who were there.[35]

Presumably God's sovereign purposes called for this immediate group to come in contact with, and be challenged by, the crucial truths concerning Jesus previously crucified but now risen. It was for this particular mission, this particular proclaiming of Jesus to these Roman officials, and to others through them, that Paul received new strength from his Lord.

In addition to holding the conviction that his imprisonment advanced the saving purposes of God and Christ, Paul is also fully convinced that he himself will be completely vindicated when Christ returns to enact judgment and confer glory. That Christ will indeed carry him far beyond the limitations of a Roman judgment can be regarded as one of the fundamental perspectives of the letter.

Paul's conviction regarding Christ's sovereign power is expressed at the outset of 2 Timothy; however, before considering his words in chapter one it is first useful to consider the continuation of the passage that has just been analyzed. After indicating that the Lord strengthened him to proclaim the message for the sake of the Gentiles, Paul then reflects concerning Christ's power to rescue him:

> So I was rescued from the lion's mouth. The Lord will rescue me from every evil and save me for his heavenly kingdom. To him be the glory for ever and ever. Amen. (2 Tim 4:17b-18a)

The first time that "rescue" appears within this passage, it refers to a past event. The second time it is used, the reference is to a rescue that will occur in the future. Significantly, Paul's experience of the first rescue is what engenders his trust regarding the rescue he anticipates in the future.

The phrase "from the lion's mouth" can refer to Paul's deliverance from Satan, from the power of the Roman Empire, from the hands of the emperor, or from death itself.[36] Paul may, however, be referring to deliverance from a *combination* of these evils.

Building upon this experience of deliverance in the present, Paul looks to the future. In the future, he will be rescued, not from one specific evil, or even from a specific combination of evils. Rather, he will be rescued "from every evil."[37]

It should also be emphasized that the Lord will *save* Paul for his *heavenly kingdom*. This concept of Jesus effecting Paul's salvation (here *sōsei)* is particularly significant in a Roman context in which "savior" has become a title for acclaiming the Roman emperor. The concept of Jesus bringing Paul into a heavenly kingdom *(ten basileian autou tēn epouranion)* also has the potential for engendering tensions in a Roman world that acknowledges only one empire and one universal ruler.

Paul's words in these verses indicate that his entry into Jesus' kingdom will take place sometime in the future. Nevertheless, the kingdom of which Jesus is the supreme ruler is in existence even as Paul writes. Manifestly, Paul has not yet entered this kingdom. But Jesus does have the sovereign power to save him and bring him there.

Paul's confidence in Jesus' capacity to rescue him is grounded in his belief that God has already used Jesus' initial appearing *(epiphaneias)* to abolish death and confer unending life. This concept of the earthly arrival of Jesus as an "appearing" that effectuates salvation is well articulated at 2 Tim 1:10, a passage whose full analysis was deferred until now. Note that the appearing of Jesus is here explicitly the appearing of a *savior*. "Savior" is, in fact, Jesus' explicit title. Paul writes that God's purpose and grace has now been manifested "through the *appearing* of our Savior Christ Jesus, who abolished death and brought life and immortality to light through the gospel."

Just as "saving" and "kingdom," two concepts with implications for the Roman world, were combined in a remarkable way at 2 Tim 4:17-18, a comparable combination can be observed in this verse. As noted, "savior" has particular meaning with reference to the cult of the emperors. So also does the term "appearing."

Five decades before Jesus' birth, Julius Caesar was acclaimed at Ephesus as "the god who has *appeared* .... the common *savior* of human life."[38] By way of comparison, Paul's claims for Jesus in this passage (and elsewhere in the letter) are far more sweeping than the claims of grandeur that the Ephesians advanced for Julius Caesar. According to 2 Timothy, Jesus has the decisive power to abolish death and confer life and immortality. Jesus' power is thus of a magnitude incomparably greater than that of any emperor.[39]

Another common feature of the two passages in 2 Timothy that refer to Jesus' second coming is that both passages mention Jesus' role as a supremely sovereign judge. Such an emphasis on the definitive judgment of Jesus his Lord is of particular significance from the standpoint of Paul's situation as a prisoner who faces the verdict of a Roman judge.

In the passage now to be considered, Paul solemnly urges Timothy to be steadfast in his preaching and in all aspects of his ministry, regardless of the circumstances:

> I charge you in the presence of God and of Christ Jesus who is to judge the living and the dead, and by his appearing and his kingdom: preach the word, be urgent in season and out of season, convince, rebuke, and exhort, be unfailing in patience and in teaching. (2 Tim 4:1-2)

Three motivating factors are cited by Paul as he adjures Timothy. The "appearing" *(epiphaneian)* and the "kingdom" *(basileian)* of Christ are cited as factors to inspire perseverance. Paul's appeal is also given in the presence of God and in the presence of Jesus, who will exercise a definitive judgment.

This image of Jesus as sovereign judge of the living and of the dead is integrally related to his final appearing and is an integral aspect of the larger plan of God in Christ Jesus.[40] In Paul's perspective, no one is excluded from Christ's sovereign assize. *All* of the living and *all* of the dead will be subject to Christ's scrutiny.

Such a perspective regarding Christ's universal judgment inevitably relativizes the meaning of any verdict that the Roman authorities might pronounce against Paul. The verdict of Paul's Roman judges fades to nothingness in comparison with the judgment about Paul that Jesus will pronounce at his final appearing.

The verdict of these authorities and *these authorities themselves* will ultimately be subjected to Christ's judgment. Like Paul himself and like all of the living and all of the dead, these Roman authorities will ultimately stand before Christ and be assessed according to Christ's own standards.

Regarding Paul's vindication, one further reference remains to be considered. In 4:8 Jesus is again imaged as a sovereign judge. That which was implicit at 4:1

is now made explicit. The judgment that Jesus will render on the day of his appearing will explicitly affirm and reward Paul's faithfulness:

> Henceforth there is laid up for me the crown of righteousness, which the Lord, the righteous judge, will award to me on that Day, and not only to me but also to all who have loved his appearing. (2 Tim 4:8)

With reference to the Christological images present in 2 Timothy, it should be observed that a new attribute of Jesus is presented here, the attribute of righteous judging. Jesus is *the righteous* judge. He will ultimately judge Paul with a righteousness that will relativize any verdict against Paul given by his Roman judges.[41] It must be underscored that Paul makes this avowal as a chained Roman prisoner to Timothy. In this passage Jesus is also *the Lord*.[42] Jesus, Paul's Lord, will decisively vindicate Paul and every other faithful disciple. He will do so in his capacity as the sovereign judge over all who are living and all who are dead.

What specifically does Paul expect to receive from Christ? On the great day of Christ's appearing, Paul expects to receive an insignia that will splendidly confirm the faithful service that he has rendered. This emblem will be "the crown of righteousness."[43] Christ will award it to him on that Day. And Christ will award it not only to Paul, but to all who have *loved* his appearing.[44]

Notes

1. This chapter is an adaptation of chapter 8, "The Circumstances of Paul in 2 Timothy" from Richard J. Cassidy, *Paul in Chains: Roman Imprisonment and the Letters of St. Paul* (New York: Crossroad, 2001). It is reprinted here with permission of The Crossroad Publishing Company.

2. See M. Prior, *Paul the Letter-Writer and the Second Letter to Timothy* (Sheffield: Sheffield Academic Press, 1989) 37-45, for a discussion of the often neglected phenomenon of co-authorship by Timothy and others within the Pauline corpus. Prior points out that within this corpus only Romans, Ephesians, and the Pastorals are authored (or said to be authored) solely by Paul.

3. Would a pseudepigrapher feign an address to Timothy and intimately mention other individuals as a part of a strategy for establishing authenticity? In an excursus, H. Conzelmann, *The Pastoral Epistles* (Philadelphia: Fortress, 1972) 127-28, discusses the relatively abundant information about Timothy and other persons that is given in 2 Timothy and concludes that the pseudepigrapher has included such detailed information in order to buttress the impression that the letter actually originated with Paul. In *The Function of Personal Example in the Socratic and Pastoral Epistles* (Rome: Biblical Institute Press, 1986) 235, B. Fiore reaches a similar conclusion, holding that this "art" of including detailed information was taught in schools of rhetoric within the ancient world.

4. Recognizing the differences between Paul's undisputed letters and the Pastorals, Prior (*Paul the Letter-Writer*, 57-59) explains these differences on the basis of three considerations. First, there is no co-authorship indicated for the Pastorals. Second (in Prior's judgment), Paul did not use a secretary in writing the Pastorals. Third, the Pastorals are ad-

dressed to individuals and are, thus, in the category of private correspondence. Prior is also persuaded that the contents of 2 Timothy bring it closer to Paul's undisputed letters than is the case for 1 Timothy and Titus. He notes (p, 168) that 2 Timothy lacks the emphasis on church structure that is found in 1 Timothy and Titus; 2 Timothy's emphasis upon Paul's sufferings also distinguishes it from 1Timothy and Titus.

5. This passage will be the focus of an analysis in section four below.

6. A scenario based on Paul's authorship and a scenario based on deutero-Pauline authorship must both be considered. To hold that Philemon was written by Paul himself *after* 2 Timothy would require that Paul later became astonishingly relaxed about the perilous and frustrating circumstances that he details in 2 Timothy. Such a sequence would also require the supposition that Demas had somehow returned to Paul's side. It is indeed surprising that the high drama of desertion and a first trial are not alluded to in Philemon if Paul had in fact already experienced these phenomena. And regarding Demas, could Paul have written so benignly in Philemon that Demas was among the co-workers sending greetings (Phlm 23-24) if earlier "Demas, in love with this present world" had deserted him and gone to Thessalonica (2 Tim 4:10)? If 2 Timothy is pseudepigraphical and if the pseudepigrapher knew the text of Philemon, the foregoing considerations continue to have validity. The letter with the desertion of Demas must "logically" be positioned after the letter in which Demas is presented benignly as a faithful co-worker.

7. A more extended analysis of the significance of Demas' departure will be given in section six below.

8. As G. Fee observes, *1 and 2 Timothy, Titus* (San Francisco: Harper & Row, 1984) 178, two dimensions of meaning relative to humiliation appear to coalesce in 2 Tim 1:8 and 1:12. Regarding undeserved humiliation, it is desirable not to be discouraged (for the humiliated person will ultimately receive divine vindication). It is also desirable to stand with the person suffering undeserved humiliation. In this context, "do not be ashamed" means "do not turn away out of embarrassment." See H. Kee, "The Linguistic Background of 'Shame' in the New Testament," in On *Language, Culture, and Religion: In Honor of Eugene A. Nida* (The Hague: Mouton, 1974) 133-47, for an analysis of the complex range of meanings that *aiscbyno* and its related forms can have within the New Testament writings.

9. In this verse the second meaning that Fee (*1 and 2 Timothy*) adduces for "do not be ashamed" seems to predominate. Timothy is encouraged to stand with two persons who have experienced humiliation: the crucified Jesus and the chained Paul. Fee comments (p. 178): "There is a stigma to being associated with a crucified Messiah (thus a state criminal) and his (political) prisoner. Yet it is 'undeserved' humiliation from which there will be vindication 'on that Day' (see V. 12)." It should also be noted that, when "Lord" (*kyrion*) in 1:8a is taken as a reference to Jesus, the meaning of "me his prisoner" (*eme ton desmion autou*) in -1:8b is not far from the meaning of similar phrases in Phlm 1 and 9 and in Eph 3:1 and 4:1.

10. The significance of this use of *epipbaneias* and *soteros* within the context of the imperial ruler cult will be elaborated in section six below.

11. There are presumably three dimensions of meaning coalesced in Paul's declarations here: (a) he is not embarrassed by what has befallen him; (b) he is in no way turning from his allegiance to Christ crucified; and (c) he trusts in his own vindication from the humiliation he presently endures. The latter two dimensions can be readily noted in the remaining clauses of 1:12.

12. A. Hultgren, *I-II Timothy, Titus* (Minneapolis: Augsburg, 1984) 116, notes that this statement gives rise to further questions. After considering whether Paul could have been disowned by Christians in Asia, Hultgren judges it more probable that certain Asian Christians *who had been in Rome* retired to . . . Asia, thereby deserting Paul. Hultgren notes a possible connection with 4: 16 where it is stated: "At my first defense, no one took my part; all deserted me."

13. Inasmuch as the present chapter on 2 Timothy (as well as the preceding chapter on Colossians and Ephesians) leaves open the possibility of deuteron-Pauline authorship, the reconstruction of the situation in Asia is made in terms of the logic of the text of the letter. Several references within the letter seem to suggest that Timothy is located somewhere within the province of Asia although probably not at Ephesus. 2 Tim 1: 16 may imply that Onesiphorus is from Asia, and in 4:19 Timothy is instructed to greet the household of Onesiphorus. The wording in 4:12, where it is indicated that Paul sent Tychicus to Ephesus, suggests that Timothy himself is not at Ephesus. Wherever Timothy is located it seemingly would not be a great detour for him to stop at Troas (4:13) in order to pick up Paul's cloak.

14. G. Knight, *The Pastoral Epistles* (Grand Rapids: Eerdmans, 1992) 384, observes that Onesiphorus' simple presence to Paul would have "refreshed" him. *Anepsyxen* may also imply that food brought by Onesiphorus refreshed him. It should be noted that the conditions of Paul's custody were such as to allow for this support by Onesiphorus.

15. See T. Lea, *The New American Commentary: 1, 2 Timothy* (Nashville: Broadman, 1992) 198, for a concise discussion of the views of commentators who are pro and con on the topic of Onesiphorus' death.

16. See especially 2 Tim 2:14-19; 3:8-9.

17. Along with the entreaty that Timothy come quickly to Rome, Prior, *Paul the Letter-Writer*, 51-64, considers these instructions regarding Timothy's faithfulness and his formation to be a principal purpose of the letter.

18. Prior, *Paul the Letter-Writer*, 91-112, surveys the scholarly discussion on this question and notes that 2 Tim 4:6-8 is a crucial text. Prior's own interpretation of 4:6-8, which is not accepted with the present study, leads him to conclude that Paul is actually confident about the future and is indeed preparing an apostolic team for further missionary activity.

19. Murphy-O'Connor (*Paul*, 359-60) observes that Onesiphorus first faced the problem of ascertaining just where Paul was among the one million plus inhabitants of Rome and then faced the problem of reaching him in a city that had no street names and no house numbers. As an illustration of Onesimus' dilemma, Murphy-O'Connor cites a passage from Terence's *The Brothers*, in which Demea experiences incredible frustration in gaining viable directions to his destination in Athens, a city much smaller in population than Rome.

20. Regarding the nuances of *hede* and *spendomai*, Knight (*Pastoral Epistles*, 4.58-59) writes: "He does not mean that his death will take place immediately, since he can ask Timothy to come to be with him (vv. 9, 21) and bring him some items (v. 13). But he does indicate its certainty and that it is near."

21. Kelly, *A Commentary on the Pastoral Epistles* (New York: Harper and Row, 1963) 207, draws attention to the various dimensions of meaning that Paul brings forward in using *spendomai* and *analyseos* in speaking about his death. Kelly suggests that *spendomai* draws from the Jewish liturgical custom of pouring out and suggests that *analyseos* evokes the picture of a ship weighing anchor or a soldier or traveler striking camp. Along with other commentators, Kelly notes that the image of Paul pouring himself out as an offering occurs

10 Phil 2:17, where *spendomai* is used. Further, the concept of Paul's "departure" also appears in Phil 1:23 where the *cognate verb analysai* is used.

22. The conjecture that Timothy would have possessed knowledge of Paul's acquittal if Paul had actually been formally tried and acquitted can be put forward if Paul is the author of this letter. If deutero-Pauline authorship is posited, it becomes difficult to determine whether a preliminary hearing or a formal trial is being imaged here.

23. Fee (*1 and 2 Timothy*, 245) believes that the Roman juridical practice of *prima actio*, a preliminary hearing before the emperor or a magistrate, is being referenced here. The actual trial would then follow although there might be a considerable interval of time between the preliminary hearing and the formal trial. Fee's interpretation on this point comports well with the sense of the letter (a) that Paul has an interval of time before him and desires to have Timothy with him and (b) that Paul definitely has the outcome of his condemnation and death in view.

24. As referenced in n. 11 above, A. Hultgren alludes to yet another possibility when he argues that Christians from Asia who were present in Rome failed to come to Paul's assistance.

25. The letter's comment regarding Luke in 4: 11 weighs against this interpretation. Luke's supportive presence is highlighted; in contrast to Demas and others he is imaged as steadfastly at Paul's side. Would Luke have been depicted in this way if he had profoundly disappointed Paul at the time of Paul's first "defense"?

26. See M. Zerwick and M. Grosvenor, *A Grammatical Analysis of the Greek New Testament* (Rome: Pontifical Biblical Institute, 1988) 645.

27. For a discussion of the possible juridical meanings, see Knight, *Pastoral Epistles*, 469.

28. *Egkataleipo* is also used in 4:10, where Paul laments that Demas "deserted" him. Thus in 2 Timothy Paul twice references desertion, and in 1:15, as previously discussed, he speaks of his experience of having others "turn away" from him.

29. As observed by various commentators, the meaning of Paul's words here are similar to the meaning of Jesus' words according to Luke 23:34.

30. Again, conjectures and influences of this type are plausible if Paul is the author of the letter. If deutero-Pauline authorship is assumed, the writer is still obviously concerned to portray Paul experiencing desertion but may not be concerned with presenting this as the act of someone who was previously Paul's co-minister.

31. See section six below for an extended reflection on the meaning that Christ's "appearing" has for Paul in 2 Timothy.

32. 2 Timothy testifies to a very strong bondedness between Paul and Timothy (indicated by such passages as 1:25; 2:1; 3:14-15). Paul does not appear to doubt that Timothy will respond wholeheartedly to *his* request.

33. On the assumption that Paul himself authored this request, various commentators have conjectured about the contents of the books/parchments that he desires to have Timothy bring. Suggestions include writings from the Old Testament, Paul's personal documents, or blank sheets of writing paper. Hultgren, *I-II Timothy*, 143, advances the idea that Paul might conceivably be referring to copies of letters that he had previously written.

34. As Fee (*1 and 2 Timothy*, 198) notes, the relationship between Paul's suffering and salvation is not dear here. Nevertheless the relationship is definitely affirmed, and it is thus vitally important that Paul endure his suffering faithfully. It will be explicated below that

this use of *soterias* had implications in reference to the imperial ruler cult. Knight, *Pastoral Epistles*, 400, emphasizes that the *salvation* brought by Jesus in the present has the decisive future attribute of "eternal glory."

35. Rom 1:5 and Gal 3:8 are among the New Testament texts in which a group that is representative of the Gentile peoples is referred to as "all the Gentiles."

36. From among these possibilities, Fee, *1 and 2 Timothy*, 246, thinks that Paul may mean deliverance from death, Fee's argument is on the grounds that there appear to be echoes of Psalm 22 within this passage on desertion, rescue, and deliverance from the lion's mouth. It should be noted that Fee considers these words to have been penned by Paul after he experienced the proximity of death. If this passage is deutero-Pauline, the author seemingly wanted to emphasize that Paul experienced a very precarious situation while under the custody of the imperial authorities at Rome

37. Knight, *Pastoral Epistles*, 472, is among the commentators who discern the similarity between these words and those in Matt 6:13 in a petition of the Lord's prayer. Knight notes that the eschatological direction of this passage makes it evident that Paul is not excluding any evil that might be done to him, but is excluding the power of evil to destroy him finally.

38. Deissmann (*Light*, 344) cites this text from *Sylloge Inscriptionum Graecarum*. For a discussion of these two terms and other terms from 2 Timothy that have significance in the imperial ruler cult, see W. Bossuet, *Kyrios Christos* (Nashville: Abingdon, 1970) 310-312. See also the excursus on these two terms in Conzelmann, Pastoral Epistles, 100-104. For an extended treatment of the various Egyptian acclamations of Augustus (and some discussion of subsequent emperors, including Nero) as "savior," see W. Otto, "Augustus Soter," Hermes 45 (1910) 448-60. Two of the entries pertaining to Nero as savior are collected in E. M. Smallwood, *Documents Illustrating the Principates of Gaius, Claudius and Nero* (Cambridge: Cambridge University Press, 1967). The first (no. 419) is an inscription from Egypt in A.D. 60 or 61. As translated by D. Braund, *Augustus to Nero: A Sourcebook on Roman History 31BC-AD68* (London: Croom Helm, 1985) 254, the initial address is as follows: "To Nero Claudius Caesar Augustus Germanicus, imperator, the saviour and benefactor of the world . . . . " The second entry (no. 142), an inscription from Cyprus in 60 or 61, is broadly similar to the Egyptian inscription, and specifically acclaims Nero as "savior."

39. The challenge to the imperial ruler cult posed by 2 Timothy should not be overlooked. If this letter is written by Paul, it represents a significant shift away from the perspective of Rom 13:1-7. If 2 Timothy is deutero-Pauline, the writer delineates a *Paulusbild* whose features are highly controversial with the context of Roman rule. It should be emphasized that the writer of 2 Timothy is presenting a far more politically charged *Paulusbild* than is commonly appreciated. Thus, for example, Conzelmann, *Pastoral Epistles*, 128, puts forward the following statements regarding 2 Timothy's imaging of Pauls "Its purpose is to portray Paul as the model of patient endurance in suffering, and thereby of the Christian life in general . . . "; and "This purpose is also served by the picture of the abandoned prisoner and the description of his exemplary attitude . . . . " From the perspective of the present study, such descriptions are neglectful of the concrete circumstances of Paul in 2 Timothy where Paul is a Roman prisoner in chains reflecting about Roman judgment from the perspective of Jesus' ultimate vindication of him.

40. This depiction of Jesus as judge of the living and of the dead in 4:1 complements

the description of him at 1:10 as the one who abolished death and brought life and immortality to light. Having himself passed from death to life, Jesus now sovereignly judges both the living and the dead.

41. As observed by Knight, *Pastoral Epistles*, 461, *ho krites dikaios* indicates that Jesus, the supreme judge, is absolutely "righteous" and "just." For this reason he is qualified to give the crown of righteousness.

Knight does not take into consideration the implied contrast between Jesus as sovereign judge and Paul's Roman judges. Will the Roman authorities give a just verdict in Paul's case? The implied meaning of 2 Timothy is that they will not do so. Yet Paul looks beyond any Roman judgment. He looks beyond any negative Roman verdict to the judgment that will be given by a sovereign judge whose righteousness is unsurpassed.

42. The implications of Paul's repeated references within 2 Timothy to Jesus as "the Lord" should not be overlooked in assessing the letter's challenge to the developing imperial ruler cult. For reflections regarding the upsurge in the use of *ho kyrios* for the emperor during Nero's reign, see R. Cassidy, *John's Gospel in New Perspective* (Maryknoll, NY: Orbis, 1992) 13-14 and notes. In this dosing section of 2 Timothy, besides 4:8, there are three other references to Jesus as the Lord who possesses full sovereignty for judgment and vindication (see 4:14; 17,18).

43. See Knight, *Pastoral Epistles*, 461, for a discussion of the range of meanings possible for *stephanos tes dikaiosynes*. Knight favors the view that this genitive is appositional and should be translated: "the crown, namely, righteousness."

44. This closing reference provides encouragement for Timothy personally, as well as for other Christians, to long for Christ's return. Kelly, *Pastoral Epistles*, 210, suggests that the outlook expressed here bears resemblance to the perspective regarding heavenly citizenship that is expressed at Phil 3:20.

Response to Father Cassidy

Patrick Quirk
Associate Professor and Associate Dean,
Ave Maria School of Law, Naples, Florida

Introduction

Some will contend that the teacher's principal task is to stamp out ignorance. In the year of St. Paul, Fr Cassidy's *Paul in Chains*[1] is indeed a first-rate manual for those seeking to remedy their lack of knowledge of Paul's relationship to Rome and the Romans. I look forward to further volumes in the years to come.

We have now had almost two thousand years to plumb the depths of St Paul's writings, and it should be obvious to all that we are still not done. I am reminded of Simon Schama's recent book on the French Revolution in which he relates the story of China's Premier (Zhou En-lai) being asked what he thought of the French Revolution. "It's too soon to tell," he is supposed to have said.[2] This may be the case with glorious St. Paul, but we press on nevertheless.

As a part-time student of Roman law, I was impressed by Father Cassidy's great knowledge of Roman customs duties, direct and indirect taxation systems, coinage, transport systems, communications systems, and merchant customs.[3] I was also taken by descriptions of the various prison types, and the assorted categories of imprisonment: incarceration, military custody, and free custody. His discussion of the tension between Paul's comments in Romans 13 ("obey lawful authority") and the effects of incarceration as reflected in the *Letter to the Philippians* is absorbing.

Like so much of Sacred Scripture, Paul's correspondence has borne enormous fruit over two thousand years of argument over Church-State relations. The following imperfect list of "Pauline problems," as written about and, indeed, lived out in person by this great Apostle, demonstrates his enduring influence:

- What does it mean to obey state authority? ("Render unto Caesar . . . ," etc.)
- What are the limits of civil disobedience?
- What are the prerequisites for revolution?
- What is treason?
- What are the rights and duties of kings?
- What are the boundaries of due process of law?

Any one of these questions could occupy us in the context of a law school conversation about St Paul.

My choice today is to focus on Paul's uncomplicated declaration that he is a Roman citizen. This claim had enormous consequences for him and for the early Church. Without this claim, Paul may never have preached at Rome, or have endured the severe hardships that have inspired Christians for two millennia. Indeed, he may not have written any more letters.

We are all familiar with the dialogue in Acts 25: 6-12 and the words of temporal authority that set Paul on his dangerous journey: "After Festus had conferred with his council, he declared: 'You have appealed to Caesar. To Caesar you will go!'" I would like to put this appeal by Paul to the privileges of Roman citizenship into a modern context, and then to consider some aspects of citizenship: What is it for? What is it to be compared with? What would we do without such an important concept?

What is a Citizen?

To be a citizen is to be many things. Experts define it as a ". . . Passive and active membership of individuals in a nation-state with certain universalistic rights and obligations at a specified level of equality."[4] Law school courses often deal with citizenship in the context of different law courses. There is rarely a course on "citizenship law," just as there is rarely a course on "the law of the motor car" or "the law of the horse,"[5] but we do find citizenship mentioned frequently in many areas: immigration law and the law of refugees, administrative law, constitutional law, human rights law, and in similar public law areas of the curriculum. Indirectly, the concept of citizenship is important for private international law concepts such as domicile and residence. The following topics are often featured as a part of these courses:

- Immigration and citizenship policies, privileges, and obligations
- Acquisition of citizenship (birth, naturalization, and descent)
- Plural citizenship(s) (belonging to more than one nation-state or to a supra-national body like the European Union)
- Loss of citizenship
- Deportation, detention, and their consequences
- Refugee and asylum issues
- Equal protection and labor issues

• The problem of statelessness

Citizenship is a prized possession, but one often over-looked in daily life. We may have cause to think about our citizenship more especially at certain times: for example, when we vote, travel overseas using our national passport, seek certain jobs or positions of public trust,[6] or meet with someone from another country.

The very word itself—"citizen"—originates from the Greek idea of allegiance to a particular "city" (not a nation or country).[7] In this time of globalization, we are told we are "citizens of the world." Being a citizen can sometimes distinguish one from being a soldier, or from being of higher or lower birth.[8] Good citizens are said to be "solid," "honest," and "upright." Citizens are said to be "from the town" rather than from the country (countrymen or peasants). Citizens are also often said to be "private citizens," as when they do or say something in their non-public capacity.

Citizens have been known to be "subjects" of a particular monarch. At other times, such as that of the French Revolution, those formerly named *Monsieur* were suddenly recast as "citizens" (*citoyens*) of France to indicate their support for the new regime. The various theories of citizenship that came out of the French Revolution would take us beyond the scope of this paper, so I offer one example. Writing in 1789, Jacques-Pierre Brissot declared:

> "All authority comes from the People. But the People can only maintain this authority through its obedience. For if it allows itself to disobey the Citizens to whom it has given power, then everything is lost, there can no longer be Laws, or peace, or public safety. The citizen who disobeys public authority disobeys himself."[9]

St. Paul knew better than this, or was at least concerned with citizenship of a higher order.

Expectations of the Citizen

We expect certain things of citizens: loyalty, the payment of taxes and other assessments,[10] law-abiding behavior, defense of the territory, etc. Frequently, we expect citizens to be "responsible" in a very nonspecific sense, and we encourage our children to be "responsible citizens." Sometimes, we are disappointed.

There are now several concepts that compete with citizenship, especially since the time of the Enlightenment: various class distinctions come to mind, and so too does the recent and ubiquitous "consumer."[11] Sometimes when we speak of a citizen, we are deliberately excluding some other role we might play in society: mother or father, brother or sister, or even statesman.

Finally, we could think on Augustine's great work *City of God* and the idea that one can be "A Citizen of the Heavenly Jerusalem, and but a Stranger and a Sojourner here."[12]

Citizenship: is there an Antonym?

In searching for the *opposite* of what it means "to be a citizen" or "to hold citizenship," we will encounter interesting terms such as "aliens" (which, it seems, can be friendly, enemy, resident, or non-resident). Indeed, Benedict XVI surprises us greatly in his Angelus speech of August 12, 2007 in which he spoke of aliens in the context of the Heavenly Jerusalem:

> This was well known to the primitive Christian community, which considered itself "alien" here below and called its populated nucleuses in the cities "parishes[,]" which means, precisely, colonies of foreigners [in Greek, *pároikoi*] (cf. I Pt 2:11). In this way, the first Christians expressed the most important characteristic of the Church, which is precisely the tension of living in this life in light of Heaven.[13]

To be considered one of a "colony of foreigners" is certainly an attention-grabbing way to speak about membership in a local parish. Other important concepts here include "banishment," "exile" (think of Dante), "expatriation," "deportation," and "expulsion." All involve the stripping away of rights and duties, the lowering of status, or the infliction of punishment.

Can we imagine a world without the idea of citizenship? Would such a world be possible? History would suggest this is out of the question. Citizenship was essential to the life of the classical world, and "[i]t was a fixture in the philosophical and psychological treatises of the ancient Greek and Roman worlds that children are to be reared for *citizenship*, and that this required systematic schooling in what is often translated as *virtue*."[14]

I submit that this is just as important to us today. And perhaps Paul, led by the Holy Spirit, had this in mind when he invoked his Roman citizenship before Festus. What follows are some suggestions as to why this is may be so.

Citizenship of Paul

Paul's identification as a Roman citizen (by birth), as well as a Tarsian and a Jew, was a colossal moment in early Christianity. It would seem that God is writing in large letters here. He wants to bring citizenship into the equation since it is so close to human experience throughout history, and is something that we all relate to as citizens of our own countries.

St. Paul's mission to the Gentiles is in part accomplished through the fact that he is a citizen of one of the world's great empires. The empire eventually kills Paul, to be sure (it did no less to his Master), but it is through Paul's dual witness by first claiming citizenship and the shield of Roman legal protection, and then suffering grievously as a result, that we understand the difference between the earthly and heavenly cities. Paul is in this sense an example for us all. He is the proto-citizen since he has an ideal understanding of the relationship between the kingdoms of heaven and earth. We also must make our own judgment about what is to be given to Caesar and what is to be rendered unto God.[15]

Citizenship also turns our mind to the question of migration. Pope Benedict XVI recently described St. Paul as a "migrant by vocation."[16] His Holiness spoke of Paul's diverse origins:

> Born into a family of Jewish immigrants in Tarsus, Cilicia, Saul was educated in the Hebrew and Hellenistic cultures and languages, making the most of the Roman cultural context. After his encounter with Christ on the road to Damascus (cf. Gal1:13-16), although he did not deny his own "traditions" and felt both esteem and gratitude to Judaism and the Law (cf. Rm 9:1-5; 10:1; 2 Cor 11:22; Gal 1:13-14; Phil 3:3-6), he devoted himself without hesitation or second thoughts to his new mission, with courage and enthusiasm and docile to the Lord's command: "I will send you far away to the Gentiles" (Acts 22:21).[17]

Paul seemed destined to transcend Greek and Hebrew culture, and then present the result ("Hellenized Hebraism") to the court at Rome.

Treason

Father Cassidy's essay also gives an opportunity to ponder briefly the charge of treason. The charge of treason was, it seems, on the statute books due to the large number of assassination attempts made on the life of the Emperor. In normal political circumstances, this might be seen as quite reasonable. But in the life of Emperor Nero, we see the development of an insane hypersensitivity and paranoia, where even the slightest offense could be manipulated into a treasonous act and punished in the most severe manner. Such is the result of a man thinking he is a god deserving of worship by other men. By way of contrast, Paul's life and witness point in another direction entirely. He is proclaiming the Man who is also God. But Paul is no traitor, at least not to the True King.

Imprisonment

Paul's imprisonment is a drastic development in the context of his citizenship. Typically, prisoners are no longer free to enjoy all the rights and privileges of full citizenship: they are often no longer able to vote (felon disenfranchisement laws), and have obvious limits on their freedom of movement. Paul's appeal to Caesar (*via* his Roman citizenship) leads him into a constriction of the very citizenship on which he is relying. This may perhaps be a sign of the stripping away of his earthly life and the beginning of his heavenly life; at the very least, it is an illustration of the exhaustion of Paul's temporal remedies.

Fr. Cassidy's essay also turned my mind to those who faithfully visited Paul during his incarceration. Scripture guarantees that to visit a prisoner is to encounter Christ.[18] Prison visitation can be dangerous even today, and this was certainly the case in Roman times.

Conclusion

Ultimately, the story of Paul's appeal to his status as a Roman citizen provides yet one more aspect to the overall message of Jesus Christ. Again, in the words of Benedict XVI:

> "Jesus Christ brought a substantial novelty, opening the way towards a more human, freer world through the reciprocal distinction and autonomy of the State and the Church, that is, between what belongs to Caesar and what belongs to God (cf. Mt 22: 21)."[19]

Thus, Paul's appeal to Roman civil law, at the apex of which stood the great Caesar, helps us, in fact, to see more clearly "the things that are *not* Caesar's."

Notes

1. Richard J. Cassidy, *Paul in Chains: Roman Imprisonment and the Letters of St. Paul* (New York: Crossroad, 2001).

2. Simon Schama, *Citizens: A Chronicle of the French Revolution* (New York: Alfred A. Knopf, 1989), xiii.

3. Cf. Cassidy, *Paul in Chains*, 13-14, 24-25.

4. Thomas Janoski, *Citizenship and Civil Society* (Cambridge: Cambridge University Press, 1998), 9

5. *See* Frank H. Easterbrook, "Cyberspace and the Law of the Horse," *University of Chicago Legal Forum* (1996), 207. Easterbrook makes the point that law school courses are divided up into convenient but limited subject areas. In reality, all law is one "seamless web."

6. For example, someone may wish to run for President, Vice-President, or for Congress.

7. 7-91 *Immigration Law and Procedure* § 91.01.

8. Citizens seem to be ranked lower than nobles, but above the peasant class; we speak of "second-class" citizens.

9. Quoted in Janoski, 52.

10. Thankfully, at this time of economic crisis, government debt cannot be legally treated as a joint and several debt of each individual citizen!

11. "Most young people are subject to the norms of a market society. The immediate satisfaction of desires is largely encouraged by advertising. The political organization of society depends on this market mentality that transforms a citizen into a consumer. The laws of economics take over from the moral laws." Fr. Tony Anatrella, Psychoanalyst, specialist in Social Psychiatry, "The world of youth today: who are they and what do they seek?" 5 – 2: The market society and liberalism, World Youth Day: From Toronto to Cologne

(Rome, 10-13 April 2003), *available at* http://www.vatican.va/roman_curia/pontifical_councils/laity/Colonia2005/rc_pc_laity_doc_20030805_p-anatrella-gmg_en.html (last visited Jan. 5, 2010). Pope John Paul II also spoke about this role in the context of communications: "The role of the non-specialist, or 'ordinary Christian/citizen[,]' in relation to media such as the audio- or video-cassette, must not be seen as that of a consumer merely. Each individual, simply by making his reactions to the media offerings placed before him known to those who produce and market them, will exercise a definite effect on the subject matter and moral tone of future offerings. The consumer must take very seriously his responsibility to make this active contribution to the protection and improvement of the media environment in which he and his dependents must exist." Message of the Holy Father for the 27th World Communications Day, Theme: Videocassettes and audiocassettes in the formation of culture and of conscience (24 January 1993), *available at* http://www.pccs.it/Documenti/HTML/Eng/GMCS/27_GMCS_Eng.htm (last visited Jan. 5, 2010).

12. Boyle, Occas. Refl. V. x. 338 (1675).

13. Benedict XVI, Angelus (Papal Summer Residence, Castel Gandolfo, Sunday 12 August 2007), *available at* http://www.vatican.va/holy_father/benedict_xvi/angelus/2007/documents/hf_ben-xvi_ang_20070812_en.html (last visited Jan. 5, 2010).

14. Daniel N. Robinson, *A Student's Guide to Psychology, ISI Guides to the Major Disciplines* (Wilmington, DE: Intercollegiate Studies Institute, 2002), 58.

15. Matthew 22:21.

16. Message for World Refugee and Migrant Day, "St. Paul Migrant, 'Apostle of the Peoples'" (Vatican City, Oct. 9, 2008) (Zenit.org). This message was written for the 95th World Day of Migrants and Refugees, held Jan. 18, 2009, *available at* http://www.vatican.va/holy_father/benedict_xvi/messages/migration/documents/hf_ben-xvi_mes_20080824_world-migrants-day_en.html (last visited Jan. 5, 2010).

17. *Ibid.*

18. *Matthew* 25:36: "Naked, and you covered me: sick, and you visited me: I was in prison, and you came to me" (Douay-Rheims Version).

19. Pastoral Visit of His Holiness Benedict XVI to Verona on the Occasion of the Fourth National Ecclesial Convention, Address of His Holiness Benedict XVI to the Participants in the Convention (Verona Exhibition Centre, Oct. 19, 2006), *available at* http://www.vatican.va/holy_father/benedict_xvi/speeches/2006/october/documents/hf_ben-xvi_spe_20061019_convegno-verona_en.html (last visited Jan. 5, 2010).

CHAPTER TWO

St. Paul, the Natural Law, and the Catholic Tradition

Robert Fastiggi
Professor of Systematic Theology,
Sacred Heart Major Seminary, Detroit, Michigan

Introduction: Paul and the Law

When we think of St. Paul and the law, we might be tempted to understand him as opposed to the law, for he writes: "We consider that a person is justified by faith apart from works of the law" (Rom 3:28).[1] Moreover, he writes in Galatians 2:16 that "by works of the law no one will be justified," and he tells the Romans, "you are not under the law but under grace" (Rom 6:14). These passages, however, must be read in their proper context. Paul is preaching the Gospel of the redeeming love of Jesus Christ and the power of His grace. In these particular passages, he is noting the inability of the Jewish cultic law to justify human beings before God. Paul, though, praises the Jewish law as "holy" (Rom 7:12), and he recognizes the importance of his own Jewish people in God's plan: "They are the Israelites; theirs the adoption, the glory, the covenants, *the giving of the law*, the worship, the promises" (Rom 9:4; emphasis mine).

For Paul, the law of the Old Covenant served as a disciplinarian or tutor (*paidagogós*), preparing the way for Christ, "that we might justified by faith" (Gal 3:25). Justification by faith and grace for Paul, however, never means freedom from the moral law. He recognizes the limits of the Jewish cultic *nomos* (law), but he is not in anyway an "antinomian," (i.e., one who espouses freedom from the moral law). Quite the contrary, he writes: "What then? Shall we sin because we are not under the law but under grace? Of course not!" (Rom 6:15). He reminds the Corinthians that "the unjust will not inherit the kingdom of God," and that "neither fornicators, nor idolaters, nor adulterers, nor catamites, nor sodomites, nor thieves, nor the greedy, nor drunkards nor robbers will inherit the kingdom of God" (1 Cor 6:9-10).

For Paul believes God has revealed these moral commands, and Christian freedom in no way exempts the faithful from moral living. Paul exhorts us to offer our bodies "as a living sacrifice, holy and pleasing to God," and he tells us not to conform ourselves to this age but to be transformed by the renewal of our minds, so we "may discern what is the will of God, what is good and pleasing and perfect" (Rom 12:2).

What about those who do not know the revealed law of God, or who do not know Christ? Are they exempt from the moral law because of ignorance? It is here that Paul introduces what we call the "natural law," especially in his letter to the Romans. We know that Paul was trained in the Jewish law as a Pharisee under Gamaliel (cf. Acts 22:3; Acts 23:6; Phil 3:6). But he was also the beneficiary of a Greek education at Tarsus, which has been called "the Athens of Asia Minor."[2] We don't know all the details of Paul's exposure to Hellenistic culture, but there is clear evidence of familiarity with Hellenistic literature. Acts 17:28 refers to the sayings of some Greek poets. Titus 1:12 repeats the saying of Epimenides, a poet from the sixth century B.C., viz., "Cretans have always been liars, vicious beasts, and lazy gluttons."[3] In 1 Cor 15:33, there is reference to the Epicurean slogan: "Let us eat and drink, for tomorrow we die."

Paul's awareness of the natural law, therefore, can be explained both in terms of his Jewish and Hellenistic training, but we must also remember that he wrote under divine inspiration. Inspiration by the Holy Spirit, however, does not take away "the powers and abilities of the human authors," as Vatican II in *Dei Verbum*, 11, reminds us. In his articulation of the natural law in Rom 2:14-15, St. Paul no doubt draws upon his Jewish awareness of Jeremiah's prophecy (Jer 31:33): that God would write His law into the human heart. It is likely, however, that he is also building upon a Hellenistic tradition of the natural law, one that goes back to Sophocles (c. 497-406 B.C.) and Heraclitus (c.535-475 B.C), who both spoke of the natural law as eternal, universal, and immutable.[4] It is also possible that St. Paul was influenced by the Stoics, who embodied the view of the natural law expressed by Cicero (c. 106- 43 B.C.): "[T]here is a true law: right reason. It is in conformity with nature, is diffused in all men, and is immutable and eternal."[5] While speculations on such influences are important, we should give primary attention to Paul's own words on the subject, composed under divine inspiration. In Rom 2:14-16, he writes:

> When the Gentiles who do not have the law (*nomon*) do by nature (*phusei*) what the law requires, they are a law to themselves, even though they do not have the law. They show that what the law requires is written on their hearts (*graptòn en tais kardias autōn*) while their conscience (*syneideseos*) also bears witness and their conflicting thoughts accuse or perhaps excuse them when, according to my gospel, God judges the secrets of men by Christ Jesus (RSV Catholic).

What does St. Paul mean when he writes that the Gentiles, by observing the moral law by nature, show that the requirements of the law are written on their hearts?" In the Bible, the "heart" is not simply the seat of human emotions, but "the vital center of life that is specifically human: sense life, the life of the will, and intellectual life."[6] The natural law for Paul is therefore a matter of the heart, which includes both the intellect and the will. This is why the *Catechism of the Catholic Church* [CCC] can describe the natural law as "present in the heart of each man and established by reason" (no. 1956).

The natural law for St. Paul (and the Catholic tradition) is distinct from conscience. In Greek, *syneidesis* (conscience) must not be confused with *synderesis*, the Thomistic term for the habitual knowledge of the first moral principles (cf. ST I, 79, 12-13), which is distinct from though closely linked to conscience. Conscience is not the natural law but the "secret core and sanctuary" of man (cf. CCC, 1776 and *Gaudium et spes*, 16) that perceives the law of God (either by the natural law or revealed law) and applies it concretely by "a judgment of reason" (cf. CCC, 1778).

For St. Paul, the law written in the heart (cf. Rom 2:15) provides a basis for the decisions of conscience, which can accuse or defend the Gentiles on the Day of Judgment when "God will judge people's hidden works in Christ Jesus" (Rom. 2:16). Moreover, because God has written the moral law (Rom 2:15) into the human heart, the Gentiles really have no excuse for transgressing the fundamental precepts of the moral law. Thus, what St. Paul says in Rom 2:14-15 resonates with what he teaches in Rom 1:19-21:

> For what can be known about God is evident to them, because God made it evident to them. Ever since the creation of the world, his invisible attributes of eternal power and divinity have been able to be understood and perceived in what he has made. As a result they have no excuse, for although they knew God they did not accord him glory as God or give him thanks. Instead, they became vain in their reasoning and their senseless minds were darkened.

For St. Paul, the natural knowledge of God attained through creation combines with the natural law written in the human heart. They both provide the Gentiles with awareness of God and his law and the possibility of salvation, because their conscience might defend them on the Day of Judgment (cf. Rom 2:15). The natural law, however, removes from the Gentiles the automatic excuse of ignorance. All human beings—Gentiles as well as Jews and Christians—are bound to God's law because it is written into the human heart.

St. Augustine and St. Thomas Aquinas on Rom 2:14-15 and the Natural Law

St. Paul's articulation of the natural law in Rom 2:14-15 plays a major role in the Catholic tradition. As is well known, the Fathers of the Church drew upon both ancient philosophy and the Scriptures. There were, however, several competing notions of the natural law in the ancient world. The Roman jurist, Ulpian (d. 228 A.D) understood the natural law as "what nature teaches all animals," i.e. "the law of nature."[7] In contrast to this instinctual or biological description of natural law, there was Sophocles' awareness of "the unchangeable unwritten code of Heaven."[8] There was also, as we have seen, Cicero's description of the natural law as "right reason." Further distinctions were made in Roman times between the civil law (*ius civile*), the law for foreigners (*ius gentium*), and the natural law (*ius naturale*), but the meanings of these were not always consistent.[9]

These Greco-Roman concepts combined with the Scripture to provide Catholic thinkers with a basic sense of the natural law. Church Fathers, such as St. Augustine (354-430) and St. John Chrysostom (c. 344-407) refer to the natural law, if not by name, at least in concept.[10]

St. Augustine (354-430) refers to an "order of nature" (*naturalis ordo*) in *The City of God* 19:15, and he also speaks of an unchangeable "rational" law that is distinct from human law and implanted in the human conscience (cf. *The City of God*, 11:27 and the *Confessions* 2.4.9). Thus, he writes, "we have another and far superior sense, belonging to the inner man, by which we perceive what things are just, and what unjust—just by means of an intelligible idea, unjust by the want of it."[11]

But despite these manifestations of Augustine's awareness of the natural law, there is not in the corpus of St. Augustine, "any extensive or systematic treatise on the role of the law."[12] Moreover, with regard to the classical Pauline text of Rom 2:14-15, Augustine, in *De spiritu et littera*, chapters 43-45 (c. 412 A.D.), offers an interpretation that would not be typical of the later Catholic tradition. In this text, Augustine argues that the observance by the Gentiles of what the law requires (Rom 2:14) shows that the Gospel has purified them and enabled them, by grace, to observe the moral law. Therefore, the Gentiles referred to in Rom 2:14-15 are those Gentiles who believe in the Gospel, "since to them, on their believing, it is the power of God unto salvation."[13] For Augustine, Rom 2:14-15 must be read in light of Rom 2:8-13, where the crucial point is that "there will be glory, honor, and peace for everyone who does good, Jew first and then Greek. There is no partiality with God" (Rom 2:10-11). Because "Greek" is the equivalent of "Gentile," Augustine maintains that

> [It] follows that such Gentiles as have the law written in their hearts belong to the gospel, since to them, on their believing, it is the power of God unto salvation. To what Gentiles, however, would he promise glory, and honor, and peace, in their doing of good works, if living without the grace of the gospel? Since there is no respect of persons with God, and since it is not hearers of the law, but the doers thereof, that are justified, it follows that any man of any nation, whether Jew or Greek, who shall believe, will equally have salvation under the gospel. "For there is no difference," as he says afterwards; "for all have sinned and come short of the glory of God: being justified freely by his grace" (Rom 3:22-22). How then could

> he say that any Gentile person, who was a doer of the law, was justified without the Savior's grace?[14]

Since observing the moral law without grace is not sufficient for salvation, Augustine believes that the Gentiles who by nature observe the moral law are those Gentiles who have become Christians. For Augustine, there is no salvation apart from the grace of Christ, so "glory and honor" can only be given to those who are justified by the Savior's grace. Of course, later Catholic theology will raise the question whether the saving grace of Christ can be communicated to those who are outside of the Church "through no fault of their own."[15]

Whether observance of the commandments via the natural law contributes in some way to salvation is a complex question. Much depends on whether those who observe the natural law are responding, in some hidden way, to the grace of Christ. The question before us now, however, is how Augustine's reading of Rom 2:14-15 compares to later Catholic articulations of the natural law. In this regard, it might be helpful to compare St. Augustine's exegesis of Rom 2:14-15 with that of St. Thomas Aquinas.

St. Thomas Aquinas (c. 1225-1274), in the *Summa theologica* I-II, 91, 2 describes the natural law as the "participation of the eternal law in the rational creature" (*participatio legis aeternae in rationali creatura*) whereby the rational creature "has a natural inclination to its proper act and end" (*naturalem inclinationem ad debitum actum, et finem*);[16] the natural law is also "an imprint in us of the Divine light" (*impressio divini luminis in nobis*).[17] For St. Thomas, "a law is something pertaining to reason" (ST I-II, 91, 2 ad 3), and therefore, the natural law always pertains to the "order of reason" (*ordo rationis*).

St. Thomas Aquinas, however, cites Rom 2:14-15 to refute the claim that there is no natural law in us. After quoting Rom 2:24 in ST I-II, 91, 2, he cites the gloss that observes: "Although [the Gentiles] have no written law, yet they have the natural law whereby each one knows, and is conscious of, what is good and what is evil."

This understanding of St. Thomas (and the medieval gloss), as we will see, becomes standard in the Catholic tradition. The natural law represents the knowledge of the moral law by natural reason distinct from the knowledge of the moral law by divine revelation or divine positive law. Reason and revelation, though, work together and often reinforce the same moral principles. In this context, St. Thomas cites Rom 2:14 in support of his claim that "the moral precepts of the Old Law" belong to the "law of nature." In other words, the basic moral teachings of the Decalogue belong to the order of reason and, therefore, to the natural law (cf. ST I-II, 100, 1). Nevertheless, for a number of reasons, it was important that God teach or reinforce these moral precepts through the revealed or divine law (cf. ST I-II, 91, 4). The divine positive law was needed, first, because human beings need laws that direct them to their final end; second, because human judgment is uncertain; third, because only God is competent to make laws pertaining to the judgment of interior, hidden matters; and finally, insofar as human law is unable to punish every evil deed, there is a need for a divine law whereby no evil deed is left unpunished.

Natural Law and the Magisterium

We have seen that Augustine and Aquinas offer different interpretations of Rom 2:14-15. But what does the Church say? To answer this question, it is helpful to survey the insights on Rom 2:14-15 and the natural law found in magisterial interventions.

In 473 A.D., the Council of Arles required the priest, Lucidus, to affirm that "over the course and sequence of the centuries, some were saved by the law of grace, others by the law of Moses, others by the law of nature (*lege naturae*), which God had written into the hearts of all [cf. Rom 2:15] in the hope of the coming of Christ; but since the beginning of the world, no one has been liberated from the bond of original [sin] except through the intercession of the sacred blood."[18] Here we see that the natural law or "the law of nature" served as a means of preparation for the reception of salvation through the power of Christ's blood in a manner analogous to the Law of Moses. In his book, *The Meaning of Grace*, [Cardinal] Charles Journet observed that in this "age of the natural law,"

> ... grace came into men's hearts by adapting itself to the movements of nature. When man obeyed the true impulses of his nature to perform good acts, when he chose the morally good, grace was there in secret, bearing him up to make contact with realities of a higher and more mysterious kind ... Grace came down into his soul in the guise of the movements of nature, drawing him towards ends far beyond those he could know by his natural powers.[19]

If the natural law could prepare human beings to receive the saving grace of Christ before the coming of the Savior, it can also serve now to move human beings to salvation "who through no fault of their own, do not know the Gospel of Christ or his Church, but who nevertheless seek God with a sincere heart, and, moved by grace, try in their actions to do his will as they know it through the dictates of their conscience."[20]

In his Bull "*Ex omnibus afflictionibus*" of Oct. 1, 1567, Pope Pius V censured the following proposition of the proto-Jansenist, Michel de Bay:

> They think like Pelagius who understand the text of Romans 2 of the Apostle: "The Gentiles, who do not have the law, by nature do what the law requires" [Rom 2:14] as referring to the Gentiles who do not have the grace of faith [D-H, 1922].

Here we see that St. Pius V rejected the argument of Michel de Bay that applying Rom 2:14 to the Gentiles lacking faith was a denial of the need for grace (i.e., the Pelagian position). Pius V affirmed the Catholic understanding of Rom

2:14 as referring to the knowledge of the divine law apart from the gift of supernatural faith, i.e. via the natural law.

Pope Clement XI, in his 1713 constitution, *Unigenitus Dei Filius*, condemned 101 errors of the Jansenist, Pasquier Quesnel. Among these errors was the denial of any true natural knowledge of God. According to Quesnel, without divine grace, any knowledge of God can only produce "presumption, vanity and opposition to God Himself." Against this error, Clement XI cites Rom 1:19 [D-H, 2441] where St. Paul states that God has made Himself known to the Gentiles. The condemnation of this Jansenist error shows the confidence the Catholic Church has in the natural knowledge of God.

The same confidence in the natural knowledge of God is manifested at Vatican I, where, in the Dogmatic Constitution, *Dei Filius*, Rom 1:20 is cited as evidence that God can be known by the natural light of human reason (cf. D-H, 3004 and 3015). The Catholic Church, therefore, affirms a twofold order of knowledge: natural and supernatural. Although natural reason cannot know the mysteries of the faith, it is sufficient to know "the one true God," and those who say that the "one true God, our Creator and Lord, cannot be known with certitude by the natural light of human reason through the things that are made" are anathematized (cf. D-H, 3026). St. Paul, we can see, provides the scriptural warrant for affirming the knowledge of God by natural reason, and the light of human reason is intimately connected with the natural law.

After Vatican I, the Pauline doctrines of the natural knowledge of God and the natural law are consistently upheld by the Magisterium. The very first affirmation of the Anti-Modernist Oath of 1910 cites Rom 1:20 to testify that, "God, the beginning and end of all things, can be known with certainty and also demonstrated by the light of natural reason (*naturali rationis lumine*)" [D-H, 3538]. Vatican II, in its *Dogmatic Constitution on Divine Revelation, Dei Verbum*, also reaffirms this infallible teaching of the Catholic Church by citing Rom 1:20 (no. 6).

The appeals to Rom 2:14-15 in support of the natural law are likewise found in the more recent Magisterium. Blessed John XXIII, in his 1963 encyclical, *Pacem in terris*, notes that: "The world's Creator has stamped man's inmost being with an order revealed to man by his conscience; and his conscience insists on his preserving it" (no. 5). He then cites Rom 2:15: "Men 'show that the work of the law is written in their heart. Their conscience bears witness to them" (no. 5). Vatican II, in its *Pastoral Constitution on the Church in the Modern World, Gaudium et spes*, also refers to Rom 2:15-16 in teaching that: "Man has in his heart a law written by God; to obey it is the very dignity of man; according to it he will be judged" (no. 16).

In his writings, John Paul II consistently appealed to Rom 2:14-15 to underscore the importance of the "law written in the human heart." We find him citing Rom 2:15 as a point of departure for his discussion of freedom and the natural law in *Veritatis splendor* [1993], no. 46. In confirming the grave immorality of the killing of an innocent human being in *Evangelium vitae* [1995] no. 57, he states that: "This doctrine, based on that unwritten law which man, in the light of reason, finds in his own heart (cf. Rom 2:14-15), is reaffirmed by Sacred Scripture, transmitted by the Tradition of the Church and taught by the ordinary and universal Magisterium."

Pope Benedict XVI has followed suite. In an address given on Feb.12, 2007 to the participants in an international congress on the natural moral law, he observed that the reliance on the empirical approach to knowledge "makes us incapable of seeing the ethical message contained in being, a message that tradition calls *lex naturalis*, natural moral law." He goes on to observe:

> It is precisely in the light of this contestation that all the urgency of the necessity to reflect upon the theme of natural law and to rediscover its truth common to all men appears. The said law, to which the Apostle Paul refers (cf. Rom 2:14-15) is written on the heart of man and is consequently, even today, accessible."[21]

Our brief survey of magisterial statements shows a consistent appreciation of Rom 1:19-20 and Rom 2:14-15 as fundamental texts for affirming man's natural awareness of God and of the moral law by means of the natural law written into the human heart. In this regard, it seems that the Magisterium has opted for a more Thomistic rather than Augustinian reading of Rom 2:14-15.[22]

Four applications of St. Paul's natural law doctrine

How do St. Paul's doctrines relating to the natural law apply to us today? I would suggest four main applications.

First, there is the knowledge of God by natural reason (cf. Rom 1:19-20), which establishes a common reference point for transcendent truth, meaning, and purpose. Thus, Vatican I, in *Dei Filius*, anathematizes those who deny that "the One, true God, our Creator and Lord, cannot be known with certainty with the natural light of human reason through the things that are created" (D-H, 3026; cf. D-H, 3004 and 3015 where Rom 1:20 is cited in support of this doctrine).

Second, the eternal law inscribed in the human heart (cf. Rom 2:14-15) provides support for universal moral norms. As we have seen, John Paul II cites Rom 2:15 as the heading above *Veritatis splendor*, 46, where he discusses the universal character of sexual moral norms.

Third, there is the unity of the human race, as testified by Acts 17:26: "and [God] made from one every nation of men to live on the face of the earth." This unity of the human race serves as the precondition for the concept of international law, the law of nations, (*ius gentium*) developed by Francisco de Vitoria, O.P (c. 1483-1546) and Francisco Suárez, S.J. (1548-1617). Vitoria spoke of a certain kinship that exists among all human beings, insofar as all share a common nature and a common end.[23] Suárez elaborates on the same theme in *De legibus*, lib. 2, cap. 19, n. 9 [published in 1612]:

> Although divided into various peoples and kingdoms, the human race always has a certain unity, which is not only that of a species, but also one that is political and moral, which the precept of mutual love and mercy proclaims, a precept that extends to all, even to strangers, and of any condition whatsoever. Hence, though each autonomous city, state or kingdom is in itself a complete community, and made up of its members, nonetheless any one of them is also a member in some way of the world, insofar as it belongs to the human race. For these communities will never singly be so self-sufficient that they will not need mutual help and fellowship, as well as communication, sometimes for a better mode of life and greater utility, sometimes indeed out of moral necessity and need, as the actual state of affairs makes clear. For this reason they will need some law, by which they can be directed and rightly ordered in this kind of communication and fellowship.[24]

The importance of Acts 17:26-27 in its application to the international law has likewise been underscored by recent popes. In his 1998 encyclical, *Fides et ratio*, John Paul II links Paul's testimony to the unity of the human race (Acts 17:26) to the universal desire of human beings to know, a desire which also "looks to the good which is to be performed" (*Fides et ratio*, 24-25). In addressing the General Assembly of the United Nations on April 18, 2008, Pope Benedict XVI pointed to "unity of the human family" and "the innate dignity of every man and woman" as truths that are affirmed in Scripture, the natural law, and by the United Nations itself. He explained that such principles of the international order have been long recognized by the Catholic Church:

> The principle of "responsibility to protect" was considered by the ancient *ius gentium* as the foundation of every action taken by those in government with regard to the governed: at the time when the concept of national sovereign States was first developing, the Dominican Friar, Francisco de Vitoria, rightly considered as a precursor of the idea of the United Nations, described this responsibility as an aspect of natural reason shared by all nations, and the result of an international order whose task it was to regulate relations between peoples. Now as then, this principle has to invoke the idea of the person as image of the Creator, the desire for the absolute, and the essence of freedom.[25]

Fourth, there is the natural structure of human acts and relations (cf. Rom 1:24-27; 1 Cor 6:12- 7:10; Eph 5:28-33), which roots human sexuality in the embodied dignity of the human person as male and female. This is not reducing human sexuality to "physicalism," as some Catholic revisionist theologians (e.g., Fr. Charles Curran) have claimed. Rather, it is applying the law of reason to the natural ordering of human sexual acts (cf. John Paul II, *Veritatis splendor*, 47-50). In this context, the true meaning of the natural law is discovered in reference to "man's proper and primordial nature, 'the nature of the human person,' which is the person himself in the unity of soul and body, in the unity of his spiritual and biological inclinations and of all the other specific characteristics necessary for the pursuit of his end" (*Veritatis splendor*, 50).

Conclusion

This brief survey of the Catholic theological and magisterial tradition shows how important St. Paul is for understanding the meaning and application of the natural law. Because the demands of God's law are written into the hearts of all human beings (Rom 2:15), and because all human beings can know God through what He has made, there is a common, universal basis for morality and human rights. Perhaps it was providential that the Year of St. Paul coincided with the sixtieth anniversary of the Universal Declaration of Human Rights by the United Nations. On Dec. 10, 2008, the Pontifical Council for Justice and Peace held a celebration of the 1948 Universal Declaration. In this regard, we can appreciate how important St. Paul has been and is for the Catholic understanding of universal human rights. The great Apostle to the Gentiles, inspired by the Holy Spirit, affirmed the natural law that unites the hearts and minds of all human beings and prepares them for the grace and truth found only in Christ Jesus.

Notes

1. All scriptural translations are from the *New American Bible* (1987) unless otherwise indicated.

2. *The New World Dictionary-Concordance to the New American Bible* (New York: World Bible Publishers, 1970), 517.

3. Many scholars today believe that Titus was written by a disciple of Paul rather than by Paul himself. Nevertheless, the letter still forms part of the "Pauline corpus."

4. See Jacques Maritain, *Natural Law: Reflections on Theory and Practice* (South Bend, IN: St. Augutnine's Press, 2001), 26.

5. Cicero, *Rep.* III, 22, 33: cited in the *Catechism of the Catholic Church*, 1956.

6. *The New World Dictionary-Concordance to the New American Bible*, 230.

7. Cf. Willam E. May, *An Introduction to Moral Theology*, Second Edition (Huntington, IN: Our Sunday Visitor, 2003), 80.

8. Cf. Sophocles, *Antigone*, ii. 452-460; cited in Maritain, 26.

9. Cf. T.A. Wassmer and S.A. Long, "Natural Law," in *New Catholic Encyclopedia*, Second Edition Vol. 10 (Detroit: Thomson Gale, 2003), 180.

10. *Ibid.*, 181.

11. St. Augustine, *The City of God*, Book XI, 27 trans. Marcus Dods (New

York: Random House, 1950), 372.

12. Richard J. Dougherty, "Natural Law," in *Augustine Through the Ages: An Encyclopedia* ed. Allan D. Ftizgerald, O.S.A. et al. (Grand Rapids, MI: Willaim B. Eedrmans, 1999), 583.

13. St. Augustine, *On the Spirit and the Letter*, chapter XLIV, in *The Basic Writings of St. Augustine*, Vol. 1 ed. W.J. Oates (New York: Random House, 1948), 495.

14. *Ibid.*

15. Cf. Vatican II, *Lumen gentium*, 16 and the *Catechism of the Catholic Church*, 847.

16. The Latin text is from the Leonine edition of 1894; the English translation here is from St. Thomas Aquinas, *Summa Theologica*, Volume II trans. Fathers of the English Dominican Province (Allen, TX: Christian Classics, 1981), 997.

17. *Summa theologica* I-II, 91, 2.

18. Denzinger, Heinrich and Peter Hünermann, *Enchiridion symbolorum definitionum et declarationum de rebus fidei et morum* 40th ed. [Freiburg: Herder, 2005]:henceforth, D-H., 341. All translations from Denzinger are my own.

19. Charles Journet, *The Meaning of Grace* trans. A.V. Littledale (Princeton, N.J.: Scepter Publishers, 1996), 95.

20. *Catechism of the Catholic Church*, 847; Vatican II, *Lumen gentium*, 16

21. Translation taken from the Vatican website (www.vatican.va).

22. Of course, some passages of Augustine harmonize better with the magisterial tradition than what we have examined in *De spiritu et littera*.

23. Cf. Robert Fastiggi, "Vitoria, Francisco de," in Michael L. Coutler et al. eds. *Encyclopedia of Catholic Social Thought, Social Science and Social Policy* (Lanham, MD: Scarecrow Press, 2007), 1125-1127. See also Francisco de Vitoria, "On the American Indians" 3, 1 where, citing Sirach 13:15, he notes that "amity (*amicitia*) between men is part of natural law;" see *Vitoria: Political Writings* ed. A Pagden and J. Lawrance (Cambridge: Cambridge University Press, 1991), 279.

24. Translation adopted with slight modification from José Pereira, "The Achievement of Suárez and the Suarezianisation of Thomism," in A. Cardoso et al. eds. *Francisco Suárez (1548-1617): Tradição e Modernidade* (Lisbon: Ediçōes Colibri, 1999), 156.

25. As cited on the Vatican website (www.vatican.va). In his more recent encyclical, *Caritas in veritate* [June 29, 2009], Pope Benedict XVI affirms the human race as "a single family working together in true communion" (no. 53), and he notes that "in all cultures there are examples of ethical convergence, some isolated, some interrelated, as an expression of the one human nature, willed by the Creator; the tradition of ethical wisdom knows this as the natural law" (no. 59).

Response to Robert Fastiggi

Brian Scarnecchia
Associate Professor,
Ave Maria School of Law, Naples, Florida

God's signature "in the things he has made,"[1] and in the natural law "written upon the fleshy tablets of our hearts"[2] provides the only firm foundation for a culture of human rights. When the laws of nature and the natural moral law are not seen as self-evident proof of God's providence directing all creation and orienting human freedom, then the great truths about human dignity are threatened with all their consequences for international relations, the rights of nations and human solidarity.

Only the Fool Says there is No God

Dr. Fastiggi writes: "For St. Paul, the natural knowledge of God, attained through creation, combines with the natural law written in the human heart. They both provide the Gentiles with awareness of God and his law . . . ."[3]

God reveals himself to us through the *works* he performs and through the *words* he speaks naturally and supernaturally. Supernaturally, through the eyes of faith, God has revealed himself through the patriarchs, priests, prophets, and kings of Israel:

> Revelation is realized by deeds and words, which are intrinsically bound up with each other. As a result, the works performed by God in the history of salvation show forth and bear out the doctrine and realities signified by the words; the words, for their part, proclaim the works, and bring to light the mystery they contain.[4]

In the fullness of time, God provided the complete revelation of himself through the words and works of his only begotten son, Jesus Christ. When asked by the followers of John the Baptist if he was the Messiah or if they should expect another, Jesus replied by pointing to his works: "Go back and report to John what you hear and see: the blind recover their sight, cripples walk, lepers are cured, the deaf hear, dead men are raised to life, and the poor have the good news preached to them."[5]

Analogous to God's supernatural revelation of himself through faith, God has revealed himself naturally through reason. Reason can detect in the mighty *work* of creation a design that makes manifest God's "invisible attributes of eternal power and divinity."[6] God, who has revealed his existence and providence in his work of creation, also speaks an interior *word*, the natural law, written upon the fleshy tablet of the human heart,[7] interpreted through the quasi-prophetic voice of each person's conscience:

> According to St. Paul, conscience in a certain sense confronts man with the law, and thus becomes a 'witness' for man; a witness of his own faithfulness or unfaithfulness with regard to the law, of his essential moral rectitude or iniquity . . . . St. Bonaventure teaches that 'conscience is like God's herald and messenger; it does not command things on its own authority, but commands them as coming from God's authority, like a herald when he proclaims the edict of the king. This is why conscience has binding force.'[8]

Reason sees the links between the unimaginably intricate design in all creation and an all-knowing and all-powerful and imaginative Designer, the recognition of which should lead to spontaneous wonder and awe:

> It is reason that recognizes direction toward an end, plan, intention, design, and purpose in nature, and it does so in ever greater measure. The more we are able to know, the more complete and detailed our knowledge of the processes of life, the greater—in my view—our wonder and admiration should become. Conversely, it becomes all the more irrational to derive all of this . . . from an 'unguided, unplanned process of random variations and natural selection.'[9]

Therefore, anyone who fails to see God in the works he has made or hear his word in the silence of their heart has, St. Paul tells, "stultified" themselves.[10] In punishment, divine retribution pays them back in their own coin. Because they made themselves stupid, having willfully denied what is self evident and exchanged "the glory of the immortal God for images representing man," God abandoned them to their lusts and to every kind of wickedness epitomized in the unnatural vice of homosexual acts "where they receive in their own bodies the penalty for their perversity."[11] Because they refused to see what their eyes could not deny, the Designer in the great design of creation, and failed to heed the natural law in the depths of their hearts, whose voice they cannot help but hear, God gave them over to unreasonable and unnatural behavior. Their public and irrational denial of God's existence merits as punishment God's abandonment of them to their irrational lusts and a public display of unnatural behavior.[12]

St. Paul's use of poetic justice serves to further substantiate natural law. It shows that God is not arbitrary and capricious, but avails Himself of the norms of reasonableness. Poetic justice underscores the fact that true law is not based on the will of the lawmaker but on an ordinance of reason that everyone, Jew and Gentile alike, can understand:

> [P]rophets who use the notion of poetic justice are implicitly appealing to a human consensus about what sort of acts are just and unjust, which is not logically derived from the revelation of moral norms by God, but rests on ideas about ethics formed by reason—which one might conveniently refer to as natural law . . . . For the moral principles which rational men can recognize are not other than the principles on which God himself works when judging the actions of men.[13]

Do Only Simpletons See Design In Creation?

In an op-ed article to the New York Times, Cardinal Schönborn defended the thesis that creation exhibits intelligent design; that the best evidence simply does not support the conclusion that creation is the product of random chance. In reply, Richard Dawkins, atheist biologist and apologist for Darwinism and author of *Unweaving the Rainbow*, labeled Cardinal Schönborn a "simpleton."[14] Cardinal Schönborn distinguished evolution, a scientific theory, from Dawkins' "evolutionism":

> What I call evolutionism is an ideological view that says evolution can explain everything in the whole development of the cosmos, from the Big Bang to Beethoven's Ninth Symphony . . . . Can matter create intelligence? This question cannot be answered scientifically, because the scientific method cannot grasp it. Here we can only argue philosophically, metaphysically or religiously. Reason can recognize that matter cannot organize itself. That it at least needs information, and information is an expression of intelligence.[15]

The Cardinal premised his opposition to evolutionism, as St. Paul did in his letter to the Romans, on the fact that when confronted with the whole complexity of life, it is unreasonable to explain it as mere random process: "No person who experiences such complexity would say that it created itself. That's the point. The second step is to ask—Ok, which intelligence? As a believer, I naturally think it is the intelligence of the Creator. And 90 percent of humanity thinks so too."[16] Cardinal Schonborn explained that he is doing what Pope Benedict XVI has repeatedly asked the church to do: "[D]efend reason against a reductionism that in the end, ideologically speaking is a kind of materialism."[17] He lamented that the ideology of evolutionism has led to ruthless reductionism in economics: "In western societies we have the model of open competition in a fully deregulated free-market economy. We overlook the fact that the economy needs first of all a model of cooperation and not a model built on the survival of the fittest."[18]

In his book, *Chance or Purpose?: Creation, Evolution, and a Rational Faith*, Cardinal Schönborn contrasts right reason with the "power knowledge" ushered in at the time of the Enlightenment when the "language of creation" and "any message from the Creator" was eliminated "so that sheer utility, with no limitations" might become the model to determine everything.[19] Power knowledge brought into a dominant cultural position the two ideologies of Marxism and Darwinism. He says, it was "no accident that Friedrich Engels, after reading Darwin's *Origin of Species*, wrote enthusiastically to Marx that here they had found the scientific basis for their theory."[20]

The Discovery of a New World Sparked the Development of Human Rights

Today a "new world" is being discovered, not by explorers, but by scientists. As in the past, with its benefits there will come dangers.[21] Dr. Fastiggi draws our attention, in his third application of St. Paul's Natural Law doctrine, to the works of Francisco de Vitoria, O.P. (†1546) and Francisco Suarez, S.J. (†1617). Goaded by the discovery of a New World and the abuses visited upon its indigenous people by colonists, these two founders of International Law fashioned a law of nations based on "a certain kinship that exists among all human beings, insofar as all share a common nature and a common end."[22]

In 1537, the reverberations of Vitoria's lectures at Salamanca on the rights of indigenous persons had produced such a positive effect that "Pope Paul III issued two Briefs wherein he upheld the fundamental equality of Indians who possess a human soul and are 'truly men.' He excommunicated Catholic colonists in the New World who deprived the Indians of life, liberty or property."[23] Although the legacy of Francisco de Vitoria was honored in 1976 by the United Nations, who claimed him as their precursor and "Father of International Law,"[24] the lessons he taught have been rejected.

The modern age has suffered at the hands of those who "worshiped and served the creature rather than the Creator."[25] In the eclipse of God since the French Revolution in 1789, human law was increasingly seen as an expression of the "general will" of Rousseau rather than a rational ordering. First, the Deists and Jacobins denied that God, the Great Architect, had any concern for the world he had set in motion. With God out of the picture except as an indifferent cosmological background, human beings had no common point of reference beyond and above their own special interests. They imagined a state of nature where persons turned on each other as wolves, and tried to create a Leviathan, an absolute State to impose order on all,[26] or power-mechanisms in a free-for-all society to secure the "survival of the fittest."[27] Then the collectivists, the Bolshevists, Fascists, and the Nazis adopted the notion of law as a manifestation of the general will to deny human dignity to certain groups and to further their special interests. Finally, and still with us today, are those who seek to dominate the world through an ideology of radical individualism and *laissez faire* economic liberalism and have "plunged humanity into the global crisis we are now experiencing in the awesome confrontation of a culture of life and a culture of death, a philosophy of love and a philosophy of hate."[28]

In the debate over creation and evolution, how we answer the questions of whether God is evident in the things he has made, and whether there is, in human nature, an inherent law concerning what is rational moral behavior, has a huge impact on the continued viability of a truly human civilization. If St. Paul is wrong and God is neither heard in our individual conscience nor seen in creation, then, as Dostoyevsky implied in *Brothers Karamazov*, all things are possible.[29] This, then, becomes the test of a culture of human rights today: "whether science can be combined with a sustainable responsibility for creation" and whether we can formulate "basic ethical guidelines capable of underpinning a high-technology civilization and its capabilities, which threaten our very existence."[30]

Pope John Paul II warned that we are witnessing an "eclipse of the sense of God" that provides a breeding ground for hedonism, utilitarianism and extreme individualism. In the penumbra of this eclipse, the world looks remarkably similar, he tells us, to that of St. Paul who rebuked the Romans for thinking they were wise when they had become fools, unable to distinguish right from wrong.[31] In the eclipse of God and the accompanying eclipse of reason, we find "the values of being are replaced by those of having" and a so-called quality of life ethic interpreted as economic efficiency, consumerism, physical beauty and pleasure are valued "to the neglect of the more profound dimensions—interpersonal, spiritual and religious—of existence."[32] We end up worshiping creatures, ourselves, in this eclipse that deforms God's image in us and tempts us to offenses against others as well; "the profound meaning of man is betrayed and communion between people is compromised."[33]

On the fiftieth anniversary of the *Universal Declaration of Human Rights* (1948), the United Nations General Assembly affirmed that the human genome would provide the new ground for human rights when it endorsed the *Universal Declaration on the Human Genome and Human Rights* (1998). While the *Declaration on the Human Genome and Human Rights* condemns certain practices, such as reproductive cloning and genetic discrimination, it failed to protect the inherent dignity of prenatal human beings who possess a complete copy of the human genome. How can the human genome be entitled to dignity while the human person from whom it comes is not?[34]

If the common ground of human rights is the purely material substance of the human genome, how can the determination of right and wrong behavior ever have binding normative value? How can we blame the Deists, Jacobins, Bolshevists, Fascists, Nazis of the past, or the international money interests of today for trampling underfoot all who oppose their special interests, while disguising it as an expression of the "general will?" As Cardinal Schönborn says, "Genes are not responsible for anything. They are not prosecuted in law when they produce cancer cells."[35]

Exalting the human genome as the common ground of human rights may legitimize a neo-eugenics movement. In the past, decisive negation of belief in creation combined social Darwinism and its cult of the strongest with pseudo-racial theories to produce a "most horrific expression in National Socialism."[36] Even Richard Dawkins admits that social Darwinism is a prescription for Fascism: "No decent person wants to live in a society which works according to Darwinian laws . . . . A Darwinian society would be a Fascist state."[37]

Discovering A Great Hope Provides The Substance Of A New World

St. Paul contrasted the great hope of Christians with the despair of those who fail to see the Creator in the things he has made, and who live under the dominion of the "elemental spirits of the universe."[38] Quoting Saint Gregory of Nazianzen, Pope Benedict XVI explained in *Spe Salvi*, that when the star-following Magi adored Christ, astrology came to an end, because the stars were now seen as moving in an orbit determined by Christ. It is not immutable blind laws of "matter and of evolution that have the final say," but a Person who loves us:

> And if we know this Person and he knows us, then truly the inexorable power of material elements no longer has the last word; we are not slaves of the universe and of its laws, we are free. In ancient times, honest enquiring minds were aware of this. Heaven is not empty. Life is not a simple product of laws and the randomness of matter, but within everything and at the same time above everything, there is a personal will, there is a Spirit who in Jesus has revealed himself as Love.[39]

As Pope Benedict tells us, faith in the meaningfulness of the universe and the value of each person's life, confirmed in the Advent of the Spirit behind the ordered cosmos, provided a new "substance" upon which the early Christians could stand firm, beyond the material substance perceptible to their senses. This new substance was faith in Christ which, as its first deposit, provided hope in eternal life, that is, in perfect happiness. That hope makes present to the believer "in embryo," so to speak, the things that are hoped for. Because perfect happiness is already present in embryo, it creates "certainty" and an interior attitude so that the present is touched by the future reality.[40] This new substance, this new *terra firma*, sets Christians free to "resist the overbearing power of ideology and its political organs," a resistance which martyrs and ascetics demonstrate so well.[41]

Pope Benedict warned that the temptation today is to lose hope in the new substance provided by faith in Christ and the perfect happiness already experienced in embryo, and return to a world dominated by belief in the laws of nature and technology's ability to save us and bring about an earthly paradise, "the kingdom of man."[42] A political realization of such false hope first surfaced in the French Revolution,[43] and then in the "scientifically conceived politics" of Marx.[44] These false hopes led to the belief that the right state of human affairs and the moral well being of the world could be guaranteed through good structures alone. But as Pope Benedict states, this is not the case:

> Even the best structures function only when the community is animated by convictions capable of motivating people to assent freely to the social order . . . . Anyone who promises the better world that is guaranteed to last for ever is making a false promise; he is overlooking human freedom . . . . If there were structures which could irrevocably guarantee a determined—good—state of the world, man's freedom would be denied, and hence they would not be good structures at all.[45]

Good structures help, but are not enough. Man cannot be saved from outside.[46] It is not science and good structures that from without will redeem man but a supernatural love with the power to transcend death that alone is capable of transforming man from within.[47] Our age needs desperately to rediscover this truth now that the hope of creating a perfect world through scientific knowledge and scientifically based politics is constantly receding.[48]

Ultimately, Pope Benedict tells us, a culture of human rights depends on a capacity for suffering that unleashes in the human spirit a sense of justice, the ability to give each their due:

> Is the other important enough to warrant my becoming, on his account, a person who suffers? Does truth matter to me enough to make suffering worthwhile? . . . [I]n truly great trials, where I must make a definitive decision to place the truth before my own welfare, career[,] and possessions, I need the certitude of that true, great hope of which we have spoken here.[49]

Conclusion

In December of 2007, I was invited by the Secretariat of State of the Holy See, together with eighty-five other representatives, to participate in the first gathering of "Non-Governmental Organizations (NGOs) of Catholic inspiration" in Rome. At the close of the meeting, Pope Benedict XVI delivered an address. He spoke in the spirit of Francisco de Vitoria, asking all NGOs of Catholic inspiration to "counter relativism creatively by presenting the great truths about man's innate dignity and the rights which are derived from that dignity."[50] He also warned that the current regime of international relations was marked "by a relativistic logic" that sought to secure peaceful coexistence and the bases for international norms not on the truth about man and his dignity or an ethic based on recognition of the natural moral law, but instead upon "consensus between states—a consensus conditioned at times by short-term interests or manipulated by ideological pressure."[51]

At the heart of the tensions in international relations is the question of sovereignty. Jacques Maritan pointed out that the rights of man and the obligations of the State require a common understanding that only God is sovereign.[52] Today, the State seeks to take the place of God and religion and dominate public life and culture.[53] In this way, the state becomes an idol and demands our ultimate allegiance. When St. Paul was taken in chains to Rome, he gave witness to Christ, and therefore, to God, evident in Creation and in conscience. In the recent past, Christians gave similar witness before a tyrant State:

> Karl Barth ... fled [Nazi Germany], not because it was tyrannical but because it was idolatrous; it put the State where God ought to be; it proposed to replace the church. It was evil because of that claim—and this quite apart from what it did.[54]

Today, reference to "a higher moral law which rests upon God" is still a point of convergence for persons from diverse cultures and an antidote to the relativistic logic which threatens international relations.[55]

In the collapse of the cultural convictions that God is knowable by reason from the things he has made and by a law written deep within the human heart, we who teach in Catholic seminaries and schools of law have a service to perform; we must strive to rekindle in our students a *great hope*. As Pope Benedict said, it is our duty to form a new generation of leaders, "animated by convictions capable of motivating people to assent freely to the social order" permeated with the "great truths about man's innate dignity and the rights which are derived from that dignity." The natural revelation of God in conscience and creation combined with his complete revelation through faith in the Person behind creation, the Logos, "born of [a] woman,"[56] provides great hope. This faith provides a firm certainty in the ultimate meaningfulness of all human life, and in ethical norms not derived from consensus, but rather non-negotiable, and inalienable. It is vitally important that we, like Francisco de Vitoria and Francisco Suarez, motivated by the new discoveries of our day, apply the natural law to those most at risk in the new world discovered by scientists, especially the human embryo, from those willfully blind to the "language of creation" and guided solely by utilitarian "power knowledge."

Thomas Jefferson warned that should firm certainty in God be undermined in the United States, the culture of human rights upon which this nation was founded would fall. "Can the liberties of a nation be thought secure when we have removed their only firm basis, a conviction in the minds of the people that their liberties are a gift from God?"[57] Therefore, like St. Paul, we must not be "ashamed of the gospel"[58] or of being called simpletons by those who, wittingly or unwittingly, threaten the foundations of a culture of human rights by closing their eyes and their hearts to the signature of God in conscience and creation. We serve our country well when we proclaim the great hope we have in the unity of faith and reason[59] exhibited in the Christian idea of the world—"that it originated in a very complicated process of evolution but that it, nevertheless, still comes in its depths from the Logos. It thus bears reason in itself."[60]

Notes

1. Romans 1:19-20,26.
2. Romans 2:15.
3. Robert Fastiggi, "St. Paul, the Natural Law, and the Catholic Tradition" in the present volume. See also Romans 1:19–20; Romans 2:14–15.
4. *Dei Verbum*, 2. Cf. *Catechism of the Catholic Church*, 53.
5. Matthew 11:2–5.
6. Romans 1:20.
7. Romans 2:14.
8. John Paul II, *Veritatis Splendor*, 57–58; cf. Vatican II, *Gaudium et Spes*, 16.
9. Christoph Cardinal Schönborn, *Chance or Purpose? Creation, Evolution, and a Rational Faith* (San Francisco: Ignatius Press 2007), 164.
10. Romans 1:22.
11. Romans 1:24-32.
12. Romans 1:24-25.
13. Alan F. Johnson, "Is there a Biblical Warrant for Natural-Law Theories?" *Journal of Ecumenical Studies* 25/2 (June, 1982), 190, citing J. Barton, "Natural Law and Poetic Justice in the Old Testament," *Journal of Theological Studies* New Series 30/1 (1979), 12-13.
14. Ibid.
15. Catholics and Evolution: Interview with Cardinal Christoph Schönborn, available at http://www.beliefnet.com/Faiths/Christianity/Catholic/2006/01/Catholics-And-Evolution-Interview-With-Cardinal-Christoph-Schönborn.aspx (last visited Jan. 5, 2010)
16. Ibid.
17. Ibid.
18. Ibid.
19. Schönborn, *Chance or Purpose*, 155.
20. Ibid., 156.
21. Fr. Joseph M. De Torre, *Contemporary Philosophical Issues in Historical Perspective* (Pasig City, Philippines: University of Asia and the Pacific Press, 2001), 150.
22. Fastiggi, footnote 24.
23. De Torre, footnote 21, p. 139.
24. Ibid., 132.
25. Romans 1:25.
26. E.g., Thomas Hobbes.
27. De Torre, footnote 21, p. 147.
28. Ibid., 148.
29. Fyodor Dostoevsky, *The Brothers Karamazov* trans. Richard Pevear and Larissa Volokhonsky (San Francisco: North Point Press, 1992).
30. Schönborn, *Chance or Purpose,* 158.
31. Romans 1:22; *Evangelium Vitae* (1995), 24.
32. *Evangelium Vitae*, 23.

33. *Evangelium Vitae*, 36.

34. Nora O'Callaghan, "Human Origins and Human Rights in the Genome Age," *Ave Maria Law Review* 3 (2005) 123, 144.

35. Schönborn, *Chance or Purpose*, 121.

36. Ibid., 157; cf. O'Callaghan, 144.

37. Schönborn, *Chance or Purpose,* 170, citing an Austrian daily paper, *Die Presse*, July 30, 2005, viii.

38. Colossians 2:8.

39. Pope Benedict XVI, *Spe Salvi*, 5; see *Catechism of the Catholic Church*, 1817-1821.

40. *Spe Salvi*, 7

41. Ibid., 8.

42. Ibid.,17.

43. Ibid.,19.

44. Ibid.,20.

45. Ibid.,24.

46. Ibid., 25; see Pope Benedict XVI, *Caritas in Veritate*, 11.

47. Benedict XVI, *Spe salvi,* 26.

48. Ibid., 30.

49. Ibid., 39.

50. Pope Benedict XVI, To Members of Catholic-Inspired Non-governmental Organizations: Counter Relativism by Truth, *L'Osservatore Romano* (12 December 2007), 5–6.

51. Ibid.

52. Jacques Maritain, *Man and the State* (Chicago: University of Chicago Press, 1951), 24..

53. Brian Scarnecchia, "The Tension Between Faith and Culture," in Federation of Asian Bishops Conference and the Pontifical Council for Culture, *Dialogue Between Faith and Culture: Towards Integral Human and Social Development* (Manila: Lucky Press 1998), 227, 233.

54. Thomas L. Shaffer, "Jurisprudence in the Light of the Hebraic Faith," *Notre Dame Journal of Law, Ethics, and Public Policy* 85 (1984),1.

55. *Final Statement*, *in* Federation of Asian Bishops Conference and the Pontifical Council for Culture, *Dialogue Between Faith and Culture: Towards Integral Human and Social Development*, 36, 40-41.

56. Galatians 4:4.

57. Thomas Jefferson, *Notes on the State of Virginia* ed. W. Peden (Chapel Hill: University of North Carolina Press, 1955), 163.

58. Romans 1:16.

59. See generally, Pope John Paul II, *Fides et Ratio* (1998).

60. Joseph Ratzinger [Pope Benedict XVI] cited in the dedication page of Schönborn, *Chance or Purpose*.

CHAPTER THREE

The Wisdom of the Greeks vs. the Wisdom of Christ in St. Paul

Rev. Earl Muller, S.J.
Professor of Systematic Theology,
Sacred Heart Major Seminary, Detroit, Michigan

Recourse to the natural law, of course, requires recourse to a philosophical basis, which is to say, to the use of human reason in abstraction from any consideration of revelation understood in the narrow sense of an appeal to Scripture or the Judeo-Christian tradition. I make this qualification because natural theology, and the natural law which is allied with it, are more broadly speaking still dependent on a revelation of God who has made himself evident in the things he has created (Rom. 1:18–23). Allied with this perspective is Paul's conviction that all things are created through Christ which in principle raises the question of the way in which the *logos* of the philosopher is to be related to the *Logos* of God who has become incarnate, died, and risen from the dead. I would propose in this essay to focus on Paul's reaction to and understanding of philosophy in general and in its relationship to Christ.

A First Look

Paul's fundamental reaction to philosophy—and here the focus is on the wisdom of the Greeks identified with the various schools of philosophy which arose in and in some measure defined the Greco-Roman world which forms the milieu in which Paul worked and wrote—can only be described as, in some sense, negative.[1] Paul was sent "to preach the gospel, and not with the wisdom of human eloquence (οὐκ ἐν πειθοῖς σοφίας λόγοις), so that the cross of Christ might not be emptied of its meaning" (I Cor. 1:17). He repeated the thought several verses later:

> When I came to you, brothers, proclaiming the mystery of God, I did not come with sublimity of words or of wisdom. For I resolved to know nothing while I was with you except Jesus Christ, and him crucified. I came to you in weakness and fear and much trembling, and my message and my proclamation were not with persuasive [words of] wisdom (οὐκ ἐν πειθοῖς σοφίας λόγοις), but with a demonstration of spirit and power, so that your faith might rest not on human wisdom but on the power of God (I Cor. 2:1–5).

Two preliminary comments can be made about this reaction. The first has to do with a fundamental difference in approach to wisdom between Paul and the Greeks. Simplistically put, the Greeks had a tendency to see true wisdom as only approachable speculatively. This is paradigmatically seen in the opposition between Socrates (or Plato speaking through Socrates), who sought a truth that transcended concrete history, and the Sophists, who used education as a means to political power. It is Socrates who was held up for special respect in the ancient world, not the Sophists. One finds a similar emphasis among Hellenistic Jews of whom Philo is renowned. Palestinian Jews, "Hebrews," among whom Paul counted himself, had a more pragmatic understanding of wisdom that was not the pragmatism of the Sophists. Wisdom, in its root meaning, is a skill. The artisans who had skill in working with various materials in the construction of the temple were deemed "wise." This notion of wisdom as skill very easily encompassed skill in human relationships. A higher form of wisdom again was skill in one's relationship with God. Here Israel did not have to rely on its human ingenuity; it did not have to figure out through a speculative use of reason how to succeed in its relationship with God. Rather, Israel knows how to deal with God because God has revealed it. Wisdom itself, God's own wisdom, has come to dwell among the sons of men (Prov. 8:31), and this wisdom is none other than the book of the Law given by Moses (Sir. 24:22). "'This great nation is truly a wise and intelligent people.' For what great nation is there that has gods so close to it as the Lord, our God, is to us whenever we call upon him? Or what great nation has statutes and decrees that are as just as this whole law which I am setting before you today?" (Dt. 4:6–8; cf. Ps. 147:20). It is this confidence that God's own wisdom has been revealed in the Law and in Jesus Christ that marks Paul's fundamental reaction to Greek wisdom: for all of their speculative prowess, the Greeks do not know the first thing about dealing with God.

To the mature, Paul does speak wisdom, "not . . . of this age" but rather "God's wisdom," which has been hidden, but is now "revealed to us through the Spirit."

> For the Spirit scrutinizes everything, even the depths of God. Among human beings, who knows what pertains to a person except the spirit of the person that is within? Similarly, no one knows what pertains to God except the Spirit of God.

> We have not received the spirit of the world but the Spirit that is from God, so that we may understand the things freely given us by God. And we speak about them not with words taught by human wisdom, but with words taught by the Spirit, describing spiritual realities in spiritual terms (I Cor. 2:6–13).

Access to true wisdom—to the wisdom which characterizes God himself and in which all merely human wisdom participates—is mediated by the Spirit of God. There are three things to note in this connection.

First, Paul's preference for presenting the gospel through demonstrations of the Spirit rather than through displays of philosophical eloquence makes perfect sense in this context. Human reason, under its own power, does not have the kind of access to the mind of God that is provided by the divine Spirit.

Second, the relevant question becomes that of how one obtains this divine Spirit which provides such access to Wisdom. The answer is not, of course, through the intellectual discipline associated with the study of philosophy. Rather, this Spirit is available only through Jesus Christ, the Son of God.[2]

The third thing to note regarding the Spirit's mediation is that Jesus Christ is the Son of God, the very Word of God. He is, in Paul's own words, "the power of God and the wisdom of God" (I Cor. 1:24). And this Jesus Christ, this very Wisdom, is proclaimed by Paul as crucified. That this seems counterintuitive, or indeed, foolish, is precisely the point that Paul makes about the Greek reaction to the gospel. Paul's speech at the Areopagus, in which he attempted to engage the Greeks on their own terms (as narrated in Acts 17:22–34), was greeted with scoffing and disinterest when he began preaching to them on the death and resurrection of Christ (17:32). Greek philosophy could not envisage a resurrection of the body. Greek philosophy could not countenance Wisdom itself, in which all its philosophy formally participated, as crucified.[3] We need to examine Paul's response in more detail lest we be tempted to exclaim, as did Tertullian, "What indeed has Athens to do with Jerusalem"?[4]

Persuasive Words of Wisdom: Literary Structure of I Cor. 1:17–3:3

Paul claimed that he did not use "persuasive words of wisdom," (I Cor. 2:1–5) that he was "untrained in speaking" (II Cor. 11:6). Still, he expected that his letters would be read aloud in the community (I Th. 5:27). Although Jews in general at this time were quite literate, the normal mode for sharing with the community such documents as the Gospels or the Pauline letters would have been through oral recitation.[5] In such an oral culture, care is generally taken to make it easier for the listener to retain what has been heard. This will be done by means of repetitions and parallelisms (synonymous or antithetical) often organized in terms of chiasms or ring structures. This can be seen fairly clearly in the text (I Cor. 1:17–3:3) we have been examining. It is worth exploring this rhetorical structuring of Paul's letter, since it will lead us to a clearer insight into how Paul handles philosophy. The displays set out in the attached figures should not be taken in any absolute fashion, as if Paul (or his amanuensis) composed in this fashion. They are simply aids allowing us (whose culture is not particularly oral) to see the various sorts of parallelism that are operative in the text. Often a given text can be displayed in more than one fashion highlighting different parallels. The English translation has been modified to reflect the original Greek more slavishly since studies of Pauline rhetorical devices must, of necessity, be based on the Greek text.

The first text to examine is I Cor. 1:17–2:2.[6] It is found in Figures 1–3. I direct your attention to Figure 1. The passage begins with a triple negation; it ends with a triple negative. There is a triple negative near the center of the passage. This establishes a simple A–A–A pattern. There is a similar (B–B–B) pattern established for the affirmation of Christ crucified. The cross of Christ is proclaimed at the beginning; Christ crucified is proclaimed at the end. Christ crucified is proclaimed near the center of the passage. The two more central passages containing the negatives and the proclamation of Christ crucified are on either side of the center of the passage and are further connected (beyond the similar A–A–A or B–B–B patterns) by the "call" (C–C). The disciples are "called" by the proclamation of Christ crucified; their "call" does *not* involve a triplet of different things. The combined pattern looks like this: AB(1:17–18)–BC(1:22–24)–D(1:25)–CA(1:26)–AB(2:1–2).

One could also point to the virtual recurrence of the "wisdom of word," which phrase opens the passage, in the closing reference to "lofty words or wisdom." "Wisdom" or a cognate occurs in virtually every verse of this passage. There is a subtle shift here that contrasts the "wise words" of the secular realm ("the world") with the word (or proclamation) of the cross that is carried on at the end of the passage. The parallelism between 1:17–18 and 2:1–2 is further cemented with the coordination between Paul's being "sent" in the opening verses and his "coming" at the end.

Verses 1:19–20a are clearly paralleled with 1:30–31. This established by the citation from Scripture in both sets of verses announced by the same "it is written." In the earlier verses, three rhetorical questions follow the scriptural citation and spell out its meaning; in the later verses, three characterizations of Christ (following his identification as wisdom) precede the Scripture citation and prepare for it. It would not be inappropriate to describe these characterizations as three "answers" to the earlier rhetorical questions. Over and against "the wise words of the debater of this age" are set "the righteousness, sanctification, and redemption available in Christ Jesus."

Verses 1:20b-21 are likewise easily seen as parallel to 1:27–28. In both cases there is the fourfold reference to "the God." The use of the article in these instances contrasts with the anarthrous references to God everywhere else in the passage (with the exceptions of the center of the passage and the closing instance in 2:1). Verses 1:20b–21 are introduced by and develop the preceding citation from Scripture. In the latter verses, with a similar message, we find: "God makes foolish the wisdom of the world" in order that mere flesh might not boast in God's presence. This prepares the way for the latter quotation from Scripture.

These parallels establish a ring structure (incorporating the previously discussed parallels):

AB – E – F – BC – D – CA – F – E – AB
(1:17–18)–(1:19–20a)–(1:20b–21)–(1:22–26)–(1:27–28)–(1:30–31)–(2:1–2).

The center of the passage (1:25—"For the foolishness of God is wiser than men, and the weakness of God is stronger than men") expands the discussion beyond the question of wisdom. This expansion has already appeared earlier in the passage; here in the center it is codified in terms of paradoxes. God's folly is wiser than human wisdom; God's weakness is stronger or more powerful than human strength or power. This coupling of wisdom and power is already found in the outer verses of the ring structure: the word of the cross is to the believer is the "power of God" (1:18); Christ Jesus has become "wisdom for you from God" (1:30). The correlation between power and strength is provided by the parallelism between verse 26 and verses 27–28: not many Corinthians Christians are wise—God shames the wise; not many are powerful–God shames the strong; not many are well-born—God makes nothing those who "are" (well-born). God is "weak"; the Corinthians are, in the eyes of the world, "weak." There is a further play on words involved in these verses. The Greek word for strength is ἰσχύς; Paul uses the related forms ἰσχυρότερον and ἰσχυρά in this passage. The verb for "to shame" is αἰσχύνω; Paul uses the cognate καταισχύνῃ. Notice in these words for shame the presence of the syllables which are the same for the words for strength: ισχυ. They are different words, but what the Greek-speaking listener is going to "hear" in this play on words is that "God chooses the foolish to de-strengthen the wise, the weak to de-strengthen the strong" (κατα–ισχύνῃ τὰ ἰσχυρά).

These two complementary areas (wisdom and power) are not equally attended to by Greeks and Jews. The Greeks (as Paul is presenting them) are primarily interested in wisdom, in wise words, in debate; the Jews, for a variety of reasons, are not interested in speculative reason but in pragmatic power. Their encounter with God has not been predominantly through the sharpening of their reasoning powers, as it had been for the Greeks, but through their experience of a God who intervenes on their behalf throughout history. Their God is a "man of war" who protects (or punishes) his people from the vagaries of history. Jews seek power, they seek signs (works of power). They are scandalized by a God or a Messiah who is manifested as weak, powerless. Paul's insight is that God's "weakness" (the cross of Christ) is incredibly powerful and is able to save those who believe. It is this power to save (the Jewish interest) that answers to the Greek interest in a speculative reason which has no power to transform one's relationship to God. But the power to save (to bring righteousness, sanctification, and redemption) is revealed to be the very wisdom which the Greek, in principle, seeks after. But that wisdom is paradoxically only available precisely because the world refused to know God through wisdom. They chose corruption and a corrupt reason to genuine knowledge of God. The point is important for our purposes. The wisdom which Paul opposes is not the wisdom available to an uncorrupt human reason; he is opposed to the wisdom of the world, which is a corrupt distortion of true wisdom. The Greek can only discover wisdom through God's folly; the Jew can only discover power through God's weakness. What they both implicitly seek is the same reality: Jesus Christ who is the power of God and the wisdom of God. In this regard, note also the parallel between 1:18 ("the word of the cross . . . to us is the power of God") and 1:30 ("Christ Jesus who became wisdom for you from God").

There are features to the passage which escape the structuring indicated in Figure 1. There is the repetition of the word "to save" in verses 1:18 and 1:21b; there is the two triplets in the latter half which are not matched by triplets in the first half of the passage. Such stylistic anomalies can, of course, simply be an indication of the finitude of the human author. Sometimes they signal additional and overlapping patterns of parallelism. Thus, in Figure 2, verses 1:17–24 manifest a distinct ring structure of two levels with a center. The references to Christ and to Paul's preaching of the cross in 1:17 are reprised in verses 1:23–24; the references to "the word of the cross," "folly," and to "being saved" in 1:18 are reprised in verse 19b—"folly," "the kerygma," and "to save." Here the preaching of the cross, the kerygma proclaimed by Paul, even though it makes no sense to the Greek, provides power for salvation.

Likewise, one can recognize a ring structure in 1:22–2:2 (see Figure 3), the second half of the passage (with some overlap of the first half). The opening reference to Christ having been crucified in 1:23 is matched by a similar reference in 2:2. In verses 1:24 and 1:30 Christ is identified as the wisdom of God. Verses 1:26 and 1:27–28 set out the notion of wisdom in the flesh. In addition these two sections are structured as triplets revolving around the themes of wisdom, power, and being someone important. The point of these parallels is obviously to contrast this wisdom in the flesh with the wisdom that is God's, namely, Christ.

I Cor. 2:1–8 (Figure 4) has been more difficult to display. One reason for this is that it serves as a bridge passage (and an overlapping one) between two more cohesive passages (1:17–2:2 and 2:6–3:3). The beginning of this passage closes out the previous passage; the end opens up the next. Still, there are elements which unify this portion of the letter and they are worth commenting on briefly. First, there is a general pattern throughout these verses: a statement of fact is followed by a negation which is followed by an alternative—a "statement—not this—but that" structure. The "statement" or the "but" are sometimes understood. A few examples will clarify this. Paul comes to the Corinthians [πρὸς ὑμᾶς] not with lofty words [but] proclaiming the mystery of God. The Greek grammar (ἦλθον οὐ καθ' ὑπεροχὴν λόγου ἢ σοφίας καταγγέλλων ὑμῖν τὸ μυστήριον [μαρτυριον]) will allow the translation found in the RSV—"When I came to you, brethren, I did not come proclaiming to you the testimony of God in lofty words or wisdom"—but it will also support the translation found in the NAB—"When I came to you, brothers, proclaiming the mystery of God, I did not come with sublimity of words or of wisdom." The RSV (which has missed the "statement-not this-but that" pattern throughout the passage) associates the "proclamation" with "lofty words," the NAB, in contrast, associates the "proclamation" with Paul's "coming."[7] Paul [the statement "in his coming" is implied] did not know anything in the Corinthians except [or but] Christ crucified. "Lofty words" are associated in this way with a puffed up "knowledge" (cf. I Cor. 8:1); in contrast, the mystery of God is found in Christ crucified. These parallels very much fill out what Paul is intending. In verses three to five Paul "becomes" to the Corinthians [πρὸς ὑμᾶς] *not* in plausible words of wisdom *but* in demonstration of spirit and power in order that their faith *not* be in human wisdom *but* in the power of God. In verses six to eight Paul speaks wisdom *not* of this age nor of its leaders *but* of God wisdom in hidden mystery [ἐν μυστηρίῳ]. God decreed this before the ages; *none* of the leaders of this age knew this; [*but*] if they had they would *not* have crucified Christ *but* eye has not seen . . . . It is instructive, then, to string the negatives together: not according to lofty words or wisdom—nothing is known—not in plausible words of wisdom—not in human wisdom—not of this age nor of its leaders—they did not know the mystery of God. The wisdom in view throughout these negatives is the wisdom of this world, a corrupt wisdom that refuses to know God (1:21). Paul refuses the "knowledge" of this world. Instead he offers an alternative found in the "but" phrases—the mystery of God—Christ crucified—demonstration of spirit and power—the power of God—God's wisdom in hidden mystery—God's decree concerning our glory and the Lord of glory. In this transition passage redemptive power is again being set over and against a vacuous and ineffectual wisdom. It is a power that is hidden behind the foolishness and scandal of the cross.

The passage is divided into three parts: verses 1–2, 3–5, and 6–8. Each of those parts is further structured; these structures are distinctive to each part. There are clear verbal parallels between the first and third parts and between the first and second parts. On this basis postulating parallelism between the second and third parts provides interesting insight into Paul's thought. A more detailed analysis of these summary reflections follows.

The first part consists of a statement of Paul's coming followed by two "negation-but" phrases. He does not use lofty words or wisdom; he knows nothing. All he does is to proclaim the mystery of God; all he focuses on is Christ crucified. This part, on the one hand, is parallel to the second part. This is established by the repetition of the notice of Paul's attitude toward the Corinthians (πρὸς ὑμᾶς) and the negatives—"not in plausible words of wisdom"—"not . . . in human wisdom"—which parallel the opening "not according to lofty words or wisdom." These parallels serve to link concepts that are not otherwise obviously linked: "the mystery of God" and "Christ . . . crucified" with "demonstration of spirit and power" and "in the power of God." The parallel between these two parts likewise clarifies Paul's assertion of the mode of his coming: "in weakness, and in fear, and in much trepidation." The use of a triplet here calls to mind a similar triplet used in the previous passage—"not wise, not powerful, not well-born"—and God's use of "the foolish, the weak, the poor born" to shame the "wise, the strong, those who *are* something." Paul's weakness, fear, and trepidation are themselves manifestations of the mystery of God in a way analogous to the cross. It is the paradoxical observation "when I am weak, then I am strong" (II Cor. 12:10). Paul begins this section speaking of his weakness; he ends it by speaking of God's power and demonstrations of the Spirit.

On the other hand the first part is parallel to the third part. In the first part Paul comes proclaiming the mystery of God and "not knowing" anything except for Christ crucified; in the third part Paul speaks and the leaders of the age are "not knowing" of the mystery of God and therefore crucify Christ.[8] There is an ironic contrast in this that carries over to the theme of wisdom. In the first part Paul does not preach according to wisdom; in the third part he does speak of wisdom. It is clearly a different wisdom that he is speaking about, a hidden wisdom inaccessible to the clever debater, to the leaders of this age whose minds have been darkened. Paul, who "knows nothing" but the foolishness of the cross, knows more (or rather, more appropriately) than the leaders of this age.

The second part has already been commented on. There is, as in the first part, a repetition of the "negative—but" sections but here the "statement" shifts. For one thing, the "statement" is not, as such, the notice of Paul's coming but the mention of "my word and my kerygma" which is balanced in the repetition by the mention of "your faith." Of course, the Corinthians' faith is precisely a response on their part to Paul's apostolic proclamation. If Paul's proclamation was not based in human wisdom but rather in divine power, then so too their faith.

The third part has also already been commented on. This part has been divided into two sections with each section ending with a reference to glory. The two sections are chiastic in structure and, in a sense, are the reverse of each other in terms of the placement of the negation—the first: wisdom—not—not—wisdom; the second: no one—knowledge—knowledge—not. Both sections speak of this age and the leaders of this age; both sections refer to the glory that (implicitly) lies hidden. The reference to glory completes a movement of thought *from* Christ crucified *through* the power of God and the demonstrations of the Spirit that lies hidden in the death of the Lord *to* the glory that awaits us in the future with the Lord of glory who has been crucified (and who has risen).

As a whole, then, this passage continues the thought of the preceding passage which pits the salvific power of the gospel proclamation of the crucified Christ against a merely human (and corrupt) wisdom that is flashy but ineffective. It does not know of the hidden purposes of God that are revealed to those who believe the proclamation and place their trust in Christ.

The next major passage is I Cor. 2:6–3:3 (cf. Figure 5). The treatment of this passage will be a bit more summary, since it does not impinge on our topic to the extent that the previous passages have. Nevertheless, it is part of the complex extending from I Cor. 1:17 to 3:3 and does confirm some of the things we have noted.

The passage opens with Paul announcing that he does speak wisdom to the mature (2:6–8); it closes with Paul telling the Corinthians that he does not have the power to speak to them in this way because they are immature, still "babes in Christ" (3:1–3). That Paul intends the ending to echo the beginning is underscored by the triple reference to wisdom at the beginning which parallels the triple reference to power at the end. There is, as well, a triple negative at beginning and end (οὐ, οὐδὲ, οὐκ—οὐκ, οὐ, οὐδὲ) as well as fourth more or less matching negatives, "no one" and the first "not yet" (οὐδεὶς—οὔπω). We see in this parallelism a continuation of the correlation between wisdom and power found in the previous passage.

The next inward segment of the ring structure are quotations from Scripture (Is. 64:3 and Is. 40:13 though cf. also Wis. 9:13 and Jer. 23:18). The closing affirmations are also parallel: "God revealed through the Spirit"—"we have the mind of Christ." The next segment has the Spirit searching "all" (2:10b) and the spiritual person judging the "all" (2:15). "The things of" a man, "the things of" God, and "the things of" the Spirit of God form the next segment, a parallelism emphasized by the double negatives. There is then the central kernel (which itself can be divided into two parts—the reception of the Spirit and teaching in the Spirit).

There is, seemingly, an extra set of negatives in verse nine—all the others seem to balance out. Such "distortions" can be a marker for other parallels not well exposed by a given display scheme. In this case it is possible to see an alternate textual unit extending from 2:6 through at least 2:14. This unit would be structured by sets of triple negatives—2:6–8, 2:9–10, 2:11–12, 2:13–14. One notes that the theme of "speaking" and "wisdom" have been reintroduced in the last set of negatives which parallels what is found in the first set. Thematically the second and third sets belong together. The reintroduction of wisdom also sets up the introduction of the theme of power with which the passage closes.

There are a few points of interest in this material for our overall topic contrasting the wisdom of the world with the wisdom of Christ. Here the contrast with the wisdom of the world is specifically identified in terms of the Spirit of God (2:13). The spirit of the world does not enable the leaders of this age to "know" the hidden mysteries of God. As we have seen the spirit of the world provides a wisdom but one that is corrupted—the truth is obscured because of the refusal of the world to know God through wisdom (1:21). Christians, on the other hand, have the Spirit of God, which searches even the depths of God (2:10). Not only, therefore, do Christians know the hidden mysteries of God, not only do Christians know how to achieve salvation, not only do they have the power to achieve salvation, but, at least in principle, they are the only ones really able to do philosophy, to know how the universe really "is." Paul does not develop this point but it is implicit in what he says. If we have the mind of Christ, the Spirit of God, who plumbs the very depths of God, in principle *we know everything!* Our minds have been healed and strengthened. We can truly *see*. This is certainly the presupposition of the patristic period: Christianity is the only true philosophy.

Implications of the Literary Structure of I Cor. 1:17–3:3 and of the Whole Letter

This survey of literary structure in I Cor. 1:17–3:3 has hopefully accomplished three things. First, it has served to reinforce the points made in the introductory summary and to expand and clarify those points. For instance, in I Cor. 1:21 Paul writes that "since in the wisdom of God the world did not come to know God through wisdom it pleased God . . . ." There is a clear presumption here, similar to that found in Rom. 1:18–23, that the Greeks could have and should have known God through the things that have been created (in Romans) or through their natural reason (in I Corinthians).[9] Since they refused true wisdom, God confounds them with a "folly."

A second and perhaps more significant reason for this survey of literary structure has been to "test" Paul's claim that he used no "wisdom of words" in proclaiming the gospel. There are a couple of similar texts in II Corinthians. Early in the letter he protests that "we have conducted ourselves in the world, and especially toward you, with the simplicity and sincerity of God, [and] not by human wisdom but by the grace of God" (II Cor. 1:12). In II Cor. 11:6 he writes that, "Even if I am untrained in speaking, I am not so in knowledge; in every way we have made this plain to you in all things." In point of fact Paul, or at least his amanuensis, was very skillful in his use of words. This is true of his letters in general (a number of studies in recent decades have detailed this). The passages we have been examining in particular demonstrate a high level of rhetorical competence.[10]

Paul gives us a clue as to how we are to understand his "way with words" in II Cor. 11:21—"But what anyone dares to boast of (I am speaking in foolishness) I also dare." Paul prefers not to entrust his message to mere eloquence (relying instead on demonstrations of Spirit and power really to make the point) but he is not going to allow the message of the gospel to be discredited on the grounds that its proclaimer (Paul) is uneducated.[11] He may well not have had an impressive speaking style, but his "knowledge" even in such mundane skills as (written) rhetoric are impressive. Scarcely a word is out of place; virtually everything is balanced; the repetitions and circular patterns of discourse manifest a keen sensitivity to an oral culture. Paul is no crude barbarian stumbling over his words as he proclaims Christ, "and this one crucified." He is powerful, he is precise, and he makes full use of all the rhetorical "tricks" available to the skilled speaker or writer of his time. What this means is that when Paul claims not to be using rhetoric to convey the gospel we need to take his claim with a grain of salt. Paul, throughout the Corinthian correspondence, is much more than a little ironic in his tone (and occasionally sarcastic, cf. II Cor. 12:13). He is shattering any Corinthian pretence to exalted learning with his own patent and considerable learning (II Cor. 11:6). The upshot of this use of rhetoric by Paul, even as he claims to have or use no rhetorical skills, is that one needs likewise to be cautious in assessing Paul's claim not to be using human wisdom (or philosophy) in his exposition of the gospel.

Third, and perhaps most important, broadening the examination of Paul's literary structuring of I Corinthians allows us to put the first two chapters into the context of the whole letter. Examination of the whole letter makes it clear that Paul intended a close parallelism between the opening chapters on the "folly of the cross" with the penultimate chapter on the resurrection, which, as I will suggest, could be labeled the "wisdom or philosophy of the resurrection."

The letter divides into roughly three sections. In the first, extending from 1:17 to 4:15, Paul examines fundamental attitudes in the Corinthian community and his own approach to them. There is a persistent theme of wisdom and folly, power and scandal. The second section is marked off by an *inclusio*, Paul's appeal to the Corinthians to "be imitators of me" (4:16, 11:1). Various issues of morality are treated with a central section (also central to the entire letter) on marriage. The third section likewise has an *inclusio*—the reference to the "traditions" (11:2, 15:1–3). Here the focus is on the community gathered together in fellowship and worship. The reference to the "traditions" leads into the final major section—Paul's teaching on the resurrection which complements his opening teaching on the cross. There are other elements which serve to tie these three sections together. If Paul comes preaching the cross not with words but with power (2:1–5) he sends Timothy to speak of the kingdom of God not in talk but in power (4:17–21). These latter verses look backward to the discussion throughout the first part of the letter; the immediately preceding reference to imitation of Paul (4:16) looks forward to the more moral part of the letter. In the first part, Paul sets out the knowledge we have through the Spirit (2:9–16); in the third part, the gifts of the Spirit are discussed in such a way as to focus things on love (12:1–14:33). The "rubric" for understanding this contrast between knowledge and love is found in the central section—"Knowledge puffs up, but love builds up" (8:1–3).

These brief indicators of the structure of the whole of First Corinthians will have to suffice. The chief point of looking at the entire letter was to highlight the structural parallels between the opening material on wisdom and folly and the cross which we have been examining with the closing material on the resurrection.

I Cor. 15 and the "Philosophy" of the Resurrection

Chapter 15, excluding the opening and closing verses, is divided into three sections each of which is further divided into three parts (cf. Figure 7). The opening and closing verses exhibit a similar structure and theme:

I Cor. 15:1–2	**I Cor. 15: 58**
Now I would remind you, brethren,	Therefore, my beloved brethren,
the gospel which I preached to you	
which also you received in which also you stand through which also you are saved	be steadfast, immovable, always abounding in the work of the Lord
to what word I preached to you	
if you hold fast except unless in vain you believed	knowing that your labor is not in vain in the Lord.

The first section is focused on the basic apostolic kerygma—first, the kerygma itself (I Cor. 15:3–4); second, the history of appearances (I Cor. 15:5–8); third, Paul's reflection on his own apostolate (I Cor. 15:9–11). There is a bit of self-positioning by Paul in his account of the apparitions in that he, in effect, places himself on the same rank as Cephas:

Cephas [Peter] (v. 5)
  the twelve (v. 5)
    five hundred brothers (v. 6)
    James [the brother of the Lord][12] (v. 7)
  all the apostles (v. 7)
Paul (v. 8)

This self-positioning Paul had already set out in Galatians 2:7–8.

The next major section runs from 15:12–34 (cf. Figure 8).[13] It is, as noted, divided into three parts. One recognizes the "logical" character of the first part, I Cor. 15:12–19, from the "if—then" structure of the discourse (the "then" is often implied) in which the mutual entailment of the general resurrection of the dead and the specific resurrection of Christ is explored.[14] The third part (I Cor. 15:29–34) is likewise clearly focused but the focus is on behavior—why people are baptized on behalf of the dead, why Paul put himself in constant peril, why Christians exercise restraint in their behavior. This focus on behavior marks this third part as having a more "ethical" character.[15]

The second part (I Cor. 15:20–28) is of yet another sort of character than "logical" or "ethical." The focus is on human origins, the "universe" (or "the all," τὰ πάντα), and the hierarchy of power and order, and the reconstitution of humanity and the universe in Christ. Here, Paul is setting out the structure of creation (compare Gal. 4:1–11, 6:15) and that is appropriately understood as a physics or a cosmology.[16] The third section (I Cor. 15:35–57), as will be examined below, expands on this physics—one sees this in the repetition of specific vocabulary and themes. In short, the last two thirds of chapter 15 articulate a "philosophy" of the resurrection in its logical, ethical, and physical dimensions. This "philosophy" of the resurrection is the necessary correlate of the "folly" of the cross. It is a "wisdom" that is not accessible to the world which seeks wisdom or demands signs but which refuses to know God through wisdom (I Cor. 1:21–22) but only to those (be they important people or insignificant) who have heard and received in faith the apostolic proclamation of the death and resurrection of Jesus.

The character of I Cor. 15:20–28 as a "physics" will strike the modern ear as odd. Modernity has, for instance, very much reduced the scope of physics and cosmology to a consideration of the dynamic of particles or waves and forces and the interplay of these in the structure of the universe. But ancient philosophy included more under its physics or cosmology than we are accustomed to include. Plato, for instance, in his *Timaeus* included the creation of humanity as well as the establishment of the fundamental elements in its consideration of the origins and structure of the universe (the "All").

Still, a work like the *Timaeus* is highly speculative in contrast to what we find in Paul. Paul is very much the Jew in seeking real power rather than mere speculative knowledge. Plato was himself aware of the speculative character of his work, and placed the account of creation, not in the mouth of his mentor, Socrates, but in the mouth of one of his disciples, Timaeus, who characterized his account with the modest claim of merely being a "likely story."[17] One ought not to be misled by such disclaimers. The vocabulary Plato uses in the *Timaeus* follows very closely that found in the *Republic* where Plato describes the intellectual ascent out of the cave.[18] The *Timaeus*, in effect, transforms Platonic epistemology into cosmology. The ascent out of the cave, however, is a very pragmatic program; it is a pedagogy, a plan for education in the ideal city-state. Such a pedagogy functions, then, in the Greek world as a "way of salvation," a way of achieving spiritual or intellectual perfection. It is an account of salvation "by reason alone." Paul's account of the "way of salvation" faces squarely the problem of sin which distorts "reason alone": "the wrath of God is revealed from heaven against all ungodliness and wickedness of men who by their wickedness suppress the truth" (Rom. 1:18); "although they knew God they did not honor him as God or give thanks to him, but they became futile in their thinking and their senseless minds were darkened" (Rom. 1:21). Salvation and perfection are not possible to a fallen reason alone. But God has broken through the darkness of fallen reason and revealed the light of Christ. Salvation and perfection are possible to those who accept the proclamation of the crucified and risen Lord in faith. They are given power to know, to know truly, and to act in love in the pattern of the crucified Christ.

Above I argued that there were specific features which link I Cor. 15:35–57 with I Cor. 15:20–28. It is time to look at some of these. In Figure 8, I Cor. 15:20–28 was displayed as coming in three parts—the Adam imagery (20–23), the delivery of the kingdom to the Father after every power has been destroyed (24–26), the subordination of all things to the Son by the Father (27–28). Each of these parts manifests a repetition in vocabulary and has been displayed in two parts. Figure 9 presents an alternative way of displaying the parallels within the text. Here the passage falls into two parts, each part a ring structure. Thus in 15:20–23, one sees the following pattern: Christ—firstfruits—through a man death, through a man resurrection – in Adam all die, in Christ all made alive – firstfruits – Christ. The second ring structure (15:24–28) is grounded by four "when" (ὅταν) clauses. These surround statements that "all" has been placed "under his feet." The very center is the notice that the last enemy destroyed is death. "The God" is repeated at beginning and end; "Father" in the beginning is matched by "Son" at the end. If one compares this twofold ring structure with I Cor. 15:35–57 (cf. Figure 10) one notices a similar twofold ring structure for each of the three parts of this section. This literary structuring merely underscores that 15:35–57 was intended by Paul to complement the ideas first raised by him in 15:20–28. The repetition of the Adam imagery (15:21–22, 44b–49) accomplishes this, as do the victory over death (15:26, 54–55) and the perspective of the *parousia* and of the *eschaton* (15:23, 24–25, 28, 50–53). I Cor. 15:35–57 thus functions as an expansion and development of the material introduced in I Cor. 15:20–28.

The question posed in 15:35, which is ultimately a question of "physics" (and a speculative one at that), sets the stage for the material in the third section (Figure 10): "But some one will ask, 'How are the dead raised? With what kind of body do they come?'" Such a person is foolish, according to Paul, not because the question is foolish, but because the answer is obvious. He uses the imagery of sowing a seed to indicate that a different kind of body is to be expected in the resurrection, one, as he will develop, which is not subject to the sort of mortality which characterizes the present body.

Paul then describes different kinds of flesh, different kinds of bodies (15:39–41)—human, animal, bird, fish, heavenly (sun, moon, stars).[19] This conception surely comes from the opening chapters of Genesis but it does also mirror the

Greek philosophical perspective. The four fundamental elements are fire, air, water, and earth and, in Plato's *Timaeus*, there are creatures made out of and for each ambience—the gods, birds, fish, land creatures. The singling out of sun, moon, and stars likewise echoes Genesis (1:16).[20] Particularly given the later contrast between the first man who was dust from the earth and the second man who is from heaven, the contrast Paul makes between bodies of heavenly regions and bodies of earthly regions (15:40) is provocative. Plato explicitly identified the stars with deities. Stoicism similarly identified fire with pure intelligence. The lights in the firmament were commonly identified with intelligent beings.[21] One finds a trace of this even in Genesis which, though it demotes the sun and moon and stars to mere keepers of time (and not of destiny) it also refers to the hosts of heaven (Gen. 2:1—πᾶς ὁ κόσμος αὐτῶν) which throughout the Old Testament are identified with angelic beings. Whatever Paul's own convictions regarding sun, moon, and stars, (and this is never set out in any detail) his answer would have resonated with his philosophical and religious culture. Terrestrial bodies are perishable, dishonorable, weak, psychical, drawn from the dust of the earth; celestial bodies are imperishable, glorious (as are sun, moon, and stars), powerful, spiritual and from (or of) heaven (I Cor. 15:42–49). Mortal bodies are of the former, resurrected bodies of the latter. The one cannot inherit the other but the perishable must put on imperishability and the mortal, immortality. How is this concretely possible, since the one has nothing to do with the other? It is accomplished in Christ. Whatever else one can say about this argument, it is surely a speculative tour de force drawn out against the backdrop of overlapping religious and philosophical conceptualities. That much alone speaks volumes about Paul's appropriation of philosophical wisdom.

A Few Concluding Remarks

There are two things of significance in this material. The first is the use that Paul makes of philosophical forms. By dividing his material on the resurrection into sections of logic, physics, and ethics he is clearly intending to set out a "philosophy" of the resurrection. The question is whether this serves merely as a metaphor or whether he intends more than this. That he tries to answer a question about the resurrection using concepts that would make sense to a Greek philosopher suggests that he intends more than a mere metaphor. It is clear, for instance, that he presumes that the laws of logic are valid; the mutual entailment of the general resurrection of the dead and the resurrection of Christ depends, at least in the argument he presents in I Cor. 15:12–18, on the validity of logical argumentation. Likewise, his conclusion in the ethics section that "if the dead are not raised, 'Let us eat and drink, for tomorrow we die'" would be recognized as valid among the Greeks as a statement of Epicurean principle.

The second thing of significance is the way that Paul transforms philosophical forms in the light of the resurrection. There are several points that can be made. First, the Epicurean principle can only be rejected if there is some sort of accountability for moral action that transcends this life. At the very least, one requires some notion of an afterlife. But the afterlife in question must be more than a vague shadowy persistence that characterizes both the Homeric world and much of the world of the Old Testament. Accountability is required, and for that a full personal existence after this life is required. Such a full personal existence, certainly a human personal existence, is not possible apart from a human body. At any rate, such a view is certainly arguable in a Greek context (perhaps more successfully with Aristotelians and their ilk).

A second point would flow from Paul's comment that "if for this life only we have hoped in Christ, we are of all men most to be pitied" (I Cor. 15:19). Why would Christians be more pitied than other men if our end is the same? Presumably this is because Christian life involves "rigors" in contrast to the pagan life which would make no sense to undertake if there were no corresponding rewards in view. What is undermined, if there is no resurrection of the dead, is the whole meaning of the cross of Christ. The wisdom behind the divine folly of the cross can only be unfolded in terms of a divine power that is victorious over death. Christ is the wisdom and power of God. All merely human wisdom participates in this divine wisdom and must, if it is to cohere with Truth Itself, also manifest the goodness and love of God which is revealed in Christ, and this one crucified and risen. A philosophy that is not in some way shaped by the cross and resurrection of he who is Wisdom incarnate is separated from Truth. True philosophy must understand itself as a servant of the mystery of God, of the mystery of Truth.

A third point, explicating the last part of the previous, is that if *all things* (the universe) have been subordinated to the Lord Jesus Christ ("through whom all things are and through whom we exist" [I Cor. 8:6]), then the intelligibility of the universe is marked by that same Lord. A philosophy that knows nothing of the mystery of God manifest in Christ crucified and risen is one that has abstracted from reality *as it concretely is*. Perhaps such a philosophy is still able to achieve genuine insight, but it is just as likely to oppose itself arrogantly to the Lord of glory as did the "intelligent" Greeks of Paul's time.

This last observation provides the basis for a final comment on natural law. We make a mistake if we think that mere reason is capable of making the case for natural law. Arrogance is arrogance; if there is no willingness to believe, no argument in the world will break through the shell of studied ignorance that characterizes many of the modern forms of philosophical thought. For his part God, according to Paul, does not pander to such arrogance. He presents instead an absurdity—wisdom nailed to the cross—and power for those who believe.

FIGURE 1

I Cor. 1:17–2:2

17 For **not** sent me Christ to baptize but to preach
not in wisdom of word in order that
not make futile the cross of Christ.

18 For the word of the cross to the on the one hand perishing folly is
and to the being saved to us power of God is.

19 For it is written "I will destroy the wisdom of the wise and the cleverness
of the clever I will thwart."
20 Where a wise one?
Where a scribe?
Where a debator of the age this?

Has not made foolish the God the wisdom of the world?
21 For since in the wisdom of the God
did not know the world
through the wisdom the God,
it pleased the God
through the folly of the kerygma
to save the believing;

22 Since also Jews signs demand and Greeks wisdom seek
23 and we preach Christ having been crucified,
to the Jews a scandal and to Gentiles folly
24 and to those called,
to Jews and to Greeks,
Christ,
of God power and of God wisdom.

25 Because the folly of the God more wise than that of men is
and the weakness of the God more strong (ἰσχυ-ρότερον)
than that of men.

26 For see your call brothers that
not many wise according to the flesh,
not many powerful,
not many well-born.

27 But the foolish of the world chose the God
in order to shame (κατα-ισχύνῃ) the wise,
and the weak of the world chose the God
in order to shame (κατα-ισχύνῃ) the strong (ἰσχυ-ρά),
28 and the poor born and the nothing chose the God, the not being
in order that the being might be made void,
29 that may not boast all flesh in the presence of the God.

30 From him you are in Christ Jesus who became wisdom for you from God,
righteousness
and sanctification
and redemption.
31 As it is written "the boaster in the Lord let him boast."

2:1 I coming toward you brothers came
not according to lofty words or wisdom proclaiming to you the mystery of the God.
2 For I did **not** judge anything to know in you
if **not** Jesus Christ and this one having been crucified.

FIGURE 2

I Cor. 1:17-24

17 For not sent me Christ to baptize but to preach not in wisdom of word in order
that not make futile the cross of Christ.

18 For the word of the cross to the on the one hand perishing folly is and to the
being saved to us power of God is.

19 For it is written "I will destroy the wisdom of the wise and the
cleverness of the clever I will thwart."
20 Where a wise one? Where a scribe? Where a debator of the age this?
Has not made foolish the God the wisdom of the world?
21 For since in the wisdom of the God did not know the world through
the wisdom the God,

it pleased the God through the folly of the kerygma to save the believing;

22 Since also Jews signs demand and Greeks wisdom seek
23 and we preach Christ having been crucified, to the Jews a scandal and to Gentiles folly
24 and to those called, to Jews and to Greeks Christ, of God power and of God wisdom.

FIGURE 3

I Cor. 1:22-2:2

22 Since also Jews signs demand and Greeks wisdom seek
23 and we preach Christ having been crucified,
to the Jews a scandal and to Gentiles folly

24 and to those called, to Jews and to Greeks, Christ, of God power and of God wisdom.
25 Because the folly of the God more wise that that of men is and the weakness of the God more strong that that of men.

26 For see your call brothers that
–not many wise according to the flesh,
–not many powerful,
–not many well-born.

27 But
–the foolish of the world chose the God in order to shame the wise,
–and the weak of the world chose the God in order to shame the strong,
28 –and the poor born and the nothing chose the God, the not being in order that the being might be made void,
29 that may not boast all flesh in the presence of the God.

30 From him you are in Christ Jesus who became wisdom for you from God, righteousness and sanctification and redemption.
31 As it is written "the boaster in the Lord let him boast."

2:1 I coming toward you brothers came not according to lofty words or wisdom proclaiming to you the mystery of the God.
2 For I did not judge anything to know in you except Jesus Christ and this one having been crucified.

FIGURE 4

I Cor. 2:1–8

1 I coming toward you brothers came
not according to lofty words or wisdom
proclaiming to you the mystery (variant: testimony) of God.

2 For not
did I judge anything to know in you
except Jesus Christ and this one crucified.

3 I
in weakness
and in fear
and in much trepidation
became toward you
4 and my word and my kerygma
not in plausible words of wisdom
but in demonstration of spirit and power,

5 in order that your faith
not may be in wisdom of men
but in power of God.

6 Wisdom we speak in the mature and wisdom
not of the age this
nor of the leaders of the age this, the ones being made void,
7 but we speak of God wisdom in mystery the hidden,

which decreed the God before the ages into glory ours,
8 which no one
of the leaders of the age knew,
for if they had known
not
the Lord of the glory would they have crucified.

FIGURE 5

I Cor. 2:6-3:3

6 *Wisdom* we speak in the mature, *wisdom*
not of the age this
and **not** of the leaders of the age this, the ones being made void,
7 but we speak of God *wisdom*
in mystery the hidden which decreed the God before the ages into glory ours
8 which ***no one*** of the leaders of the age this knew (ἔγνωκεν) for if they had known (ἔγνωσαν),
not the Lord of the glory would they have crucified.

9 But as it is written
"What eye has **not** seen (εἶδεν)
and ear **not** heard
and upon the heart of man **not** come up
what has prepared the God for those who love him."
10 And to us revealed the God through the Spirit;

for the Spirit all searches,
even the depths of the God.
11 For who knows (οἶδεν) of men the things of the man
if **not** the spirit of the man, the one in him.
The things of the God
No one knows (ἔγνωκεν)
if **not** the Spirit of the God.

12 And we **not** the spirit of the world received
but the Spirit, the one from the God in order that
we might know (εἰδῶμεν)
the by the God having been grace gifted to us;

13 and what we speak **not** in teaching of human wisdom words
but in teaching of Spirit by the spiritual spiritual
things explaining.

14 And psychic man **not** receives
the things of the Spirit of the God. For folly to him they are
and **not** powerful to know (γνῶναι)
because they are spiritually judged up.
15 And the spiritual judges up the all;
and himself by ***no one*** is judged up.

16 For "who knows (ἔγνω) mind of Lord which instructs him?"
And we mind of Christ have.

3:1 And I, brothers,
not am *powerful* to speak to you
as to spirituals
but
as to the fleshly,
as infants in Christ.
2 Milk you I gave to drink
not solid food,
for ***not*** yet you were *powerful*.
But
not yet now are you *powerful*,
3 for still fleshly you are.

FIGURE 6

First Corinthians

1:1–17	Introduction
1:17–2:2	The folly of the cross
2:1–5	Paul comes preaching the cross not with words but with power
2:6–8	Paul does impart divine wisdom to the mature
2:9–10	It is written: the Spirit
2:11	Comprehending the things of God
2:12	Knowing the gifts not with the world's spirit but by the Spirit
2:13	Paul imparts wisdom not with words but by the Spirit
2:14–15	Comprehending the things of the Spirit
2:16	(It is written): the mind of Christ
3:1–3	Babes in Christ; there is jealousy and strife
3:4–9	Paul and Apollos
3:10–15	Paul the master builder; the foundation is Christ
3:16–17	You are God's temple
3:18–20	Wisdom and folly; it is written
3:21–22	You are Christ's
4:1–5	Paul the servant of Christ; judged by the Lord
4:6–7	Paul and Apollos
4:8–15	Paul is their father; they are puffed up
4:16	"Be imitators of me"
4:17–21	Timothy sent; kingdom of God not in talk but in power
5:1–12	Immorality
6:1–11	Lawsuits
6:12–20	Immorality
7:1–40	Marriage
8:1–13	Idol food
9:1–27	Paul's "legal" defense of himself
10:1–33	Idol food
11:1	"Be imitators of me"
11:2	The traditions
11:2–16	Women praying and prophesying; the image (וּנמֵלְצַ)
11:17–22	Unworthy celebration of the Lord's supper
11:23–26	The Eucharistic narrative of institution
11:27–34	Unworthy celebration of the Lord's supper; the body
12:1–31	Spiritual gifts; the body
13:1–13	Love
14:1–33a	Spiritual gifts; praying and prophesying
14:33b–40	Women; the silence (וּנתֵוּמך)
15:1–3	The traditions
15:4–58	The (wisdom) philosophy of the resurrection
16:1–24	Closing

FIGURE 7

I Cor. 15: 1–58

	3–4: The basic kerygma	12–19: If Christ has not been raised—the logic of the resurrection The "Logic"	35–41: Different kinds of bodies—terrestrial and celestial The "Physics" expanded	
1Now I would remind you, brethren, in what terms I preached to you the gospel, which you received, in which you stand, 2by which you are saved, if you hold it fast—unless you be-lieved in vain.	5–8: The appearances	20–28: Adam and Christ—the order of the resurrection The "Physics"	42–49: Adam and Christ—psychical and spiritual, dust and heaven The "Physics" expanded	58Therefore, my beloved brethren, be steadfast, immovable, always abounding in the work of the Lord, knowing that in the Lord your labor is not in vain.
	9–11: Paul's ministry	29–34: The resurrec-tion and Christian behavior The "Ethics"	50–57: Transfor-mation and victory in Christ The "Physics" expanded	

FIGURE 8

I Cor. 15:12–34: Christian Philosophy of the Resurrection

Logic

15:12 Now if Christ is **preached** as raised from the dead, how can some of you say that
there is **no resurrection of the dead**?

13 But if there is **no resurrection of the dead**, then Christ has not been raised;
14 if Christ has not been raised, then our **preaching** is in vain and your faith is in vain.

15 We are even found to be misrepresenting God, because we testified of God that
he raised Christ, whom he did not raise if it is true that the dead are not raised.

16 For if the dead are not raised, then Christ has not been raised. 17 If Christ has not
been raised, your faith is futile and you are still in your sins.

18 Then those also who have fallen asleep in Christ have perished. 19 If for this life
only we have hoped in Christ, ***we are of all men most to be pitied***.

Physics

20 But in fact Christ has been raised from the dead, the *first fruits* of those who have fallen asleep.
21 For as by a man came death, by a man has come also the resurrection of the dead.
22 For as in Adam all die, so also in Christ shall all be made alive. 23 But each in his
own order: Christ the *first fruits*, then at his coming those who belong to Christ.

24 Then comes the end, when he delivers the *kingdom* to God the Father after *destroying* every rule
and every authority and power.
25 For he *must reign* until he has put all his enemies under his feet. 26The last enemy
to be *destroyed* is death.

27 "For God has put *all things* in *subjection* under his feet." But when it says, "*All things* are put in
subjection under him," it is plain that he is excepted who put [the] *all things* under him.
28 When [the] all things are *subjected* to him, then the Son himself will also be *subjected*
to him who put [the] *all things* under him, that God may be *everything* to everyone.

Ethics

29 Otherwise, what do people mean by being **baptized on behalf of the dead**?

If the **dead** are not raised at all, why are people **baptized on their behalf**?

30 Why am I in peril every hour? 31 I protest, brethren, by my pride in you which I
have in Christ Jesus our Lord, I die every day! 32 What do I gain if, humanly
speaking, I fought with beasts at Ephesus?

If the **dead** are not raised, "Let us eat and drink, for tomorrow we die." 33 Do not be deceived:
"Bad company ruins good morals." 34 Come to your right mind, and *sin* no more.

For some have no knowledge of God. ***I say this to your shame***.

FIGURE 9

I Cor. 15:20–28:

20 Now *Christ* has been raised from [the] dead, *first fruits* of the ones who have fallen asleep

21 For as through a man death, also through a man the resurrection of [the] dead.

22 For as indeed in the Adam all die, so also in the Christ all shall be made alive.

23 But each in the own order; *first fruits Christ*, then the ones of the Christ in (the) his parousia;

24 Then the end,
when he delivers the kingdom to *the God* and *Father*,

when he destroys all rule and all authority and power.
25 For it is necessary for him to reign until

"he has put all the enemies *under (the) his feet*,"

26 [the] last enemy to be destroyed is death.

27 "For all he has subordered *under (the) his feet*."

But **when** it says, "All have been subordered,"
it is plain that excepted the one subordering to him the all

28 **When** subordered to him the all,
then himself the *Son* will be subordered to the one subordering to him the all,
that may be *the God* the all in all.

FIGURE 10

I Cor. 15:35–57

35 But some one will ask, "How are the dead ***raised***? With what kind of **body** do they come?"
36 You foolish man! What you ***sow*** does not come to life unless it dies.

37 And what you ***sow*** is not the **body** which is to be, but a bare kernel, perhaps of wheat or of some other grain.

38 But God gives it a **body** as he has chosen,
and to each kind of seed its own **body**.

---

39 Not all flesh is the same flesh,
but there is *one kind* (ἄλλη) for men, *another* (ἄλλη) for animals, *another* (ἄλλη) for birds, and *another* (ἄλλη) for fish.

40 There are *heavenly* bodies and there are *terrestrial* bodies;
but the glory of the *heavenly* is one, and the glory of the *terrestrial* is another.

41 *There is one* (ἄλλη) glory of the sun, and *another* (ἄλλη) glory of the moon, and *another* (ἄλλη) glory of the stars;

for star differs from star in glory.

---

42 So is it with the resurrection of the dead. What is **sown** is ***perishable***,
what is **raised** is ***imperishable***

43 It is **sown** in dishonor, it is **raised** in glory.
It is **sown** in weakness, it is **raised** in power.

44 It is **sown** a physical body, it is **raised** a spiritual body.

If there is a **psychical** body there is also a *spiritual* body.

45 Thus it is written, "The first man Adam became a living **psyche**"; the last Adam became a life-giving *spirit*.

46 But it is not the *spiritual* which is first but the **psychical**, and then the *spiritual*.

47 The first man was from the **earth**, a man of **dust**; the second man is from *heaven*.

48 As was the man of **dust**, so are those who are of the **dust**; and as is the man of *heaven*, so are those who are of *heaven*.

49 Just as we have borne the image of the man of **dust**, we shall also bear the image of the man of *heaven*.

---

50 I tell you this, brethren: flesh and blood cannot inherit the kingdom of God, nor does the **perishable** inherit the **imperishable**.

51 Lo! I tell you a mystery. We shall not all sleep, but ***we shall all be changed***.

52 in a moment, in the twinkling of an eye, at the last *trumpet*.
For the *trumpet* will sound, and the dead will be raised imperishable,

and ***we shall be changed***.

53 For this **perishable** nature must put on the **imperishable**, and this mortal nature must put on immortality.

54 When the **perishable** puts on the **imperishable**, and the mortal puts on immortality,

---

then shall come to pass the saying that is written: "Death is swallowed up in **victory**."

O death, where is your **victory**?
"O ***death***, where is your ***sting***?"

56 The ***sting of death*** is sin,
and the power of sin is the law.

57 But thanks be to God, who gives us the **victory** through our Lord Jesus Christ.

Notes

1. Various attempts have been made to identify the wisdom which was the subject of Pauline criticism. Suggestions have ranged from the Jewish wisdom tradition to Hellenistic Judaism to apocalyptic philosophical strains to Gnosticism. Raymond F. Collins, *First Corinthians, Sacra Pagina* 7 (Collegeville, Minn.: The Liturgical Press/Michael Glazier, 1999), 97 suggests that trying to identify a specific philosophy operative in the Corinthian community is probably futile and that most likely Paul was "writing about wisdom as it was taught in the rhetorical schools and exploited by popular rhetoricians, whose speech was appealing to the Hellenists of Paul's day (1:22)." In short, we are probably dealing with a philosophical eclecticism that was endemic to the Hellenism of the time. Gordon D. Fee, *The First Epistle to the Corinthians*, The New International Commentary on the New Testament (Grand Rapids, Mich.: William B. Eerdmans, 1987), 64–65 (cf. n. 79), mentions sophist traditions in particular given the emphasis on rhetoric.

2. One might parenthetically note that a similar perspective is provided by Thomas in the first article of his *Summa theologica*. Thomas observes that since, on the one hand, the end of man exceeds the grasp of his reason, while on the other hand, the knowledge of God attainable by human reason is prone to error and available only to few, it follows that a special revelation by God is required if all men are to achieve salvation.

3. Fee, *First Epistle*, 77 (cf. n. 43), would object to this characterization of Christ as Wisdom itself, at least in the Corinthian context, insisting that the reference to Christ as the "wisdom of God" is *not* a christological statement . . . . Rather, it is a soteriological statement." That it is a soteriological statement is without dispute; still, Paul is making the point that the real object (Wisdom itself or redemptive power) that Greeks and Jews seek is to be identified with Jesus Christ, "and this one crucified"—this, however, is a properly christological thought.

4. Tertullian, *Prescription against Heretics* 7.

5. Cf., for instance, Justin Martyr, *I Apol.* 67: "And on the day called Sunday, all who live in cities or in the country gather together to one place, and the memoirs of the apostles or the writings of the prophets are read, as long as time permits; then, when the reader has ceased, the president verbally instructs, and exhorts to the imitation of these good things. Then we all rise together and pray, and, as we before said, when our prayer is ended, bread and wine and water are brought, and the president in like manner offers prayers and thanksgivings, according to his ability, and the people assent, saying Amen; and there is a distribution to each, and a participation of that over which thanks have been given, and to those who are absent a portion is sent by the deacons."

6. Collins, *First Corinthians*, 90–91, analyzes this passage in a fashion compatible with what is presented here.

7. Barrett, *A Commentary on the First Epistle to the Corinthians*, Harper's New Testament Commentaries (New York: Harper & Row, 1968), 62, will argue that the later reference to mystery (μυστήριον) in v. 7 influenced copyists to substitute mystery for testimony (μαρτύριον) at the beginning of the passage. Fee, *First Epistle*, 88 (n.1), 91, comes to a comparable conclusion. This argument disappears as soon as one notes the sort of literary styling that Paul has engaged in. Barrett's conviction that Paul has rejected rhetoric makes it difficult for him to recognize this. Hans Conzelmann, *1 Corinthians: A Commentary on the First Epistle to the Corinthians*, Hermeneia (Philadelphia: Fortress Press,

1975), 53, n. 6 argues this as well though he admits that μαρτύριον could just as well be a copyist insertion from 1:6. Collins, *First Corinthians*, 118, comes down firmly in favor of "mystery."

8. Whether these leaders (ἄρχοντες) are demons or political powers is debated. Conzelmann, *1 Corinthians*, 61, argues that the "mythical context" suggests demons. One could as well point to the reference to the ἀρχαί in I Cor. 15:24 which more clearly has spiritual powers in mind. See Conzleman, 271–72. Cf. also Collins, *First Corinthians*, 129. What is of interest in this question is Paul's "cosmic" rather than "political" interest. Fee, *First Epistle*, 103–4 rejects any reference to the demonic in favor of "those responsible for the crucifixion" but expands it to include leaders in a broader sense, i.e., those "'wise ones' of 1:20 and 26." This is certainly possible but he overstates the case in saying that "the linguistic evidence, the context, and Pauline theology all argue against it."

9. This is in sharp contrast to the view of Fee who sets up a complete disjunction between human wisdom and the message of the cross. A few examples from his commentary will illustrate this point: "But the more urgent concern is between *sophia* itself and the message of the cross. To have come with the former, Paul says, in effect would have been totally to negate the latter"; "the cross stands in absolute, uncompromising contradiction to human wisdom" (66); "left to themselves mere creatures cannot find out the living God" (72); "Wisdom (their thing) and the cross (God's thing) stand in absolute contradiction one to the other" (74). The absoluteness of the opposition between human wisdom and the message of the gospel is a staple in some Protestant circles. Rom. 1:18–32 does not speak of any incapacity to know at least something of God but of a willful suppression of the truth. They *could* know God and they *should* have known how to behave from God's revelation in creation; they chose not to. Paul makes a similar point in I Cor. 1:21. They *could* have known God through human wisdom; because they *did* not God has confounded them with the folly of the cross.

10. Cf. Collins, *First Corinthians*, 91: "Although Paul had professed that he did not use cleverness of speech in his proclamation of the gospel (v. 17) his exposition of the message of the cross is fraught with powerful literary and rhetorical devices . . . the message of the cross is phrased in powerful rhetoric."

11. Thus I think C. K. Barrett overstates things when he writes that Paul preached "without rhetorical skill" and that he "rejects *wisdom* (σοφία) as a rhetorical device," *The First Epistle to the Corinthians*, 49. Barrett divides the references to wisdom into good senses and bad senses (cf. p. 53), which is to a certain extent justifiable, but it leaves him unable to recognize Paul's use of philosophical forms in I Corinthians fifteen. Conzelmann, *1 Corinthians*, 54 takes a similar stance: "Everything is discarded which could provide additional human support for the message. For otherwise the latter would be subjected to human criteria and would no longer be revelation." Such a thought is particularly Protestant in its reluctance to see properly human activity as coordinated with the divine initiative. It strikes such commentators as allowing a place for "works."

12. Cf. Barrett, *First Epistle to the Corinthians*, 343.

13. Collins, *First Corinthians*, 547, divides this passage into the same three parts as well. He sees an A-B-A' pattern and there is some point to this.

14. This logical character is generally acknowledged by the commentaries. Cf. William F. Orr and James Arthur Walthar, *I Corinthians*, The Anchor Bible, vol. 32 (Garden City, New York: Doubleday, 1976), pp. 325–27 or Collins, *First Corinthians*, 542, who speak

even of a syllogistic logic.

15. Cf. Barrett, *First Epistle to the Corinthians*, 362 speaks of Christian ethics though he characterizes this whole section in terms of *ad hominem* arguments as does Fee, *First Epistle*, 761–62. Collins, *First Corinthians*, 557–58, speaks of Paul's use of diatribal style here which is a feature of Hellenistic moral discourse. "The use of the formulaic 'humanly speaking' . . . , the moralistic language of v. 33, and Paul's diatribal style coalesce to suggest that it is philosophical moral discourse that provides the rhetorical *heurēsis* of v. 32a." Cf. also 560, n. 33, "The exhortation 'don't go astray' is a classic formula of moral exhortation . . . . The language of 'going astray' . . . is characteristic of the discourse of Hellenistic moralists." Fee, 770, notes that the metaphor of fighting wild beasts is the sort of metaphor common "in the moralistic literature of Hellenism."

16. This is generally missed by the commentators who focus rather on the apocalyptic character of the material. Of course, apocalyptic material is frequently cosmological in scope.

17. Plato, *Timaeus*, 29c–d.

18. Ibid. 27d–29d; *Republic* VII, 517b–c, 524c–525a, 533b–534e.

19. Fee, *The First Epistle*, 783, sets these verses out in the same chiastic pattern as presented here.

20. Cf. Collins, *First Corinthians*, 563–64.

21. Cf. Conzelmann, *1 Corinthians*, 282, n. 23.

Response to Fr. Muller

Patrick Gillen
Assistant Professor,
Ave Maria School of Law, Naples, Florida

Fr. Muller has laid out for us St. Paul's complex argument for truth and its foundation in an acute appreciation for the intimate relationship between the revealed and natural law. By making the rhetorical strategy St. Paul employed to appeal to his sophisticated audience more accessible to us, and by giving us greater insight into St. Paul's carefully crafted argument, Fr. Muller has helped us understand St. Paul's message more fully. I am grateful for the knowledge he has kindly shared with us and delighted to have this opportunity to offer a few thoughts by way of response.

Upon reviewing Fr. Muller's piece, I recalled that the medieval scholastics regarded theology as the queen of the sciences. It struck me that the preeminence given theology reflects this idea Fr. Muller has described—that wisdom consists in learning how to rightly order our relationship to God, our ultimate end and greatest good. In this sense, we who see ourselves as heirs of the Judeo-Christian tradition evaluate all knowledge in light of our ultimate end—just like the Jews of St. Paul's day—and theology necessarily informs this all-important inquiry. Similarly, many of us who come together to study law at Ave Maria proceed on the premise that we will apply our talents to a career in the legal profession, and we describe our work as a vocation or "calling" to a particular kind of service. We seek to live the rightly ordered life through service to individuals who need our help and, more broadly, the common good of our society.

So I believe that Fr. Muller's lecture inevitably presents a question we must ask ourselves as we pursue our calling in the law: what does the wisdom that Fr. Muller brings to our attention mean for each of us as members of the legal profession? In an age when our profession often seems terribly removed from the wisdom St. Paul offered to the ancient Greeks, what can we do with the knowledge Fr. Muller has shared with us? Here are a few thoughts along these lines that I wish to offer by way of response.

Meeting together about two millennia after St. Paul engaged the Greeks, we citizens and lawyers find ourselves in a situation with remarkable parallels. For one thing, our current situation, frequently called post-modern and post-Christian, features a proliferation of philosophical theories which, if they purport to offer wisdom at all, rely upon extremely abstract formulations that are wholly divorced from any realistic view about the human person and the good towards which our lives should be directed.[1] Indeed, the lack of wisdom (understood as how to live life well) produces undesirable consequences all around us. The "right to choose" is the euphemism for abortion, the "right to die" or "death with dignity" is the euphemism for euthanasia, "dignity" is the catch phrase of the "gay"-rights movement, including its effort to redefine marriage and family, gender is a social construct we are told, and human sexuality is understood without any reference to procreation, the natural family, or for that matter, much more than fleeting pleasure. Things that were once unmentionable have become the topic of daily discourse, whether same-sex sexual activity or arguments made for clone-and-kill medical research. In sum, we encounter views of liberty that amount to license, aberrant conduct that is exalted as a means of self-realization, and vice that is passed over in the name of autonomy.

Significantly, a great deal of the vice and foolishness we see around us has been accepted because it is dressed up in (dare we say blessed by) philosophical theories held out as the wisdom of our day. Unfortunately, these philosophical theories, positing hypothetical original positions and the like, rely upon abstractions that lack any meaningful connection to history and experience. This brings to mind the situation St. Paul confronted in Athens: speculative reason, with all its strengths, obscured a larger truth revealed in Scripture. So I believe our current situation gives us good reason to agree with St. Paul's stated skepticism for the more speculative strain of philosophy he encountered in Athens. We, like St. Paul, cannot afford to set aside the great tool of good philosophy; but we, like St. Paul, must be aware of its severe limitations.[2]

In the face of these pernicious cultural developments, we propose the wisdom provided by the Judeo-Christian tradition. But here again, our situation often parallels that of St. Paul in Athens, for our reliance upon the Judeo-Christian tradition is increasingly met with scoffing. Worse still, we are told that such wisdom is a private affair that has no place in civil discourse. How far we have come from St. Paul's day, in which philosophy was seen as being concerned with wisdom, understood as the way to live rightly, and religion was seen as sharing that concern!

Nevertheless, I believe there are concrete things we should do in an effort to ensure that our culture is not cut off from the wisdom contained in the Judeo-Christian tradition. The first thing we can do in our larger role as lawyers in civil society is to defend the valuable contribution that the Judeo-Christian religious tradition has played in our history.

I say this because I believe that our effort to enlighten civil society with wisdom mediated through the Judeo-Christian religious tradition is complicated by a deplorable lack of historical consciousness at best, and a false telling of our history at worst. According to this post-modernist "narrative," our current prospect became possible only after civil society freed itself from religion and the "Enlightenment" ensued. Since that time, civil society, freed from the limitations of religion and served by science (understood to be the highest expression of unfettered reason), has ascended to the current pinnacle of human progress. In time, the deficiencies of the simple-minded views that characterize this modern period became evident, and the subjectivity of human experience and the need to create meaning became apparent. This is the current project of the academy—to help create meaning in an otherwise meaningless world. Those who advance this "narrative" of the development of Western Civilization believe that religion is an impediment to progressive society, a form of ignorance and source of division. Thus, they seek to exclude religion and its ancient store of wisdom from public life even as they busy themselves constructing a variety of theories that are designed to serve as wisdom.

We must see that this effort to minimize the contribution of the Judeo-Christian tradition to our history is groundless and destructive. Historians have long noted the importance of religion to the progress of civil society.[3] Indeed, it was once commonplace that the claim for religious liberty advanced by early Christians made possible a sphere of autonomy from the state that served the cause of individual liberty.[4] The positive role that Christianity has had in formation of the traditional family and the resulting benefits for society at large is undeniable.[5] And against the current myth that religion impedes scientific inquiry, we must cite the work of those historians who have shown how the "creationist" mindset engendered by Christian revelation provided the seed bed for modern science.[6]

Likewise, we must bear witness to the importance of religion in our national experience. A desire for religious liberty informed the colonization of this continent and the American Revolution.[7] A concern for religious liberty explains in no small measure the drafting of the Bill of Rights; in fact, the religious liberty provision was perhaps the most remarkable feature of the Constitution to the people of the day.[8] Furthermore, historians have long identified the role that religious inspiration has played in the great reform movements of our national experience.[9] With these facts in mind, we can work to preserve the role of religion in civil society with reference to its many positive contributions.

The second thing we must do is to retain a lively faith in reason, just like St. Paul, and participate earnestly in the public discussion of important issues. We must not withdraw from a world that seems blind to the most important truths about the human person. Instead, we, like St. Thomas so long ago, must give witness to the universality of the Truth by pointing to its presence in our midst.[10] In this regard, we must appreciate how fortunate we are to live in a nation built upon recognition of the natural law; we must preserve that tradition, and we must build upon it. We must insist that the natural law tradition is given its full due as the philosophical foundation for our politics and show that this contribution loses none of its luster because that philosophy remains ultimately dependent upon Revelation in creation, as Fr. Muller has noted today. We must build upon this philosophical foundation in our role as citizens and lawyers by tying our program to the intrinsic dignity of the human person–properly and fully understood.

As we engage our culture, we must give full due to the genuine contributions the modern world has made to our understanding of the human person. Fr. Muller has shown us how St. Paul adopted a skeptical stance toward reason in order to secure a fair hearing for the wisdom contained in religious tradition, while seeking to build upon the fruits of reason in service of the larger truth. We must do the same. In this regard, we must remember that the Judeo-Christian tradition has always been open to the *semina Verbi*, the seeds of the Word that have been discerned by reasoned inquiry and found their way into culture. There is no question that Modernity has yielded genuine insights into human dignity that are the *semina Verbi* of our day, and we must be open to these insights just as the early Church was open to the good fruit of classical culture. And here, the Church's engagement with the larger world can serve as our example; for when the Church enters public debate, it musters both the fruits of Christian Revelation and reasoned inquiry.

By combining the best of these traditions, wisdom as accessed by speculative philosophy and wisdom as mediated through the Judeo-Christian tradition, we can hope to have a positive impact upon our culture. By focusing attention on the concrete and often positive role that religious wisdom has played in our history, we can help others see that just as the life of the law has been shaped by experience, not logic, the law has drawn truth from religious wisdom (and experience) much more than speculative (and often sterile) philosophical inquiry.[11] As for the claims made by modern philosophers who offer wisdom of their own making, we must remind them that there is good reason to believe that the synthesis of religious wisdom and realist philosophy forged in the Middle Ages remains the single most powerful way to understand the human experience.[12]

Another way we can provide a much needed counter to the current hegemony of post-modern "wisdom" is by diligently bringing to light the harmful consequences that follow from foolish ideas that are presented as wisdom. Over thirty years after the Supreme Court enshrined the abortion license as liberty, evidence of the tragic personal and social harm caused by abortion has become all but irrefutable, human experience confirming what right reason held with certainty. It is not surprising then that current polls provide hopeful signs that people once beguiled by false claims for liberty have come to see through bitter experience (of their own or someone else) the terrible consequences of this false conception of liberty.

Sadly, a survey of our current situation points to many other areas where we appear destined to go through a painful period of relearning by experience the lessons that religious wisdom long provided. While the wake of personal and social disaster arising from the post-modern understanding of human sexuality, marriage, and family increases, there is no sign of a willingness to reconsider the issue.[13] Quite the contrary, the logical implications of the post—modernist view are being worked out with catastrophic consistency in the current effort to redefine marriage with terribly predictable and tragic consequences.

I note these examples only to show why it is important for us to catalogue the pernicious consequences of foolish ideas. By doing so, we can help others learn something St. Paul already knew from his encounter with the Greeks–speculative reason has blessed any number of foolish notions. Despite the current situation, we can collect evidence about the pernicious consequences of foolish ideas with the hope that once these are made manifest, the resulting search for wisdom may lead people of good will to consider again the wisdom mediated through the Judeo-Christian religious tradition.

Another thing we must do in an effort to serve the truth is to preserve religious liberty. We must protect our liberty to speak the truth as we see it, including the truth as mediated by religious tradition, so that we can harness the fullness of wisdom in order to shape civil society for the good.

More fundamentally, we must recognize that it is essential for us to vigorously defend our religious liberty, understood as our ability to order our lives wisely in relation to God. Recent events confirm that while appeals to dignity, tolerance, and diversity were employed to legitimize post-modern wisdom, those who relied on those ideals to secure their place in the public square, once in power, brook little difference of opinion. Rather, they demand that we observe the wisdom they preach on their own authority as if it were . . . gospel-truth.

This is no overstatement. We live in a time when the proponents of the abortion license insist that medical professionals must provide abortions despite conscientious objection[14] and recently, the California Supreme Court held that a doctor violated civil law when she refused to artificially inseminate a lesbian who wished to raise the child with her same-sex partner.[15] We live in a time when Catholic Charities of Boston was forced to cease adoption placement because it refused to place children in same-sex households and an institution inspired by the Baptist faith is sued for firing a counselor based on her openly gay lifestyle, an example the institution did not wish to hold out as healthy to the children in its care.[16] We live in a time when Catholic Charities of New York and Sacramento are forced to provide contraceptives to employees in contradiction to the teaching of the Catholic Church.[17] We live in a time when parents are not even given notice and opportunity to remove their children from instruction that violates their religious conviction.[18] We live in a time when public high schools and universities deny the right of religious clubs to insist that members conduct themselves in a manner consistent with the religious wisdom that provides the purpose for their association.[19]

These examples show that we must act if we wish to preserve what St. Paul knew to be wisdom in terms of the Old Testament and what the Founders understood to be our first liberty, i.e., the wisdom to rightly order our relationship with God. We would have to be naive or blind not to see the gravamen of current events.

And make no mistake: by taking these steps, we do a service for society. By taking these steps, we preserve an alternative vision that provides a useful counterweight to the claims of reigning post-modern orthodoxy. We preserve a wisdom that is a resource to all people of good will and, hopefully, our lives provide an example of wisdom. In this regard, we must remember that it was the natural attractiveness of the Christian way of life, not sophisticated theological formulations (no matter how necessary), which led others to join the people of "the Way."

This last point about the need to preserve religious liberty leads to another that is equally important. We must have the courage of our convictions and be prepared to act upon them in the public sphere. Like St. Paul, we must always be prepared to persuade people of good will. At the same time, we must not deceive ourselves. We need to recognize the reality of sin and the will to power. We need to see that for many the will to power and desire to define the meaning of human existence creates a "will to disbelieve."[20] We need to recall the consequences that such hubris has produced in the past and appreciate the way in which current events demonstrate a similar trajectory. In the face of such claims, we must be prepared to defend our way of life. We must not retreat behind the fashionable relativism and skepticism of our day. We must not allow false claims for tolerance to rob us of the courage of our convictions or become an excuse for cowardice in our personal or professional lives.

By making St. Paul's inspired rhetorical strategy more accessible to us, Fr. Muller has encouraged us to think about how we might use our calling in the law to serve the common good. I am grateful to Fr. Muller for his presentation and this opportunity to share with you my thoughts about how we may serve both human and divine wisdom in our professional and personal lives.

Notes

1. The terms modern and post-modern are variously defined. Here I use "modern" as chiefly referring to the Enlightenment with its characteristic confidence in reason and ability to know an objective reality, including philosophical or moral truth, a related commitment to the scientific knowledge epitomized by Newtonian Physics, and a concomitant faith in human progress. I use "post-modern" to encapsulate the deterioration of that view, including the conviction that there is no objective and fixed reality such that truth claims are inevitably subjective and relative with the resulting view that meaning is created and imposed on experience by the individual or society in the form of narrative. I see this post-modern mindset as capturing the academy and exerting significant influence on culture by the turn of the twentieth century as a result of various developments, including biblical criticism, Freudian psychology, radical skepticism in philosophy yielding logical positivism, the linguistic turn in literature, an over-extrapolation from insights derived from anthropology and sociology, and developments in science (such as Darwin's theory of evolution, and later,

the theory of relativity and non-Euclidean geometry). I realize that this periodization may be contested, but believe it is a fair and useful characterization overall.

2. There is, perhaps, no more poignant testimony to the promise and pitfalls of speculative philosophy in the Western canon than St. Augustine's Confessions. See St Augustine, *Confessions* trans. Henry Chadwick (New York: Oxford University Press, 1991).

3. Christopher Henry Dawson, *The Making of Europe: An Introduction to the History of European Unity*. (New York: Sheed and Ward, 2001).

4. Numa Denis Fustel Coulanges, *The Ancient City: A Study on The Religion, Laws And Institutions Of Greece And Rome* [1874] (Baltimore: The Johns Hopkins University Press, 1980).

5. David Herlihy, *Medieval Households* (Cambridge, MA: Harvard University Press 1985).

6. John Hedley Brooke, *Science and Religion: Some Historical Perspectives* (Cambridge: Cambridge University Press 1991).

7. J. Clark, J., *The Language of Liberty, 1660-1832* (Cambridge, Cambridge University Press 1994).

8. Mark A. Noll, *The Old Religion in a New World: The History of North American Christianity* (Grand Rapids, MI: Eerdmans, 2001).

9. William G. McLoughin, *Revivals, Awakenings, and Reform* (Chicago: University of Chicago Press, 1980).

10. See John Paul II, *Fides et Ratio*, 44; see also John Paul II, *Veritatis Splendor*, 35-82 (passim).

11. For a discussion of the fruitful interplay between the wisdom literature of the Bible and the larger Judeo-Christian tradition, see Joseph Koterski, S.J., "*Fides et Ratio* and Biblical Wisdom Literature," in *The Two Wings of Catholic Thought: Essays on Fides et Ratio* ed. David R. Foster and Joseph W. Koterski (Washington, D.C.: Catholic University of America Press, 2003), 129-162.

12. Alasdair Macintyre, *Three Rival Versions of Moral Enquiry: Encyclopaedia, Genealogy, and Tradition* (Notre Dame: University of Notre Dame Press, 1991).

13. Mary Eberstadt, "The Vindication of Humanae Vitae," *First Things* (August/September 2008), *available at* http://www.firstthings.com/article.php?year=2008&month=07&title_link=002-the-vindication-of-ihumanae-vitaei-28 (last visited Jan. 6, 2010).

14. Association of American Physicians and Surgeons, Inc., "Medical civil liberties threatened by rollback of Provider Conscience Clause" (March 17, 2009); available at: http://www.aapsonline.org.

15. *North Coast Women's Care Medical Group, Inc. v. Superior Court*, 44 Cal. 4th 1145, 1161 (Cal. 2008).

16. Fr. Robert J.Carr, "Boston's Catholic Charities to stop adoption service over same-sex law," available at http://www.catholic.org/national/national_story.php?id=19017 (last visited Jan. 6, 2010). *Pedreira v. Ky. Baptist Homes for Children, Inc.*, 186 F. Supp. 2d 757 (W.D. Ky. 2001).

17. *Catholic Charities of Sacramento, Inc. v. Superior Court*, 32 Cal. 4th 527 (Cal. 2004); *Catholic Charities of Diocese of Albany v. Serio*, 2006 NY Slip Op 7517, 1 (N.Y. 2006).

18. *Parker v. Hurley*, 514 F.3d 87 (1st Cir. Mass. 2008).

19. *Truth v. Kent Sch. Dist.*, 542 F.3d 634 (9th Cir. Wash. 2008), *Christian Legal Soc'y*

v. Kane, 2006 U.S. Dist. LEXIS 27347 (N.D. Cal. Apr. 17, 2006), *Christian Legal Soc'y Chapter. of Univ. of Cal. v. Kane*, 2009 U.S. App. LEXIS 5654 (9th Cir. Cal. Mar. 17, 2009) (affirming District Court's ruling). Christian Legal Society Chapter of Univ. of Cal. v. Martinez 130 S.Ct. 2971 (2010) affirming North Circuit.

20. Mary Eberstadt, "The Will to Disbelieve," *First Things* (February 2009), available at http://www.firstthings.com/article.php?year=2009&month=01&title_link=002-the-will-to-disbelieve-20 (last visited Jan. 6, 2010).

CHAPTER FOUR

The New Man: Nature, Sin, and Grace in St. Paul

Eduardo J. Echeverria
Professor of Philosophy,
Sacred Heart Major Seminary, Detroit, Michigan

"Ego, in Christo regeneratus, etiam cogitans ex Christo vivo."[1]

The main title of this essay refers to St. Paul's teaching in 2 Corinthians: "If then, any man is in Christ, he is a new creature. The former things have passed away; behold, all things are made new" (5:17). Elsewhere St. Paul expresses the same teaching. He describes the "new *man*" as one "who is renewed in knowledge according to the image of Him who created him" (Col. 3:10). How should we understand "*new* man" here in St. Paul's presentation of the whole gospel with respect to the goodness of creation, its corruption by the Fall into sin, and redemption in Christ? Is the man in Christ rendered a "new creation" unintelligible without the presupposition of the original creation of man by God?

The answer to this last question must be "yes." What is good by nature remains good even when shattered and broken under present sinful conditions in which grace is required. Indeed, its goodness is in fact enhanced and restored by the grace of Jesus' redemptive work. St. Paul's teaching emphasizes the radical nature of this transformation in Christ for the individual, who is now renewed in the spirit of his mind, but that transformation also has at the same time supra-individual, that is, corporate, significance. Humanity, subjected to original sin in virtue of being the descendants of the first Adam, having lost the original unity of man with God and among men, in Jesus Christ became perfectly subjected to God and united to him, and thus became a new humanity. To be rooted in Christ, God's second Adam (1 Cor. 15:20-28, 45-49), means that humanity is reconstituted in Christ as the "new humanity," the new being of the Church called "the new man" (Eph. 2:15), spoken of as the "perfect man" (Eph. 4:13), and as the "one" man in Christ Jesus (Gal. 3:28). To have put off the "old man," then, our Adamic humanity, that is our fallen state, with its darkened understanding, alienation from God, and blindness of heart, as a consequence of original sin, is the transforming event that results from having put on the "new man," the new humanity in Christ, "created according to God, in true righteousness and holiness" (Eph. 4:22-24).

Now, the relationship between nature, sin and grace must be correctly lived and comprehended in order to understand the Pauline teaching that any man who is in Christ, is a new creature. What, then, is the proper understanding of that relationship? In this essay, I, first, sketch four accounts of that relationship in the following order: 1) "grace against nature," 2) "grace above nature," 3) "grace alongside nature," and 4) "grace infuses and restores nature."[2] Having provided an account of these types, I will then argue that "grace infuses and restores nature" best fits the teaching of St. Paul helping us to make theological sense of the teaching that any man who is in Christ, is a new creation. Second, I will briefly lay out St. Paul's Christian anthropology in the light of that type and the foundational biblical themes of creation, fall, redemption, and consummation. In this connection, I will give brief accounts of the following notions: outward and inward man, body, flesh, nous, heart, soul and spirit, corruption and the bondage of sin in light of those themes. My concern here is to say something about the noetic effects of sin upon the unregenerate man's natural moral knowledge and virtue? Third, and lastly, I will explore the relation between the moral and theological virtues, as well as the problem of Christian freedom, in light of the Pauline understanding of the relation between nature, sin and grace.

I. Nature, Sin, and Grace

Three quarters of a century past, Jacques Maritain significantly remarked regarding the question of the relation of nature and grace that it is erroneous to ignore both the distinction between nature and grace as well as their union.[3] There are four types of ways in which that relation has been understood.

The first type understands grace and nature to be opposed to each other. Nature has been rendered a corrupt vessel by the fall into sin, and needs to be replaced altogether with something new by grace. One influential account of this relation sees human nature as capable of nothing but sin, with the accompanying loss or destruction of the natural power of the will. The will itself, as a consequence of the fall and the fallen state, is "capable of nothing except . . . malicious, empty self-seeking . . . possessing an insuperable bent toward evil."[4] The fall eliminates all natural inclination to goodness in the will, on this view, and also tempts us to disparage natural virtue as well as our natural capacity for contrary moral choice between good and evil—that is, the will's power to choose good over evil, or vice-versa. In short, on this view of the relation between nature and grace, the very nature of the will as God created it is disparaged in order to magnify grace. In this sense, nature would be the very opposite of grace, and hence could not be united with grace; rather nature has to struggle against grace and be replaced altogether with something new by grace, namely, a supernatural life of faith and a consequent supernaturalized freedom. Thus, supernatural freedom is to be construed as a "superstructure" added to natural freedom, rather than as something that determines and elevates our whole being, including our natural, but fallen, will. In short, on this view the Christian withdraws from the corrupt vessel that is human nature and seeks a salvation that is separate from it because human nature in its fallen condition is, essentially, irreclaimable. Against this view, John Henry Newman cogently writes,

> [The Church] does not teach that human nature is irreclaimable, else wherefore should she be sent? [N]ot that it [human nature] is to be shattered and reversed, but to be extricated, purified, and restored; not that it is a mere mass of evil, but that it has the promise of great things, and even now has a virtue and a praise proper to itself. But in the next place she knows and she preaches that such a restoration, as she aims at effecting in it, must be brought about, not simply through any outward provision of preaching and teaching, even though it be her own, but from a certain inward spiritual power or grace imparted directly from above, and which is in her keeping.[5]

The second and third types understand the relation between nature and grace to be such that grace is a "plus factor," a mere "add on" to the natural level. Consider, say, the relationship between the natural virtues (e.g., prudence, justice, fortitude, temperance) and the supernatural virtues (i.e., faith, hope and charity) in light of these types. The *Catechism of the Catholic Church* teaches that "The theological virtues are the foundation of Christian moral activity; they animate it and give it its special character. They inform and give life to all the moral virtues" (no. 1813). Now, I want to show that neither of these types can make sense of what the *Catechism* claims here, namely, the grace of the supernatural virtues directs and orders nature from *within* rather than alongside or above nature as if those virtues merely add on to the excellencies of virtuous man.[6] The reason that neither type can make sense of this claim is that they view the relationship between the natural and supernatural virtues in a dualistic and hence extrinsic fashion. In short, thinking in terms of "two-tiers," we can say that, on these types, the upper-level of grace was lost because of original sin, leaving the lower-level relatively intact and integrally unaffected by sin. Thus, both types view the redemption accomplished through the saving work of Christ as something that merely *supplements* or *parallels* our created nature. On this "two-tier" relationship between nature and grace, the latter is merely added (*donum superadditum*) to a nature that has not been integrally affected by sin, and hence human nature requires little or no internal healing and restoration.

The chief problem with these types is that by limiting the scope of man's fallen condition, they in turn limit the scope of Christ's redemptive work. The dualism between faith and life is one of the practical implications of this limitation and it is well expressed by Vatican II. "This split between the faith which many profess and their daily lives deserves to be counted among the more serious errors of our age." In critical response to this bifurcation, the council Fathers teach, "Since they have an active role to play in the whole life of the Church, laymen are not only bound to penetrate the world with a Christian spirit, but are also called to be witnesses to Christ in all things in the midst of human society."[7] The Fathers add to this, "The good news of Christ continually renews the life and culture of fallen man."[8] Years later the newly established Pontifical Council for Culture states in the same vein, "[This view] gives Christ, the redeemer of man, center of the universe and of history, the scope of completely renewing the lives of men 'by opening the vast fields of culture to His saving power.'"[9] A practical implication of the Pontifical Council's understanding of the relation between nature and grace for living the Christian life, as the Church, is well stated years earlier by Pius XII is an address to newly-made cardinals on February 20, 1946. The pope said:

> Before all else the Church progresses in depth, only thereafter in extent. In the first place she seeks man himself, using all her endeavors to form and fashion him, to perfect God's likeness in him. She does her work in each one's heart, but it affects the whole of life and every individual activity. In men thus formed, the Church provides a secure foundation for human society. . . . And now, what follows for the Church. Today more than ever she must live her mission; more energetically than ever she must repulse that narrow and false conception of her spirituality and inward life which would confine her, blind and dumb, to the recesses of the sanctuary. The Church cannot shut herself up, inactive, in the privacy of her churches and thus neglect the mission entrusted to her by divine Providence, the mission to form man in his fullness and so ceaselessly to collaborate in building the solid basis of society. This mission is of her essence. Looking at her from this standpoint, it can be said that the Church is the society of those who, under the supernatural influence of grace, in the perfection of their personal dignity as sons of God and in the harmonization of every human bent and energy, build up the mighty framework of the community of men. From this aspect the faithful, more precisely the laity, are in the front line of the Church's life; through them, the Church is the vital principle of human society. Consequently, they particularly must have an ever more clear consciousness, not only of belonging to the Church, but of *being* the Church.[10]

These words of Pius bring us to the fourth type of how nature, sin and grace are related. This type understands "nature" to mean the deepest foundations of human nature after the fall, a nature that has been savagely wounded by the fall, but still remains what God originally made them to be. These foundations are not totally corrupted, destroyed. Rather, sin corrupts God's good creation but the order of creation persists. The good news is that God's salvation in Christ restores the whole fallen creation from *within*. Consider, for example, the *Catechism's* teaching on marriage in light of creation, the fall into sin, and the redemption. Marriage is grounded in the order of creation: "The intimate community of life and love which constitutes the married state has been established by the Creator and endowed by him with its own proper laws . . . . God himself is the author of marriage." Yet, marriage as it actually functions in its fallen state is under the regime of sin and hence no longer properly functioning. Significantly, the *Catechism* applies an Augustinian principle that "the natures in which evil exists, in so far as they are natures, are good. And evil is removed, not by removing any nature, or part of a nature . . . but by healing and correcting that which had been vitiated and depraved."[11] In this light, we can easily understand the teaching of the *Catechism* on the relation between sin and nature: "According to faith the disorder we notice so painfully does not stem from the *nature* of man and woman, nor from the nature of their relations, but from *sin* . . . . Nevertheless, the order of creation persists, though seriously disturbed . . . . In his mercy God has not forsaken sinful man . . . After the fall, marriage helps to overcome self-absorption, egoism, pursuit of one's own pleasure, to open oneself to the other, to mutual aid and to self-giving."

Furthermore, the Catechism states:

> In his preaching Jesus unequivocally taught the original [i.e., creational] meaning of the union of man and woman as the Creator willed it from the beginning . . . . By coming to restore the original order of creation disturbed by sin, [Jesus] himself gives the strength and grace to live marriage in the new dimension of the Reign of God.[12]

On this view, then, of the relation between nature and grace, the relation is therefore such that grace penetrates and transforms and perfects fallen nature from within, and thus nature is redeemed in its own domain. In this connection, let me cite several key passages on the relation between nature and grace from a remarkable book by Etienne Gilson, *Christianity and Philosophy*, written in 1931. Gilson writes:

> The true Catholic position consists in maintaining that nature was created good, that it has been wounded, but that it can be at least partially healed by grace [here and now] if God so wishes. This *instauratio*, that is to say, this renewal, this re-establishment, this restoration of nature to its primitive goodness, is on this point the program of authentic Catholicism.

And he continues:

> To say that grace is necessary to restore nature is quite other than to suppress that nature to the profit of grace: it is to confirm it by grace. Grace presupposes nature, whether to restore or to enrich it. When grace restores nature, it does not substitute itself for it, but re-establishes it; when nature, thus re-established by grace, accomplishes its proper operations, they are indeed natural operations [now transformed] which it performs.

Finally, as Gilson also says later:

> Catholicism teaches that before everything the restoration of wounded nature by the grace of Jesus Christ. The restoration of nature: so there must be a nature, and of what value, since it is the work of God, Who created it and re-created it by re-purchasing it at the price of His own Blood! Thus grace presupposes nature, and the excellence of nature which it comes to heal and transfigure.[13]

Thus, grace restores and transforms nature from within its own domain. Indeed, this is how the late philosopher-pope John Paul II describes the Church's mission of evangelization and, in fact, "the purpose of the Gospel," which is namely . . .'to transform humanity from within and to make it new.' Like the yeast which leavens the whole measure of dough (cf. Mt 13:33), the Gospel is meant to permeate all cultures and give them life from within, so that they may express the full truth about the human person and about human life."[14]

Shortly before his death, the Holy Father, John Paul II, published his final book, leaving the Church, and indeed the whole of humanity, the beautiful gift of his reflections entitled, *Memory and Identity*. Relevant to the question of the indivisible unity of nature and grace is the following passages from this work:

> The resurrection of Christ clearly illustrated that only the measure of good introduced by God into history through the mystery of Redemption is sufficient to correspond fully to the truth of the human being. The Paschal Mystery thus becomes the definitive measure of man's existence in the world created by God. In this mystery, not only is eschatological truth revealed to us, that is to say the fullness of the Gospel, or Good News. There also shines forth a light to enlighten the whole of human existence in its temporal dimension and this light is then reflected onto the created world. Christ, through his Resurrection, has so to speak "justified" the work of creation, and especially the creation of man. He has "justified" it in the sense that he revealed the "just measure" of good intended by God at the beginning of human existence. This measure is not merely what was provided by him in creation and then compromised by man through sin; it is a superabundant measure, in which the original plan finds a higher realization (cf. Genesis 3:14-15). In Christ, man is called to a new life, as son in the Son, the perfect expression of God's glory.[15]

At the core of the Christian worldview is an interlocking set of life-orienting beliefs regarding the Creation, Fall and Redemption (i.e., Incarnation, Passion,

Resurrection, and Ascension).

First, God created the world good. Given the cultural mandate to subdue and have dominion over created reality, this "goodness" extends to the work of man's hands when accomplished in the light of "the truth about ourselves and about the world."[16] Indeed, the totality of creation, especially man who is its crown, actually manifests God's goodness, being created in the image and likeness of God. This manifestation of goodness is God's thesis, His affirmation, His *Yes* to the creation (Genesis 1:31).

Second, all creation (i.e., nature, culture, history, society) is fallen through original sin. Human nature as a whole has lost its original harmony, and man is wounded at the very root of his being. He is estranged from God, from himself, and from his fellow man. His humanity exhibits the marks of being sinful, prone to sin, with sin being a violation of God's will and purpose. This sinfulness denies God's thesis and has its beginnings in Genesis chapter 3. God's response to man's sin is *Yes*, but also *No*. *Yes*, because God, full of love, mercy and grace, does not abandon the fallen creation. Indeed, Genesis 3:15 contains the first proclamation of the Messiah, the *proto-evangelium*. But also *No*, because God, judging man in the light of His perfect justice and holiness is the author of the antithesis, of the sign of contradiction between good and evil, between the seed of the woman and the seed of the serpent.

Third, the Redemption accomplished through the mystery of the Incarnation and Christ's finished work—His life, passion, death, resurrection, and ascension—abrogates the antithesis between sin and creation. Put differently, the Incarnation, Passion, and Resurrection in Jesus Christ means that his grace restores an original good creation. God's original thesis is reasserted and reestablished, but also, as John Paul II asserts in the quote above, is enriched, fulfilled, and perfected. This Redemption restores the very heart of human nature, causing the rebirth of the human self in Christ (Col. 2:13; 2 Cor. 5:17). John Paul further writes: "Christ alone, through his humanity, reveals the totality of the mystery of man . . . The key to his self-understanding lies in contemplating the divine Prototype, the Word made flesh, the eternal Son of the Father." "Without the Gospel," John Paul adds, "man remains a dramatic question with no adequate answer. The correct response to the question about man is Christ, *Redemptor Hominis*."[17] This rebirth manifests itself in the integral redemption of the whole man in Christ through the fellowship of the Father, Son and Holy Spirit, and with one another in them, which has been given to us in grace (Romans 5:5). Indeed, this redemption in Christ becomes a vision of cosmic redemption for the whole creation, including the life of culture. For God's grace in Christ *restores all life to its fullness, penetrating and perfecting and transforming the fallen creation from within its own order*, bringing creation into conformity with His will and purpose.[18]

Only the fourth type can do justice to the relation between creation, sin, and the grace of restoration. Grace is seen as a healing power that infuses the fallen creation from within the domain of nature and restores all of it from the sin that corrupts it. Unlike the first type, it does not regard nature as a corrupt vessel that is irreclaimable. Unlike the second and third type, grace is not a mere "add-on" to nature but nor does it simply exist side-by-side with the natural realm. Rather, God's grace in Christ *restores all life to its fullness, penetrating and perfecting and transforming the fallen creation from within its own order*, bringing creation into conformity with His will and purpose.

II Pauline Anthropology

Characteristic of St. Paul's anthropology is his conception of sin as a universal mode of human existence.[19] This conception is expressed by St. Paul in Romans 1:18-3:20. Both Jew and Gentile alike are included in the scope of sin's universality: "For there is no distinction: for all have sinned and fall short of the glory of God" (Rom. 3:22-23). In St. Paul's explanation of sin's universality he refers to the evidence of experience in his account of the depraved Gentiles (Rom. 1:18ff.) as well as to the Jews themselves who stand condemned under the law of God (2:17-3:8). Drawing these together, he concludes: "None is righteous, no, not one; no one understands; no one seeks for God. All have turned aside; together they have become worthless; no one does good, not even one" (Rom. 3:10-12). In this connection, St. Paul doesn't enumerate the separate sins of men, but rather in speaking of the charge that he is making against all men, namely, that they are all under sin (Rom. 3:9), he is expressing a leading Pauline idea regarding the paramount power of sin that has a hold upon all men.[20]

The universality of sin in man's history has twisted every aspect of the good creation made by God such that, in the words of the *Catechism*, "the consequences of original sin and of all men's personal sins put the world as a whole in the sinful condition aptly described in St. John's expression, 'the sin of the world'."[21] In particular, man's sinful condition is such that the "man in his sin, and the coinciding of being human and being a sinner" is expressed by St. Paul with the term "flesh" (*sarx*). This use of the term "flesh" is distinct from another Pauline usage, namely, when it signifies "what is human in its weakness, dependence on God, and perishable in itself."[22] In other words, the former usage of "flesh" refers to the description of man in his sinfulness and depravity. The latter usage does not refer as such to human sinfulness but rather to human limitation, the transitory, and weakness.

Now, regarding the first usage, St. Paul writes: "for while we were living in the flesh, our sinful passions . . . were at work in our members" (Rom. 7:5). "I am of the flesh, sold under sin" (Rom. 7:14). "For those who live according to the flesh set their minds on the things of the flesh, but those who live according to the Spirit set their minds on the things of the Spirit. To set the mind on the flesh is death, but to set the mind on the Spirit is life and peace. For the mind that is set on the flesh is hostile to God, for it does not submit to God's law; indeed, it cannot. Those who are in the flesh cannot please God" (Rom. 8:6ff.). Significantly, living according to the flesh stands for what is sinful, but that does not mean that "matter or the material part of man is inherently and irremediably evil, in contrast with the soul or spirit."[23] Hence, flesh in this sense does not represent "a part of man," such as his physical materiality or a lower element in man, "but man as a whole—unregenerate, fallen, sinful man."[24] So this meaning of the flesh represents man in his religious and moral weakness before God. "Now the works of the flesh are evident: fornication, impurity, sensuality, idolatry . . ." (Gal. 5:19). "For the one who sows to his own flesh will from the flesh reap corruption" (Gal. 6:8). ". . . among whom we all once lived in the passions of our flesh, carrying out the desires of the flesh . . . and we were by nature children of wrath" (Eph. 2:3). In short, living according to the flesh is the epitome of sin, of man in his fallenness, in his being being unregenerate and hence opposed to God—reflecting a worldview that distorts the fundamental relationship of the creature to God, denying man's dependence on him, while man puts his ultimate trust in what is of human effort or origin. "Cursed is the man who trusts in man and makes flesh his strength, whose heart turns away from the Lord" (Jer. 17:5). In this connection, we cannot fail to mention "a sharp and absolute contrast" St. Paul draws "between being 'in the flesh' (unregenerate) and being 'in the spirit' (regenerate)."[25] As Ladd explains,

> While a struggle remains in the Christian between the Spirit and the flesh, Paul knows the way of victory for the Spirit. The flesh of the body comes within the orb of sanctification (1 Thess. 5:23). But the flesh as unregenerate human nature can only be put to death. Here we meet the familiar Pauline tension between the indicative and the imperative. Paul views the death of the flesh as something that has already happened in the death of Christ. Those who belong to Christ have put off the body of the flesh in the circumcision of Christ, that is, in the circumcision of the heart, which is accomplished by Christ (Col. 2:11). Paul says, "I have been crucified with Christ" (Gal. 2:20), and "our old self was crucified with him" (Rom. 6:6). The identity of the flesh and the self is further supported in this teaching of crucifixion, for Paul means the same thing by the crucifixion of the flesh as he means when he says, "How can we who died to sin still live in it?" "We have been united with him in death." "We are buried with him by baptism into death" (Rom. 6:2-4). It is I, myself, who have died with Christ.[26]

Regarding the second usage of the term "flesh," St. Paul writes that the gospel that he has received and now preaches is not man's gospel, that is, flesh and blood did not reveal it to him (Gal. 1:16). Furthermore, it is not flesh and blood that shall inherit the kingdom of God (1 Cor. 15:50), and we do not wage war against flesh and blood (Eph. 6:12). Moreover, no flesh may boast in the presence of God (1 Cor. 1:29). Regarding this second meaning of St. Paul's usage of the term flesh, W. Gutbrod writes: "As the whole man, man is therefore sarx, absolutely distinct from God, i.e., he has nothing divine in him, which is not yet to say that he is evil, but simply that he is man, who is created, and not God, who created him."[27]

Significantly, St. Paul's theology of the body does not always identify "body" with the material corporality of man. There is a shift in meaning in the use of "body" from the visible and tangible "exterior" of man to "man himself." In other words, "body" sometimes refers more fundamentally to man himself in the totality of his existence, or the whole man in his temporal bodily existence. Rather than referring to "something external to a man himself, something he *has*," this usage of "body" refers to "what he *is*."[28] We find such a comprehensive use of the "body" when St. Paul says, for example, "present your bodies as a living sacrifice" (Rom. 12:1). "Your body is a temple of the Holy Spirit. . . . So glorify God in your body" (1 Cor. 6:19f). "So husbands ought to love their own wives as they love their own bodies; he who loves his wife loves himself" (Eph. 5:28): here "himself" and "his body" are used interchangeably. "Therefore do not let sin reign in your mortal body. . . . And do not present your members as instruments of unrighteousness to sin, but present *yourselves* to God as being alive from the dead" (Rom. 6:12-13): first the "body" is mentioned, then in conjunction with it, "your members," followed by, "yourselves," which is a synonym of the former two terms. In sum, as Ridderbos puts it:

> One finds the same comprehensive use of body in those places where body means approximately the earthly human life with the inclusion of death; so, e.g., when Paul says (2 Cor. 4:10) that he at all times bears about in his body the dying of Jesus, that the life also of Jesus may be manifested in his body; or when in Philippians 1:20 he expresses the earnest hope that Christ will be magnified in his body, and adds to this: whether by my life, or by my death (cf. also Col. 1:22). When Paul, moreover, speaks repeatedly of the human 'members' (*melĕ*), the same thing is expressed. But the members point still more concretely to the different possibilities of acting, obeying, sinning, which man possesses in his bodily existence."[29]

The significance of the body in this comprehensive use, and its distinction from "flesh," is also made clear by St. Paul in that, the body not only was created by God but also it is redeemed by him and will therefore be saved and sanctified by him from death (1 Cor. 15:50ff.). St. Paul does not promise the resurrection of the flesh, and that is because man as "flesh" (sarx) cannot inherit the kingdom of God (1 Cor. 15:50). Rather, he proclaims the resurrection of the body: we eagerly await the "redemption of our body," which means the redemption of the whole man himself in the totality of his existence.

Furthermore, there is another sense in which St. Paul uses the term "flesh," namely, the sense in which "body" (*sōma*) and "flesh" are used synonymously to refer to the whole man in his external, physical existence (Gal. 4:13; 2 Cor. 12:7), or the concrete material corporeality of man. For example, this usage is expressed when St. Paul speaks of "the circumcision of the flesh," in the outward, physical sense of the word (cf. Rom. 2:28ff.), or of being present or absent "after the flesh"

(Col. 2:1-5). The "flesh" in this sense corresponds to "the outward" (Rom. 2:28f), "the outward man" (2 Cor. 4:16), "the things which are seen" (2 Cor. 4:18), "the letter" (Rom. 2:27, 29; 7:6; 2 Cor. 3:6). Moreover, the "outward man" is opposed to the "inward man" (Rom. 7:22; 2 Cor. 4:16; Eph. 3:16), "describing the outward, visible, physical and the inward, invisible, spiritual side of human existence."[30]

Looking back to the universality of sin in man's existence, corresponding to the distinction between "inward man" and "outward man" is the corruption of sin (Romans 1 and Ephesians 4) and the bondage of sin (Romans 7:14ff.), respectively. "First of all," says Ridderbos, "the corruption of sin in the 'inward man,' the *nous*, the 'heart,' which from there extends itself in the (sinful acts of the) 'outward man,' in his 'body,' and in his 'members.'" By contrast, adds Ridderbos, "the reverse sequence is in the foreground: the external man, the body, the members, appears to have been brought under the control of sin in such a way that the inner man, too (the nous, the heart, the will), is unable to offer resistance to the superior power of sin in the body."[31] Moreover, the "inward man" is specifically described by St. Paul as "understanding" (*nous*), "heart" (*kardia*), "will" (*thelēma*), "soul" (*psychē*), "spirit" (*pneuma*), and "conscience" (*syneidēsis*).[32] Space does not permit an analysis of all these concepts, but I do want to say a few words about "heart" and "*nous*."

The "heart" is the concentration point of human existence, the real center of man's being, which in the biblical sense is, then, the central religious depth dimension of one's being, where the person decides for or against God.[33] The "heart" of man, Ridderbos writes, denotes man in his capacity for being addressed by, and in his susceptibility to, the divine revelation, as well as in his self-determination with respect to that revelation. Therefore, the heart is on the one hand the point of impact of the Holy Spirit, and it is there that the great decisions fall; but it is also clear that renewal by the Spirit does not confine itself to the heart of the inward man, but intends from thence to determine his entire humanity as well.[34]

The heart is, then, the root and center of human existence, in other words, of the whole man, and expresses itself in decisions, speaking, thinking, affections, aspirations, and believing regarding man's relationship to God, to his fellowman, and to the world surrounding him.[35] Indeed, one of these modes of expression is the nous in which the whole man is seen under the multifaceted aspect of understanding, judgment, self-determination, mind, thought, thinking—yes, the biblical sense of *nous* is that rich and varied—expressing that which man knows and wills with respect to the truth and the good according to man's deepest self-determination.

Now, regarding the corruption of sin in the inward man, we would do well to see that this corruption, according to St. Paul in Romans 1 and Ephesians 4, influences the human heart and understanding. Regarding Romans 1, St. Paul tells us that men have received in their *nous* a general revelation of God—that is, God's revelation of himself in and through the works of creation, including man himself—and thus they naturally know of God (1:19-20).[36] Having resisted the evidence of God's general revelation, however, men became futile in their thinking, and their foolish hearts become darkened (1:21). As Ridderbos puts it:

> In this [futility] of the inner man, this abandonment of the *nous* as the possibility for knowing God, and in this darkening of the heart, the wrath of God is being revealed. God gives him up to the evil lusts of his heart (v. 24), to a "reprehensible *nous*" (*eis adokimon noun*), to do that which is not fitting (v. 28). For not only is the inward man given up to darkness and ignorance in his relationship to God, but he is also perverted and inclined to all unrestraint and reprehensible activity in his moral self-determination.[37]

Similarly, St. Paul writes in Ephesians 4:17-19, urging believers not to walk as the gentiles do, namely, "in the futility of their minds [*nous*]." Paul continues:

> They are darkened in their understanding, alienated from the life of God because of the ignorance that is in them, due to their hardness of heart. They have become callous and have given themselves up to sensuality, greedy to practice every kind of impurity.

The cause of alienation and subsequent moral degradation is ignorance (*dia agnoian*), lacking true knowledge, which is again linked with the futility of the *nous*, the hardening of man's heart. Since *nous* describes that by which man is most deeply determined in his thinking and willing, we can understand the relation between it and conversion. Says Ridderbos,

> Likewise the word "conversion," occurring only very seldom in Paul (*metanoia, metanoein*), denotes a reversal of the nous, i.e., a radical turning about of man in all his thinking, willing and acting (cf. 2 Tim. 2:25; 2 Cor. 12:21), the secret of which lies in turning to God with contrition (2 Cor. 7:9ff), and which manifests itself in turning away from sin.[38]

Now, in light of St. Paul's teaching on the noetic influence of sin, what is the implication of that teaching for the moral life of the unbeliever and thus the moral knowledge of the Christ-believer? Without the special revelation in Christ and hence without the understanding (*nous*) having been renewed by the operation of the Spirit, is the unbeliever bereft of any natural moral knowledge and natural virtue? The point at issue here is the natural knowledge of God's law. And the verses in question are Romans 2:12-16, but especially verses 14-15:

> For when Gentiles, who do not have the law, by nature do what the law requires, they are a law to themselves, even though they do not have the law. They show that the work of the law is written on their hearts, while their conscience also bears witness, and their conflicting thoughts accuse or even excuse them.[39]

St. Paul says that it is by *nature*, not by saving grace, that unbelievers—those who do not have the Mosaic law—do the works of the law, or what the law requires. By doing the work required by the law they are, says St. Paul, "a law to themselves" (Rom 2:14). Ridderbos correctly remarks,

> These last words do not thus denote human arbitrariness or that man is his own law, but rather the superior power of the will of God, from the knowledge of which man cannot entirely fall away. Even in the absence of the written law [of Moses], he must inevitably set before himself the will of God himself expressed in it. For this reason the passive voice of the words "the work of the law [or, what the law requires] written in their hearts" is also to be understood as: written by God.[40]

Let us take note that St. Paul says that it is the *works* of the law that is written in men's hearts, not that the law is written there. He speaks of their *doing* by nature what the law requires. Does doing by nature what the law requires mean that man knows what is right and wrong? That is, does he know the moral truths man can know by thinking about what is right and what is wrong? Furthermore, is St. Paul implying that, given that moral knowledge, man's conscience will accuse him when he does wrong and excuse him when he does right?

The single answer to all these questions has to be "yes." The unbeliever's "suppression of the truth is," says John Frame, "never complete." He adds:

> He can never eradicate the truth completely from his consciousness. If he could, he could not live at all. For this is God's world, and the world's structure, order, and meaning is God's work. . . . In ethics, non-Christians often reveal knowledge of God's law. Apologists like C.S. Lewis and J. Budziszewski have pointed out that principles like "Play fair," "Don't murder," "Be faithful to your spouse," and "Take care of your family" are universally recognized. Although many people violate these principles, they show they know them by making excuses or rationalizations, and by accusing others of violating the same principles.[41]

This seems to be the most reasonable interpretation of this Romans passage. Although I cannot argue the point here, I think this interpretation gains its plausibility because of both *general revelation*—the expression "natural law" refers especially to God's general moral revelation—and *common grace*—a non-saving grace that restrains the destructive power of sin and sustains the orders of creation, especially man's nature; common grace is a matter of God's mercy, a grace that restrains the power of evil and sin from having its full way with creation—that enables man "by nature" to do the works of the law.[42]

Furthermore, what about moral motivation? Given the noetic influences of sin, is man entirely unable to do any good and inclined toward all evil unless he is reborn in Christ through the power of the Spirit? The answer to this last question has to be "no." Otherwise, original sin and its effects on human nature and natural freedom would be such that the latter is by nature capable of nothing except malicious, empty self-seeking. But that is obviously not the case. Furthermore, if it were the case, then, freedom of will would be destroyed and lost in the fallen state. But in accord with historic Catholic teaching on the freedom of the will, even in its fallen state, the will retains both the inclination to goodness besides a new inclination to evil, as well as the natural capacity for contrary moral choices between good and evil, a capacity which is now corrupted but not destroyed. It was not the freedom of the will that was entirely taken away by the fall; rather supernatural gifts of grace were taken away, and the will itself was consequently only weakened and corrupted, hence its misuse in developing vices, as well as its inability to turn back to God without grace. But also—given nonsaving, common grace—we can explain why, as Berkouwer puts it, "man still has some discernment with respect to that which the believer knows to be the law and the orderings of God for human life."[43] Berkouwer elaborates,

> It is indeed remarkable that human life, in manifesting an innate aversion to God and his holy will and in manifesting that it cannot subject itself to the law of God, (the "natural man"—Rom. 8:7 and 1 Cor. 2:14) still stands for right and justice, for punishing that which is evil and rewarding that which is good (cf. Rom. 13:3-4). There is still an appreciation of associating with one another and of the boundaries of the human community. There is still a searching for truth and knowledge. In short, there is still a *working* of the law written in human hearts which neither know God nor serve him. This doing of the work of the law implies that the eye still *observes* as it is being compelled to notice, and that it, in noticing, *cannot* withdraw itself from the goodness of the preserving and ruling activity of God and his holy law. Only in this light can we understand that there is still some contact with civic virtue.[44]

So a properly qualified moral virtue and moral knowledge persists after the fall. Properly qualified since there is not, after the fall, a realm of "pure nature" in human life, thought, and action that is essentially unimpaired by sin—both because of the fallen condition and personal sin—and hence unaffected by the renewal and restoration of Christ's redemptive work.[45] The view I am defending presupposes the understanding of nature and grace discussed earlier: "graces infuses nature and transforms it from within restoring it to its proper ends," that is, grace neither destroys nature nor is it merely added (the *donum superadditum*) to a human nature that requires little or no internal renewal within the order of nature. Rather, because of the noetic effects of sin, nature is corrupted (not destroyed), and hence grace takes fallen nature into its service and restores it within its own domain to its proper functioning. I turn now to illustrate briefly—indeed, much too briefly—how the idea that supernatural grace infuses and transforms fallen nature helps us to understand the relationship between the natural and supernatural virtues, as well as the Pauline reality of Christian freedom, in the life of the New Man.

III True Virtue and Ordered Spiritual Liberty

In this concluding section of my essay, I especially want to focus on the following claims: one, a virtuous life that is not properly ordered to man's true and final end—the beatitude of eternal life—is "false virtue"; and two, an act of human freedom that is not worthy of the calling that a believer has received in Christ is not "true freedom" but rather "false or illusory freedom." Let us consider two major proponents of these claims: St. Thomas Aquinas and John Paul II.[46]

Before discussing the former claim, let me briefly identify six points that this claim does not bring into question. For my purpose here, I follow Sokolowski's formulation of these points:

> [1] What is good by nature is not set over against what is good by grace but is integrated into it. And what is good by grace is not simply a matter of convention and arbitrary decision; rather it builds on nature and shares in the reasonableness associated with nature. [2] God's grace is of an order different from human excellence; and [3] if it is wrong to make grace depend on human achievement, it is equally confused and confusing to let grace turn virtue into vice, arrogance, or hypocrisy, and to deprive the well-ordered soul of its strength and exemplarity. [4] Grace and the theological virtues do not obliterate the distinction between virtue, vice, and self-mastery, and they do not destroy the fact that virtuous action emerges as a middle between two possible ways of failing, by excess and by defect, and that this course of action may be more excellently achieved the more virtuous the agent is. [5] They do not circumvent the need for the actual performance of actions as the only way to establish character, and they do not eliminate the need for prudence, for practical reason, in knowing what should be done when a situation calls for action. The determinations of natural virtue remain what they are. [6] Grace and the theological virtues must be so understood that natural virtue and the essentials of the moral life retain their integrity when involved with the Christian action.[47]

The first point fits well with the understanding of nature and grace that I set forth in the first section of this paper. Let's call it a version of the Thomistic axiom:[48] grace neither abolishes nature nor leaves it untouched, but builds on it—*not* by being a "plus factor," a mere "add on," but in the sense of "confirming what is good by nature, and in appreciating that what is good according to nature is not simply good in itself but also good because created and [loved and redeemed, and] therefore willed by God."[49] Of course this view does not confuse or somehow equate God's grace, the theological virtues, and the infused moral virtues—infused fortitude, temperance, courage, prudence—with the natural virtues and their achievements; but neither does it disparage or replace altogether natural virtue and the essentials of the moral life. Aquinas explains the difference between the theological virtues of faith, hope, and charity, and the infused moral virtues. He says, [T]he theological virtues are enough to shape us initially to our supernatural end, that is, to God himself immediately and to none other. Yet the soul needs also to be perfected by the infused moral virtues in regard to created things, though as subordinate to God."[50]

In other words, the theological virtues relate the believer directly to God alone as the absolutely supreme end of man. The infused moral virtues, however, relate directly to the temporal order, to every area of human life, marriage and family, schools, business, the state, and so forth. These temporal things have real ends and are not mere means with respect to the attainment of that supreme end. They are, as God's creation, possessed of an inherent goodness in themselves, and hence their ends are worthy of attainment in themselves. Yet, because we live in a fallen world and sin has battered these institutions, the grace of God, which is mediated through the infused moral virtues, transforms these institutions from *within their very order* so that they might be perfected, and in turn be properly ordered to man's supernatural end.[51]

The question remains to be asked: What, then, is the relation, in particular, between the two levels of moral virtue, the natural and the infused? Aquinas distinguishes between natural moral virtues that are acquired and the moral virtues that are infused, that is, supernatural gifts of God's grace. The crucial difference between these two sets of moral virtue is, as Sokolowski puts it, "that the infused virtues enable man to act toward his true and final end, while the others enable him to act toward an end which is final only in one restricted area."[52] In Aquinas' own words,

> It is possible by means of human works to acquire moral virtue, in so far as they produce good works that are directed to an end not surpassing the natural power of man: and when they are acquired thus, they can be without charity, even as they were in many of the Gentiles. But in so far as they produce good works in proportion to a supernatural last end, thus they have the character of virtue, truly and perfectly; and cannot be acquired by human acts, but are infused by God. Such like moral virtues cannot be without charity.[53]

Four points are made here by Aquinas: one, the natural moral virtues are acquired by man; two, those acquired virtues, for example, fidelity and trustworthiness in marriage, issue forth in good works that may attain the ends of marriage; three, good works of this sort and others may be accomplished by nonbelievers without the supernatural virtue of divine charity and the infused moral virtues; and four, without the infused moral virtues, which are gifts of the Holy Spirit in the life of the believer that is suffused with faith, hope, and charity, man cannot properly order his life toward his true final end, because, as Romanus Cessario remarks, it is those virtues that "enable the believer to live that complete transformation of human life into which the Christian mysteries, especially baptism, inaugurate us."[54] That is, Cessario adds, the infused moral virtues are "the virtues that build up the City of God, that mark the lives of those who 'are citizens with the saints and also members of the household of God, built upon the foundation of the apostles and the prophets, with Christ Jesus himself as the cornerstone' (Eph 2:19-20)."

Implicit in Aquinas' claim that acquired moral virtues do not enable man to attain his true final end is the biblical teaching that good works do not provide salvation: "For by grace you have been saved through faith, and that not of yourselves; it is the gift of God, not of works, lest anyone should boast" (Eph 2:8-9). Therefore, without the supernatural gifts of faith, hope, and charity, and, in particular, without the infused moral virtues of fidelity and trust that are a fruit of those gifts, we lack the resources necessary to order internally our marital life to God, and realize the call to beatitude, which is eternal life with God, and this is so even if our good works enable us to achieve the ends of marriage.

Yet, there is more: Aquinas distinguishes analogous senses of virtue: with the primary, indeed perfect, sense being found in infused virtue and the secondary, derived sense, being found in natural moral virtue. Moreover, as Sokolowski puts Aquinas' point, "Yet Aquinas does not stop with this shift in the primary sense of virtue; he goes on to quote the statement from Romans 14:23, 'For all that is not from faith is sin,' and he mentions Augustine's gloss, 'Where there is no recognition of the truth, virtue is false, even in good habits,'"[55] Aquinas has already told us that that natural virtues, and hence good deeds, exist in many pagans, even without saving grace. "They direct a man well in respect to what is final in some particular field, not in the whole of life," that is, not with respect to man's "absolutely ultimate end."[56] So he does not mean that they are false virtues in every sense. So what does Aquinas mean? Well, says Sokolowski, "from the point of view of the final end of man, good dispositions that fail to serve the final end do somehow seem to be bleached of their goodness. How is this to be understood?"[57] The question, then, is what does "falsity" mean when it is used theologically to say that natural virtue is false virtue with respect to man's absolutely ultimate end. Briefly, we can answer this question by explaining what makes natural virtue true virtue in this theological sense. True virtue is true if the choices we make, as the one who has put on the new man, are worthy of the calling we have received in Christ, extend Christ's lordship of the world, are manifestly Holy Spirit-filled, and show God's redeeming presence in the world in every dimension of human life transformed by God's saving grace.

In conclusion, I want to answer a question similar to the question about the meaning of "false virtue," but this time it is about the idea of "false freedom." I want to end this essay on the "New Man" in Christ with the claim that the Christ-believer "who acts fully under the movement of grace achieves the highest exercise of freedom."[58] The Crucified Christ reveals the authentic meaning of freedom," writes John Paul II, "he lives it fully in the total gift of himself and calls his disciples to share in his freedom."[59] The gift of freedom in and through Christ effects, Cessario says, "in the believer a sort of ordered spiritual liberty that characterizes New Testament existence."[60] Ordered spiritual liberty—that is the freedom to which we have been called by Christ.

New Testament freedom is, then, radically different from the freedom of autonomy, of a formal power of man to self-determination. With the idea of freedom as autonomous self-determination comes the notion that freedom is, indifferently, authentically manifested in either of two ways, to choose good or evil. This implies that "God gave man the freedom to choose his own way according to his own will," and hence that he placed man before a neutral and indifferent choice. But in the New Testament, particularly in St. Paul's Letter to the Galatians, the choice for sin perverts true freedom by enslaving free will. In this connection, John Paul II writes, "True human freedom is not realized in decisions made against God."[61] Berkouwer similarly writes: "Man's sin is not a manifestation of his freedom, but its perversion."[62] We find a similar line of thought in the Catechism: "There is no true freedom except in the service of what is good and just. The choice to disobey and do evil is an abuse of freedom and leads to 'the slavery of sin' [cf. Rom 6:17]" (italics added). Elsewhere in the Catechism we read: "By deviating from the moral law *man violates his own freedom*, becomes imprisoned within himself, disrupts neighborly fellowship, and rebels against divine truth" (italics added).[63] In other words, true human freedom is not found in exercising the mere formal possibility of choosing either good or evil, as if to say that choosing either of the two is as such indifferent to the normative question of true human freedom.

John Paul II rebuts the view that the choice for sin is a manifestation of true human freedom and thus is not in conflict with and a perversion of true creaturely freedom. He asks, "For how could it be an exercise of true freedom to refuse to be open to the very reality [God] which enables our self-realization?"[64] The answer is obvious: "There is no tension or competition between the freedom of the believer and his submission to Christ," says Berkouwer. He elaborates in a passage worth quoting in full:

> Indeed, it is precisely that man who stands in community with Him and who submits fully to Him who is referred to as free. The restoration in Christ, the new man, refers to our restoration from the enslaved will (servum arbitrium) to the free will (libera voluntas). . . . Freedom in the New Testament is not a formal possibility or a formal power which enables the believer to choose either of two ways. On the contrary: it is no possibility but rather an actuality, the actuality of being free (cf. Gal. 3:13, 4:4). It is materially qualified and made concrete through the relation to Christ, and is identical with coming into the service of God (Rom. 6:22), with all the wealth that is implied therein. The depth and completeness of this freedom become visible. It does not compete with or limit the acts of God, *as if the more powerfully God's acts affect our lives, the narrower our freedom becomes!* Or, *as if the accentuation of our freedom should limit the power of the grace of God!* Anyone who thinks in such categories should realize that the New Testament knows no such opposition. The New Testament pictures it in precisely the opposite way: the more communion with God fills our life, the more free our life becomes.[65]

Ordered spiritual liberty is the true freedom of man that is realized precisely in his submission to God in Christ through the power of the Holy Spirit. Of course submitting to God is itself a free act in the sense that it is possible for man to do otherwise and hence to reject him, saying yes or no to sin. Yet, although the freedom to do otherwise is a condition for the possibility of submitting to God in Christ, freedom in this sense, speaking biblically, is not the highest exercise of freedom. Indeed, the biblical perspective on freedom makes clear that sin, guilt, alienation, and rebellion perverts our freedom. "Divine grace forgives this perversion of freedom, this rebellion, and annihilates its effects, and so renders man once again truly free."[66] This truth is revealed in the reality of the new freedom in Christ, which is a gift of God's grace, in the reality of the man who is made new.

Notes

1. "I, made alive again in Christ, so think from within the living Christ." So rightly says the Dutch neo-Calvinist philosopher Herman Dooyeweerd (1894-1977) in his gloss on Galatians 2:20: "I live, yet no longer I, but Christ lives in me." For the full context, see Dooyeweerd, *De Wijsbegeerte der Wetsidee*, Boek I, De Wetsidee as Grondlegging der Wijsbegeerte (Amsterdam: H.J. Paris, 1935), 472. ET: *A New Critique of Theoretical Thought*, Vol. I, The Necessary Presuppositions of Philosophy, Translated by David H. Freeman and William S. Young (Philadelphia: Presbyterian and Reformed Publishing Co., 1969), 506.

2. I am indebted to Albert Wolters for this succinct way of formulating the various possibilities of relating nature, sin, and grace. For an introduction to his thinking, see *Creation Regained* (Grand Rapids, MI: Eerdmans, 1985). For my own analysis of these various possibilities with respect to a Catholic theology of culture, see *Slitting the Sycamore: Christ and Culture in the New Evangelization* (Grand Rapids, MI: Acton Institute, 2008).

3. Jacques Maritain states, "There is one error that consists in ignoring [the] distinction between nature and grace. There is another that consists in ignoring their union," *Clairvoyance de Rome* (Paris, 1929), 222. Cited in Henri de Lubac, "Apologetics and Theology," *Theological Fragments* (San Francisco: Ignatius Press, 1989), 91—104, and for this citation at 103, n. 28.

4. Cf. Matthias Joseph Scheeben, Matthias Joseph Scheeben, *Natur und Gnade. Versuch einer systematischen, wissenschaftlichen Darstellung der natürlichen und übernatürlichen Lebensordnung im Menschen* (Mainz 1861). ET: *Nature and Grace*, trans. Cyril Vollert, S.J., S.T.D. (St. Louis/London: B. Herder Book Co., 1954), 308.

5. John Henry Newman, *Apologia Pro Vita Sua* (London: J.M. Dent & Sons LTD., 1912 [1864]), 222.

6. Robert Sokolowski, *The God of Faith & Reason, Foundations of Christian Theology* (Washington, D.C.: Catholic University of American Press, 1995 [1982]), 72.

7. Vatican II, *Gaudium et Spes*, December 7, 1965, Pastoral Constitution on the Church in the Modern World, no. 43.

8. Ibid., no. 58.

9. *Towards Pastoral Approach to Culture*, Pontifical Council for Culture, 1999, no. 6. The quotation inside this quotation is from John Paul II, "Homily of the Enthronement Mass," *L'Osservatore Romano*, October 22, 1978.

10. As cited in Yves Congar, *Laity, Church and World*, trans. Donald Attwater (Baltimore, Maryland: Helicon Press, 1960), 48-49.

11. St. Augustine, *The City of God*, Book XIV, Chapter XI, http://www.ccel.org/ccel/schaff/npnf102.iv.XIV.11.html.

12. All the quotations in this paragraph, except the quotation from St. Augustine's *The City of God*, are from the *Catechism of the Catholic Church*, nos. 1603, 1606-1609, 1614-1615.

13. Etienne Gilson, *Christianity and Philosophy*, trans. Ralph MacDonald, C.S.B. (New York/London: Sheed & Ward, 1939), 21, 24, and 111, respectively.

14. John Paul II, *Evangelium Vitae*, March 25, 1995 Encyclical Letter, no. 95. The quote within this quote is from Paul VI, 1975 Apostolic Exhortation, *Evangelii Nuntiandi*, no. 18. Paul VI adds, "The purpose of evangelization is therefore precisely this interior change, and if it had to be expressed in one sentence the best way of stating it would be to say that the Church evangelizes when she seeks to convert, solely through the divine power of the message she proclaims, both the personal and collective consciences of people, the activities in which they engage, and the lives and concrete milieu which are theirs."

15. John Paul II, *Memory & Identity, Conversations at the Dawn of a Millennium* (New York: Rizzoli, 2005), 25.

16. John Paul II, *Memory & Identity*, 81.

17. John Paul II, *Memory & Identity*, 110, 114.

18. Portions of these three paragraphs were recently published in my book, *Slitting the Sycamore, Christ and Culture in the New Evangelization*, 57-60.

19. On the theme of the "presence and *universality of sin in man's history*," see *Catechism of the Catholic Church* (hereafter *CCC*), nos. 401-405. For a theological analysis consistent with the teaching of *CCC*, see Herman Ridderbos, *Paul: An Outline of His Theology*, trans. John Richard De Witt (Grand Rapids, MI: Eerdmans, 1975), 93-95, 100-104, 114-130. I am much indebted to Ridderbos' analysis of St. Paul's anthropology. Also extremely helpful is the study by the Anglican bishop and New Testament scholar John A.T. Robinson, *The Body: A Study in Pauline Theology* (London: SCM Press LTD, 1952). See also, George Eldon Ladd, *A Theology of the New Testament* (Grand Rapid, MI: Eerdmans, 1974), Chap. 33, "The Pauline Psychology," 457-478.

20. Alister E. McGrath argues that there are several biblical models of sin: sin is like an illness, like moral guilt, like an enslaving force, and like existential alienation, with its imagery of death and life, darkness and light, sin and grace, being lost and being found. In sum, "The power of sin is broken, and its moral guilt canceled, through the saving death of Christ" (*Intellectuals Don't Need God & Other Modern Myths* [Grand Rapids, MI: Zondervan, 1993], 134-137).

21. *CCC*, no. 408. John Paul II holds that our world is shattered to its very foundation and the root of this "is to be found in a *wound* in man's inmost self. In the light of faith, we call it sin: beginning with *original sin*, which all of us bear from birth as an inheritance from our first parents, to the sin which each one of us commits when we abuse our own freedom" (*Reconciliatio et Paenitentia*, Post-Synodal Apostolic Exhortation, December 2, 1984, no. 2). See also, *Dominum et Vivificantem*, Encyclical Letter, May 30, 1986, "When on the eve of the Passover Jesus speaks of the Holy Spirit as the one who 'will convince the world concerning sin' [Jn. 16:8], . . . this statement must be given *the widest possible meaning*, insofar as it includes all the sin in the history of humanity" (no. 29).

22. Ridderbos, *Paul*, 93.
23. Robinson, *The Body*, 24.
24. Ladd, *A Theology of the New Testament*, 472.
25. Ibid., 473.
26. Ibid., 474.
27. W. Gutbrod, *Die Paulinische Anthropologie*, 99, as cited in Ridderbos, *Paul*, 94.
28. Robinson, *The Body*, 28.
29. Ridderbos, *Paul*, 116.
30. Ridderbos, *Paul*, 115.
31. Ibid., 114.
32. I am closely following the analysis of these concepts in Ridderbos, *Paul*, 117-126.
33. See *CCC*, no. 368.
34. Ridderbos, *Paul*, 228. See also, *CCC*, "The heart is the dwelling-place where I am, where I live; according to the Semitic or Biblical expression, the heart is the place 'to which I withdraw.' The heart is the hidden center, beyond the grasp of our reason and of others; only the Spirit of God can fathom the human heart and know it fully. The heart is the place of decision, deeper than our psychic drives. It is the place of truth, where we choose life or death. It is the place of encounter, because as image of God we live in relation: it is the place of covenant" (no. 2563).
35. Ridderbos, *Paul*, 119. See also, Dooyeweerd, *De Wijsbegeerte der Wetsidee*, Boek I, 472. ET: *A New Critique of Theoretical Thought*, Vol. I, 502, "The heart in its pregnant Biblical sense as religious root and centre of human existence. . . is the *fullness of our selfhood* in which all our temporal functions find their religious concentration" (506). Joseph Ratzinger also affirms the heart, in its Biblical sense, to be the root and center of our whole human existence. The heart refers to the whole man, or, as Ratzinger says, "the inner person, the entirety of the self" (Joseph Ratzinger [Benedict XVI], *A New Song for the Lord: Faith in Christ and Liturgy Today*, trans. Martha M. Matesich [New York: Crossroad, 1996], 177). For Ratzinger's reflection on the philosophical anthropology and theology of the heart in the Holy Scripture and the Fathers of the Church, see "The Mystery of Easter: Substance and Foundation of Devotion to the Sacred Heart," in *Behold the Pierced One: An Approach to a Spiritual Christology*, trans. Graham Harrison (San Francisco: Ignatius Press, 1986), 47-69. See also, Walter Principe, C.S.B., "Affectivity and the Heart in Thomas Aquinas' Spirituality," in *Spiritualities of the Heart*, edited by Annice Callahan, R.S.C.J. (New York: Paulist Press, 1990), 45-63.
36. John Paul II writes in the opening words of his marvelous 1993 Encyclical Letter, *Veritatis Splendor*, "The splendor of truth shines forth in all the works of the Creator and, in a special way, in man, created in the image and likeness of God (cf. Gen 1:26)."
37. Ridderbos, *Paul*, 122.
38. Ibid., 118-119.
39. Helpful to me in discussing these verses are the following works: G.C. Berkouwer, *De Algemene Openbaring* (Kampen: J.H.Kok, 1951), 146-194. ET: *General Revelation*, trans. (Grand Rapids, MI: Eerdmans, 1955), 175-230. Dewey J. Hoitenga, Jr., *John Calvin and the Will, A Critique and Corrective* (Grand Rapids, MI: Baker Books, 1997), 111-113. J. Budziszewski, *What We Can't Not Know* (Dallas: Spence Publishing Co., 2003). Ridderbos, *Paul*, 123-124.
40. Ridderbos, *Paul*, 107.

41. John Frame, "Unregenerate Knowledge of God," http://www.thirdmill.org/files/english/hall_of_frame/Frame.Apologetics2004.UnregenerateKnowledgeofGod.pdf. In a similar way, John Paul II writes in *Veritatis Splendor* (no. 1): "As a result of that mysterious original sin, committed at the prompting of Satan, the one who is 'a liar and the father of lies' (John 8:44), man is constantly tempted to turn his gaze away from the living and true God in order to direct it towards idols (cf. 1 Thess 1:9), exchanging 'the truth about God for a lie' (Rom 1:25). Man's capacity to know the truth is also darkened, and his will to submit to it is weakened. Thus, giving himself over to relativism and skepticism (cf. John 18:38), he goes off in search of an illusory freedom apart from truth itself. But no darkness of error or of sin can totally take away from man the light of God the Creator. In the depths of his heart there always remains a yearning for absolute truth and a thirst to attain full knowledge of it."

42. On common grace, see Dooyeweerd, *De Wijsbegeerte der Wetsidee*, Boek I, 472. ET: *A New Critique of Theoretical Thought*, Vol. I, "The Biblical motive of creation, fall into sin, and redemption in Jesus Christ in the communion of the Holy Spirit. This implies the conflict between the Kingdom of God and the kingdom of darkness in the root and the temporal coherence of our cosmos. It implies, too, the recognition of the checking of the disintegrating activity of sin by common grace, because of the regenerate human that is accepted and sanctified by God in Christ as the Head (particular grace). . . . It also leads to a thankful recognition of all the gifts and talents that God has left to fallen humanity" (507).

43. Berkouwer, *De Algemene Openbaring*, 169 [200].

44. Ibid., 171 [202-203].

45. Dewey J. Hoitenga, Jr., *John Calvin and the Will,* 113.

46. St. Thomas Aquinas, *Summa Theologiae*, I-II q. 65, art. 2. John Paul II, *Fides et Ratio*, 1998 Encyclical Letter, no. 13. Extremely helpful to me in dealing with these two claims have been G.C. Berkouwer, *De Mens Het Beeld Gods* (Kampen: J.H. Kok, 1957), especially 346-389. ET: *Man: The Image of God*, trans. Dirk w. Jellema (Grand Rapids, MI: Eerdmans, 1962), 310-348; and Sokolowski, *The God of Faith & Reason, Foundations of Christian Theology*, 69-103.

47. Sokolowski, *The God of Faith & Reason*, 76-77.

48. St. Thomas Aquinas, *Summa Theologiae*, I, q. 1, art. 8, resp. 2. See also, W.D. Hughes, O.P., Appendix 3, "The Infusion of Virtues," in the Blackfriars translation of the *Summa Theologiae*, Vol. 23, 247-248: "For St Thomas grace permeates nature, neither destroying nor leaving it alone. His is not what Fr Karl Rahner describes as the 'standard' teaching, that 'the relationship between nature and grace is thought of as two layers laid carefully one on top of the other.'"

49. Sokolowski, *The God of Faith & Reason*, 83.

50. St. Thomas Aquinas, *Summa Theologiae*, I-II q. 63, art. 3.

51. Jacques Maritain, *On the Philosophy of History*, Edited by Joseph W. Evans (New York: Charles Scribner's Sons, 1957), 130-131.

52. Sokolowski, *The God of Faith & Reason*, 78; cf. also 77, 145.

53. St. Thomas Aquinas, *Summa Theologiae*, I-II q. 65, art. 2.

54. Romanus Cessario, O.P., *Christian Faith & The Theological Life* (Washington, D.C.: Catholic University of American Press, 1996), 4, and 3.

55. Sokolowski, *The God of Faith & Reason*, 78-79. In another translation of Augustine's gloss on Romans 14:23, we read, "He that fails to acknowledge the truth, has no true

virtue, even if his conduct be good."

56. St. Thomas Aquinas, *Summa Theologiae*, I-II q. 65, art. 2.
57. Sokolowski, *The God of Faith & Reason*, 79.
58. Romanus Cessario, O.P., *Christian Faith & The Theological Life*, 168.
59. John Paul II, *Veritatis Splendor*, no. 85.
60. Romanus Cessario, O.P., *Christian Faith & The Theological Life*, 169.
61. John Paul II, *Fides et Ratio*, no. 13.
62. Berkouwer, *De Mens Het Beeld Gods*, 358 [321]
63. *CCC*, no. 1733, and no. 1740, respectively.
64. John Paul II, *Fides et Ratio*, no. 13.
65. Berkouwer, *De Mens Het Beeld Gods*, 359-360 [321-322]; italics in original.
66. Ibid., 359 [321]

Response to Eduardo Echeverria

Charles Lugosi
Visiting Professor of Law, 2007-2009
Ave Maria School of Law
Ann Arbor, Michigan

Eduardo Echeverria has provided a profound and detailed discussion of the relation of human nature to both sin and grace. From a legal viewpoint, this theological discussion is not irrelevant, for only a fallen human nature, it seems, can explain some of the more disturbing trends of contemporary jurisprudence. In particular, I have in mind the "jurisprudence of legal positivism" that has led to the denial of the right to life of the unborn. In what follows, I will argue that such a legal philosophy threatens the rational and religious foundations of the Constitution. Moreover, it reveals just how corrupt and blind human beings can become without the grace and light of God.

As human beings, we recognize in our consciences that the murder of the innocent is a grave injustice. This is a self-evident truth, for it is a natural law that is inscribed in our hearts, enabling our consciences to distinguish the difference between right and wrong. A human law that punishes the wicked for murder is in harmony with divine law and natural law, for there is justice in the result. A human law that permits the killing of innocent human beings, however, is a perversion, for it lacks moral authority and is a void law, because it is contrary to the divine law that is integral to the natural law. Dressing up murder in the clothing of a lawful act does not transform its underlying character of naked lawlessness and injustice. An unjust law is an act of violence, for it is contrary to both the divine law and natural law. A human law that permits the killing of the innocent is hostile to God. It results from living in the flesh, and is the epitome of sin.

In America, human laws that permit abortion provide proof that our courts and legislatures have supplanted God's laws by succumbing to the temptation to be like God. Ignored is God's warning that "from man in regard to his fellow man

I will demand an accounting for human life."[1]

Instead, a jurisprudence of legal positivism reigns, where law needs no validation other than the coercive ability of the state to enforce its rules. Law is not the servant of justice; rather, law imposes the coercive political will of human beings who are legally defined as persons and thus hold the balance of power, for good or for evil. For the legal positivists, the source of the law is not God, but man. In this model lies the seed of tyranny, for man puts his trust into what is of human effort or origin.

Historically, the common law of England was inseparable from natural law. William Blackstone imparted natural law principles to his law students at Oxford, teaching them that God's eternal unchanging laws comprehensively addressed good and evil, that these laws were discoverable by human reason, and applicable to all human conduct. So long as human laws (positive law) conformed to natural law (including the divine commandments of the Decalogue), individual happiness was assured. The pursuit of happiness was thus linked to natural law, which protects the family and parental authority (Fourth Commandment), human life (Fifth Commandment), the unity of a man and a woman in marriage (Sixth Commandment), property (Seventh Commandment), and honor (Eighth Commandment); and which also protects us from the greed, jealousy, and wrongful desires of others who covet what we possess and enjoy (Ninth and Tenth Commandments).[2]

Our founders, including Alexander Hamilton and George Mason, were schooled in the works of Sir Edward Coke and Sir William Blackstone, for their writings echoed the common law jurisprudence that any human laws that were contrary to natural law were void and of no effect. The Ten Commandments are the cornerstone of American civilization because they articulate the law of obligations and responsibilities that govern the freedom of individuals.

Remembrance of the Ten Commandments and their place in American jurisprudence is fundamental to ensure God's future blessings upon America, for the alternative is to live by the works of the flesh: reaping corruption, and embracing a world view that denies man's dependence upon God.

As a matter of current American constitutional law, the word "person" does not have the same meaning as "human being" until the process of live birth has been completed. Until then, legalized abortion permits parents, doctors, scientists, and judges, amongst others, to openly discriminate between human beings that are chosen for birth and those that are not. Even though in the United States the Fourteenth Amendment to the Constitution offers a right of equal protection and due process so that no person is deprived of his or her life or liberty, this right is denied to any human being who is not defined as a person—thus, all unborn human beings.

"I contend that the Fourteenth Amendment is not confined to its historical origins and purposes, and was always available to protect all human beings that are defined as non-persons, including all unborn human beings, individually and as a class. It is a matter of judicial interpretation. The Supreme Court can define 'person' to include all human beings, born and unborn. The justices simply choose not to do so."[3]

I maintain that there cannot be the "rule of law" if the Constitution is interpreted to perpetuate a legal caste system of "separate and unequal," in which there is no justice for the unborn. I contend there is no justice for the unborn human being so long as there is denial of equality, respect, dignity, liberty, life and due process of law. Since the word "person" in the Fourteenth Amendment is capable of being interpreted liberally in an objective manner consistent with the rule of law to include all human beings, not to do so violates the spirit of the Declaration of Independence, natural law, and the core liberal ideals of equality and human dignity.

Since we are called to live by the Spirit, we cannot permit abortion, for to do so is to live in the flesh, which ends in death: physical death of the unborn human being; spiritual death of those responsible for abortion.

The legal grievances that led to the American War of Independence offer hope that the United States is a nation founded upon the rule of law, and that at the root of the American Constitution is the objective truth that "human beings" and "human persons" are indistinguishable from one another. For it is only when there is spiritual harmony and proper alignment in the meaning of human being and person that our universe will attain a measure of peace and be free of discrimination and inequality that inevitably result so long as objective truth is ignored. "If all of humanity is created equally at conception, and if each member of the human race has the inalienable right to life, liberty and the pursuit of happiness, there is no place in today's world for extinguishing embryonic and fetal life."[4]

Until the legal definition of "human person" and "human being" merge, resulting in harmony between science, theology and the law, the current dissonance between truth and fiction will increase, rather than diminish. The cruel paradox will continue that as science adds more convincing proof that human life begins at conception, judges will continue to decide that healthy babies in healthy mothers may be killed with legal immunity as a matter of choice. It is law that must conform to the objective truth of science, and the law of God.

In his letter from the Birmingham Jail, Dr. Martin Luther King Jr. stated:

> Injustice anywhere is a threat to justice everywhere. We are caught in an inescapable network of mutuality, tied in a single garment of destiny. Whatever affects one directly affects all indirectly . . . . We know through painful experience that freedom is never voluntarily given by the oppressor; it must be demanded by the oppressed . . . . [T]here are two types of laws: just and unjust . . . . I would agree with Saint Augustine that "An unjust law is no law at all."[5]

Any law that degrades human personality is unjust. All segregation statutes are unjust because segregation distorts the soul and damages the personality. It gives the segregator a false sense of superiority, and the segregated a false sense of inferiority. Segregation, to use the terminology of the Jewish philosopher, Martin Buber, substitutes an "I-it" relationship for an "I-thou" relationship, and ends up relegating persons to the status of things. Hence, segregation is not only politically, economically and sociologically unsound, it is morally wrong.

I believe that the legal segregation of unborn human beings from the rest of the human family degrades and depersonalizes the humanity of the unborn, stigmatizing non-persons as inferior to persons, who assert legal but not moral superiority over non-persons. This legal segregation substitutes an "I-it" relationship for the "I-thou" relationship between a mother and her unborn child, relegating her baby to the status of a thing that may be killed with impunity. As legally inferior human beings, non-persons are at the mercy of those legally superior human beings who literally hold an arbitrary power of life or death over the unborn. Civil liberty is interpreted by persons as natural liberty—unrestrained freedom to exercise one's absolute will even if it is detrimental to other human beings and society at large. This kind of corrupt thinking is repugnant to a just society governed by the rule of law where every human life is treasured and unborn babies are welcomed as persons.

I define the "rule of law" as government by laws that people of moral conscience are willing to obey because the laws are inherently just. The ideal of the "rule of law" is to live in a democratic society that places constitutional limits on the power of government, permanently protects inalienable human rights and fundamental freedoms from undue encroachment and provides equality before laws administered by an independent judiciary. I define "rule *by* law" as the antithesis of the "rule *of* law": it means to be governed by unjust laws in any society—including democratic societies—in which the government may exercise arbitrary powers and may abridge inalienable human rights at will and remove from constitutional protection the inalienable civil rights of any human being, such as by creating a class of non-persons. The main difference between these opposite concepts is that *justice* is the defining characteristic in a society governed by "rule of law," and *deferential coerced obedience* is the defining characteristic in a "rule by law" society. Without a moral component that squares with the eternal and natural law of God and that objectively sets up a standard of righteousness, there can be no rule of law, but only the tyrannical imposition of rule by law.

"Linkage of the rule of law and the supremacy of God is foundational for the flourishing of truth and justice."[6] Truth and justice do not exist in a vacuum; they exist in a society of human beings, organized into a political state. Unfortunately, a state may become tyrannical such that truth and justice can disappear or be stifled. The solution is respect for every human being as a person. The person becomes paramount, not the state. The state exists for the benefit of every human being; not that every human being exists for the benefit of the state.

America was founded upon the rule of law, anchored in the common law infused with Christian morality.[7] Conformity to the rule of law means conformity to setting the mind on the Spirit. The resolution to the current cultural, political and legal war over abortion, and to the derivative battles over embryonic stem cell research and cloning, is found in the universal truth anchored in the concept of the rule of law that we are all created equal and that we all possess an inalienable right to life and liberty. Explicitly interpreting "person" in the Fourteenth Amendment to mean all human beings, including the unborn, from the time of conception to the time of natural death will fulfill the promise and vision of the signers of the Declaration of Independence. For there can be no rule of law, so long as the word "person" is legally manipulated to exclude and segregate classes or individuals from the human family and to discriminate against legally created castes in order to legally justify the killing or enslavement of innocent human life. Not until this legal manipulation of the word "person" ends will there exist the rule of law in America.

While in theory it may be conceded that the unborn are just as human as those people who are born, the reality is that the unborn are segregated from the born. They are invisible and inferior to those who are born. The unborn, particularly in their earliest stages of development, do not look human, and we cannot readily psychologically identify with an object that does not look like us when we look in the mirror. The unborn, and indeed newborns, are helpless creatures because they cannot survive on their own without maternal and/or medical assistance. The unborn are penniless, powerless, and depending on their age and stage of development, socially, culturally, physically, and mentally different and inferior from the rest of humanity. The unborn, and even the newborn, do not meet the global personhood criteria of segregationist philosophers who sanction the destruction of embryos and fetuses.

Those who prescribe to this argument must conclude that the unborn are thus separate and unequal. The unborn are not just segregated from the constitutional rights to life, liberty and equality guaranteed by the Fourteenth Amendment—they are excluded. It is thus permissible to discriminate against the unborn individually and as a class, for until they are born, the unborn do not attain legal protection under the Constitution. It is only over time and with continued physical development that children gain with maturity and age, political, physical, social and legal power.

The unborn are depersonalized and dehumanized, not fit for classification on the lowest rung of social hierarchies reserved for born human beings.

The depersonalization and dehumanization of human beings so they can be aborted violates the core values of American constitutional law. In a free society, where there is liberty and justice for all, government by rule of law forbids human authority in any circumstances to deprive any class of human beings of their inalienable right to life.

"The alternative choice of an expedient pragmatic rule by law approach to give effect to abortion on demand sets a dangerous precedent, for a person's former inalienable rights become insecure, with the denial of natural law, like a transient entity that is here today and gone tomorrow."[8] If the state is supreme to decide who is a person and who is a non-person, the state no longer serves the individual, but the individual the state. The state's historic role in protecting and preserving human life is replaced by a new goal to permit legal persons to dominate the lives of legal non-persons.

Failure to conform to the rule of law results in judicially legislated inequality designed to legally justify mass genocide of innocent human beings who have no say in their destiny and whose lives are devalued by operation of law.

We face the stark choice of siding with the rule of law and the opportunity to declare the unborn human being a person within the meaning of the Fourteenth Amendment, or to live according to the flesh and exclude an entire class of human beings from constitutional protection, leaving the unborn at the mercy of laws sanctioning their destruction in accordance with rule by law.

There can be no rule of law when one class of human beings is legally empowered to play the role of gatekeeper to life or death to an inferior caste of human beings. The Constitution was never intended to bestow a constitutional right of privacy to legally permit one person to take the life of an innocent human being stripped of constitutional protection.

There are limits to constitutional liberties, which begin when there is a collision with or an effect upon the constitutional rights of other human beings.[9] These limits can be removed by dehumanizing those other human beings by impersonal language and by legally redefining persons as non-persons. Once reclassified and removed from legal protection, the judiciary or the government is free to legislate and permit either a restricted or unrestricted license to kill or enslave an entire class of depersonalized human beings, just like any other class of non-persons.

There is a widely held assumption by students entering law school today that the word "person" in the Fourteenth Amendment applies only to human beings that are born alive. Personhood is identified with citizenship, which is conferred upon natural human beings by operation of law at birth.

As non-persons, the unborn today have less legal protection than slaves had prior to the adoption of the Fourteenth Amendment. It is both tragic and ironic that after the passage of the Fourteenth Amendment, not only has the Supreme Court with the *Roe, Doe* and *Casey* decisions permitted the substitution of one form of slavery for another, but it has granted legal immunity to those who kill the unborn with impunity.

For the restoration of the rule of law, there is no alternative; faithfulness to the Constitution demands nothing less. Nothing in the text of the Constitution gives anyone the private unrestrained liberty to violently override another human being's inalienable and inherent right to life. America is the envy of the world because of its commitment to the principles of justice, equality and human rights. But when rule by law does violence to those principles, society pays the price and injustice triumphs. The social war on abortion among Americans will be resolved only when opponents of the personhood of the unborn recognize the truth that the only hope for resolution is to set our minds on the Spirit, to live by grace, and to abide by the Golden Rule[10] and conform to the rule of law so that "human being" and "human person" mean the same thing.[11]

Then those who once formerly performed abortions, like Dr. Bernard Nathanson, now a Roman Catholic, will, like the former slave ship captain, John Newton, be able to sing: "Amazing Grace, how sweet the sound, that saved a wretch like me. I once was lost; but now I'm found; was blind, but now I see."

Notes

1. Genesis 9:5 (New American Bible).

2. Deuteronomy 5:6-21.

3. Charles I. Lugosi, "Conforming to the Rule of Law: When Person and Human Being Finally Mean the Same Thing in Fourteenth Amendment Jurisprudence," *Georgetown Journal of Law & Public Policy* 4 (2006), 361, 364.

4. Ibid., 372-73.

5. Martin Luther King, Jr., "Letter from a Birmingham Jail" (April 16, 1963): available at: *http://www.Africa.upenn/articles_Gen/Letters_Birmingham_htl.*; Cf. Augustine, *De Lib. Arb.* I, 5, cited in St. Thomas Aquinas, *Summa theologica*, I-II, q. 96, a. 4.

6. Lugosi, 375.

7. See, e.g. *Church of the Holy Trinity v. United States,* 143 U.S. 457, 471 (1892).

8. Lugosi, 425.

9. *See Prince v. Massachusetts*, 321 U.S. 158, 177 (1944) (Jackson, J., concurring).

10. This is a universal code all people in a diverse and pluralistic society can support, for it transcends religious affiliation. "Do to others whatever you would have them do to you." *Matthew* 7:12 (New American Bible) (Christian); "Hurt not others in ways that you yourself would find hurtful." *Udana-Varga* 5, 1 (Buddhist); "This is the sum of duty; do naught onto others what you would not have them do unto you." *Mahabharata* 5, 1517 (Hindu); "No one of you is a believer until he desires for his brother that which he desires for himself." *Sunnah* (Muslim); "What is hateful to you, do not do to your fellowman." *Talmud, Shabbat* 3id (Jewish). *See* The Universality of the Golden Rule in the World Religions, *available at* http://www.teachingvalues.com/goldenrule.html (last visited Dec. 28, 2009).

11. See generally Robert P. George, "Public Reason and Political Conflict: Abortion and Homosexuality," *Yale Law Journal* 106 (1997), 2475.

CHAPTER FIVE

The Western Legal Tradition: Its Contemporary Crisis, and Pauline Diagnosis

Philip Blosser
Professor of Philosophy,
Sacred Heart Major Seminary, Detroit, Michigan

The Crisis

In 1984, one year after the publication of his magisterial work, *Law and Revolution: The Formation of the Western Legal Tradition*, Harold Berman (1918-2007) gave an address at the Boston College Law School entitled "The Crisis of Legal Education in America."[1] Although that was over a quarter of a century ago, Berman's concerns strike the reader today as uncannily prescient and perhaps even more timely today than when they were first given voice.

We have been overwhelmed, he said back in 1984, by the belief that law is politics, that law is something made by politicians, legislators, judges, administrators and those in power to accomplish their will, a pragmatic device for enacting policy or an instrument for social engineering. In some sense, of course, law is all of these things, but it is also more: it is also morality, conscience, and history. It is not only something *made* by those in power, but also something *received* by them. Legislators and judges are not only its *masters*, but its *subjects*. What is being lost is the view the law is rooted in something bigger than the people who hand it down, that it is rooted in history and the transcendent moral fabric of the universe.

In the past, American lawyers learned their law chiefly from William Blackstone's (pronounced "Blexstun") *Commentaries on the Laws of England*, in which the eighteenth century English jurist wrote: "[T]he law of nature ... dictated by

God himself . . . is binding in all countries and at all times; no human laws are of any validity if contrary to this; and such of them as are valid derive all force and all their authority, mediately or immediately, from this original."[2]

In a striking statement, Berman says: "Without the fear of purgatory and hope of the last judgment, the Western legal tradition would not have come into being."[3] Yet in most American law schools today, one is not likely to hear any reference to the sources of our legal tradition in the Judeo-Christian convictions of our ancestors. Within the space of fifty years—Berman says within his own lifetime—the public philosophy of the United States has shifted from a religious to a secular theory of law, from a moral to a political or instrumental theory, and from an historical to a pragmatic theory. Berman writes:

> … We still use cases, but since there is not a belief in the ongoing historical development of law over generations and centuries, the doctrine of precedent has grown weaker and weaker, and the law that a case stands for no longer seems to have objectivity. It is taught by some that any case can be decided any way—that law is, basically, an argumentative technique. The judge, it is thought, decides on the basis of his political, economic, or psychological prejudices; legal reasons are merely rationalizations.[4]

Berman provides an interesting survey of the evolution of the opening statements of Harvard Law School catalogues since 1900. The 1900 catalogue says that "… the design of this school is to afford such a training in the fundamental principles of English and American law as will constitute the best preparation for the practice of the profession in any place where that system of law prevails."[5] Legal history provided the transcendent reference point for the definition of justice. The 1930 catalogue, when Roscoe Pound was dean, is even more explicit: "The school seeks as its primary purpose to prepare for the practice of the legal profession wherever the Common Law prevails. It seeks to train lawyers in the spirit of the common legal heritage of the English-speaking people."[6] In 1970 this sentence was dropped, and in 1983 the phrase "common law" disappeared altogether. But the catalogue of 1970 [nearly forty years ago] went on to say:

> No law school can today teach with certainty the law which will be practiced by its graduates throughout their professional lives. The school does seek to provide its students with a solid base of knowledge, analytical skills, and insight which will enable them to perform effectively as laws and legal institutions continue to change around them.[7]

Gone are the phrases "fundamental principles," "common legal heritage," and "common law." Berman comments: "There you have the contemporary crisis in American legal education. We are unable to identify a common purpose other than needed to 'perform effectively' as lawyers. . . . "[8]

This represents nothing less, in Berman's view, than the triumph of the positivist theory of law—the view that law is the will of the lawmaker—and the decline of rival theories, such as the moral theory that law is reason and conscience, or natural law, and the historical theory that law is an ongoing tradition in which *both* politics *and* morality play important roles. The result is a disorienting value-vertigo in legal education.

Law schools may continue offering courses in case law, but they hardly even touch upon the doctrine of precedent. They may continue offering basic courses in contracts and torts in the first year, but teachers often spend considerable time demonstrating that there really is no such thing as a "law of contracts" or a "law of torts."

To illustrate the nature of this change in legal education, Berman notes that when he first joined the Harvard Law School faculty in 1948, *all* courses in the first and second year were *required* courses, and at least one course in the third year was required. By contrast, only thirty-five years later, the 1983-84 Harvard Law School catalogue lists over 240 different courses and seminars in virtually 240 different legal subjects! Berman comments: "We have moved beyond the legal pragmatism of Justice Holmes, who said that law is a prediction of what courts will do, to the ultimate in legal pragmatism that law is a prediction of what *lawyers* will do."[9]

Now Berman says this crisis must not be mistaken, simply, for a crisis in legal philosophy. It is a crisis, he says, in *law itself*. The question as to what constitutes the precise foundations of law has always been a matter of philosophical debate; that legal systems themselves have always presupposed the validity of certain beliefs or postulates is not a matter of debate, but of historical fact. Yet, as Berman notes, in *Law and Revolution*:

> Today those beliefs or postulates—such as the structural integrity of the law, its ongoingness, its religious roots, its transcendent qualities—are rapidly disappearing, not only from the minds of philosophers, not only from the minds of lawmakers, judges, lawyers, law teachers, and other members of the legal professions, but from the consciousness of the vast majority of citizens, the people as a whole; and more than that, they are disappearing from the law itself. The law is becoming more fragmented, more subjective, geared more to expediency and less to morality, concerned more with immediate consequences and less with consistency or continuity. Thus the historical soil of the Western legal tradition is being washed away in the twentieth century, and the tradition itself is threatened with collapse.[10]

Periods of social upheaval and disintegration are not new in Western history, and such periods have strained traditional legal institutions, values, and concepts in the past. What is new today is not the threat to particular elements within the legal tradition, but the threat to the survival of that tradition as a whole. If it were merely a matter of an ideological challenge, such as Marxism or socialism, Western society would be able to accommodate it within its legal tradition and to adjust. What cannot be accommodated, however, is the disintegration of the very foundation of that tradition itself. What is undermining those foundations, says Berman, "is the massive loss of confidence in the West itself, as a civilization, a community, and in the legal tradition which for nine centuries has helped to sustain it."[11] The crisis of the Western legal tradition, therefore, is ineluctably linked to the crisis of the West as a whole.

The Tradition

It used to be said—as recently as the seventh edition of Sir Carleton Kemp Allen's *Law in the Making* (1964)—that there are four sources of law: (1) legislation (or rule), (2) precedent, (3) equity (or justice), and (4) custom (or policy). Inasmuch as any of these is disregarded, let alone disparaged, the proper significance of the others is diminished. These sources are differently weighted by different legal theories. A political and analytical jurisprudence may focus on legislation (or rule), a historical and socio-economic jurisprudence may focus on precedent and custom (or policy), and both may neglect the sources of equity (or justice) in natural law, which dominated the philosophical and moral jurisprudence of Catholic and classical tradition.

"Analytical" jurisprudence, or, as it is now more commonly called, "legal positivism," arose on the Continent under the influence of Rudolf von Jhering and Hans Kelsen, and in the English-speaking world under the influence of Thomas Hobbes, Jeremy Bentham, John Austin, John Chipman Gray, and others. In one form or another, legal "positivism" prevails throughout the West today, although it is perhaps most fastidiously identified by its Anglo-American partisans with their own legal history. "Natural law theory," with roots in Hebraic as well as Greco-Roman (and notably Stoic) traditions, arose in the Middle Ages under the influence of Aristotelian philosophy and Catholic theology and exerted a decided influence upon the formative period of the Western legal tradition. Although it experienced periodic revivals under Neo-Thomist influence, it is not identified exclusively with any one national legal history. "Historical" jurisprudence, although embedded in the English legal system since the English Revolution in the seventeenth century, only took root as a legal philosophy in Germany, under the influence of Friedrich Karl von Savigny, Otto von Gierke, and others.

"Positivism" tends to think of law as substantially little more than an expression of the law-maker's will in the form of rules and sanctions—what Max Weber called the "logical formalism" or "formal reality" of Western law. "Historical" jurisprudence thinks of law primarily as an outgrowth of custom, which derives its meaning and authority from the past history and values of the people whose law it is. "Natural law theory" thinks of law, ultimately, as an expression of conscience derived from moral standards apprehended by natural reason. Each of these perspectives apprehends only part of the total picture, and insofar as that partiality itself is ignored or treated as though it were the whole, it undermines even the partial insight of its own perspective.

The Catholic thinker may be inclined to ask, at this point, whether natural law theory should be placed on a common footing, in this manner, alongside positive or analytical law theory and historical or socio-economic law theory, as though it were just one piece of the whole puzzle. Shouldn't natural law be considered the foundation of the Western legal tradition? St. Thomas Aquinas says, after all, that all creatures participate in God's eternal law and that rational creatures do so by means of their access to the precepts of natural law. Furthermore, he also shows that when human laws are reformed, such reforms are made in by reference, whether tacit or overt, to the light of natural law.[12] Does not natural law theory offer more than just one complementary insight among these many schools and traditions of Western jurisprudence?

Part of the answer to this question, of course, is that *theories* of natural law are not the same thing as the *natural law*. "The doctrines of natural law," as Max M. Laserson writes, "must not be confused with natural law itself."[13] Natural law does not come from Hugo Grotius, or Suarez, or Francisco de Vitoria, or even St. Thomas Aquinas, or St. Augustine, or the Church Fathers, or even St. Paul, or Cicero, or the Stoics. Jacques Maritain calls Antigone the "eternal heroine of natural law" because she was aware that in transgressing the human law and being crushed by it, she was obeying the obligations of a higher law, which, she says, "live always and forever and no man knows from where they have arisen."[14]

The point is that natural law is unwritten. It is the eternal law as apprehended by natural human reason. It is what J. Budzieszewski calls, in a book by that title, *What We Can't Not Know*.[15]

Precepts of natural law are *first* principles, not in the order of time but in the order of presuppositions. "The technical expression," Budzieszewski notes, "is that the precept, though not innate, is *per se nota*, 'known in itself,' 'underived.'"[16] Like knowledge of the multiplication table, it must be learned. Hence, it is *not innate*; but, as soon as it is understood, it is seen that it cannot be otherwise. Budzieszewski writes:

> Even though the elementary principles of moral law are known by nature, they are elicited, elucidated, and elaborated by tradition. The notion that it could be otherwise expresses not the classical view of natural law, but a modern distortion of the classical view which took hold only in the Enlightenment. This distortion led to such silliness that eventually serious people gave up on natural law altogether.
>
> Nature dependent on tradition—does this sound inconsistent? It shouldn't. Even insights into "what we can't not know" require the assistance of others, for a good deal of what we know is latent: we may not realize *what it is* that we know, and we are certainly unlikely to know all its presuppositions and implications. Most of the "others" on whose assistance we rely will belong to previous gener-

> ations, because people of our own time are likely to have the same blind spots that we do.[17]

Thus, although the principle precepts of natural law are underived and known in themselves (rather than discursively), they are not innate, and their knowledge can be greatly hindered or helped by *external* factors in the culture such as traditions and laws and mores, and by *internal* factors in one's character such as intellectual or moral virtues and vices.

The Pauline Diagnosis

St. Paul offers additional insights on this question of law in the New Testament, in passages so familiar that their profundity may at times escape us. His words in Romans chapters 1 and 2 are often cited as the *locus classicus* for natural theology or natural law because Paul is speaking about the Gentiles who do not have the revelation of God in Scripture, yet nonetheless *know* about God. In chapter 1, he argues that what is known about God is evident to them and understood by them through creation ("clearly perceived in the things that have been made"), so that they are "*without excuse*" (Rm. 1:20). In chapter 2, he says that when the Gentiles who do not have the Law of Moses (the *Torah*) nevertheless do by nature what the law requires, they show that what the law requires is "written on their hearts" (Rm. 2:14-15). Nevertheless—and this is the really interesting point—he says that this knowledge is *suppressed* by them by their wickedness (Rm. 1:18). Wickedness is understood by Paul, thus, as having *epistemic* consequences: "For though they knew God," he says, "they did not honor Him or give thanks but became futile in their speculations and their foolish heart was darkened, and professing to be wise, they became fools" (Rm. 1:18-22).

This means that a certain *duplicity* is possible in people's knowledge of the truth, in their knowledge of natural and moral law, in their knowledge of "what we can't not know." For example, if St. Paul is right, there may be no such thing as a *bona fide* atheist, even if there are people who have convinced themselves, on some level of their consciousness, that they are atheists. By the same token, just as sin can darken people's understanding, so faith and virtue can serve as corrective lenses to clarify and illumine their vision. While natural law is available to all, it is not properly appropriated by all. There are cultural as well as personal factors that can help or hinder such appropriation. Just as Sacred Tradition assists the Church in interpreting Scripture, so traditions of historical jurisprudence can assist our institutions of law in retrieving the historical sources vital to Western law. A culture that fosters social virtue and decency promotes the character formation required for more readily discerning and acting upon the first principles of natural law. By the same token, the opposite is also true: neglect of history, tradition, virtue, and those things central to the cultural identity of the West have the effect of undermining its legal foundations, as well.

Let me offer a couple of illustrations of relevant duplicitous reasoning by two prominent legal theorists.

First, Oliver Wendell Holmes declared in 1897 that the object of the study of law is simply the prediction of what the courts in fact will do. Nothing more. This expresses Holmes's pragmatic view of law: law is just whatever the courts will in fact do.[18]

Yet as Robert George points out, when Holmes, as a dissenting judge, held that the courts decided a case incorrectly, as he often did, he clearly supposed that the law was something more than merely a prophecy of what the courts would in fact decide. He assumed that the judges in the majority "got the law wrong"; and, in those cases, he assumed, despite himself, the reality and pre-existence of the law as something more than a mere prophecy of what the courts would in fact do.[19] In fact, he appealed tacitly to law as some kind of a standard transcending both his own opinion and that of the court, a standard he expected the court to be aware of, and by reference to which his judgment of the court's opinion could be adjudicated. This standard, of course, is none other than what we call *natural law*.

Second, Jerome Frank, as a partisan of the so-called *legal realist* movement drawing its inspiration from Holmes, took a position so extreme in his denial of legal objectivity that in the 1931 edition of his book, *Law and the Modern Mind*, published before the Second World War, he declared himself a "fact-skeptic."[20] He was notorious for his skepticism about any objective basis for law.

Yet, in his 1949 Preface to the sixth edition of the same book, *Law and the Modern Mind*, in the aftermath of the revelation of Nazi atrocities in Europe, Frank declared himself to be a follower of the natural law teaching of St. Thomas Aquinas on the basic questions of law and morality. Nothing in his earlier writings, he insisted, was ever meant to suggest otherwise.[21]

How would St. Paul assess such duplicity? I think he would argue that the duplicity represented by Holmes's dissenting opinion and by Frank's post-war approval of the natural law teachings of St. Thomas Aquinas both have the effect of tipping the hand of these would-be legal agnostics. Both cases show how, when push comes to shove, people will readily embrace the existence of an objectively binding law-order when it is in their practical interest to do so.

How would St. Paul address those "in denial," those who have duplicitously repressed such knowledge of an objective law-order, of transcendence, of even their own duplicity? I think the answer to this question is amply illustrated by his own speech to the Council of the Areopagus in Acts 17. Paul is only too-well acquainted with the duplicity of the human mind. He knows that his pagan audience has culturally repressed the knowledge of that which, as J. Budzieszewski says, "we can't not know," including the natural knowledge all people have of God. So how does he address these skeptical Greek thinkers in Athens?

In contrast to some Protestant biblical commentators like William M. Ramsay and Martin Dibelius, who have suggested that Paul's speech was a failed experiment in natural theology that left him "disillusioned," J. Daryl Charles argues, in *Retrieving the Natural Law: A Return to Moral First Things*, that "nothing in Acts 17:16-34 suggests that Paul's strategy in Athens is misguided."[22] While it is true that St. Luke, the author of the Book of Acts, spends no time prefacing Paul's speech to the Council, this is not because Luke regarded it as a trivial or insignificant encounter. Says Charles:

> Much to the contrary, the council was an elite and prestigious body that deliberated over educational, legal, and social issues. The contemporary reader would have understood the import of Paul's invitation to address this esteemed body. It is supremely unfortunate that virtually all of this is lost on the modern reader.[23]

In fact, what impresses the reader today with even the slightest knowledge of Hellenistic culture is how carefully Paul nuances his address, as well as how shrewdly St. Luke gets every detail right in his account.[24] Paul starts by building upon pagan concepts and illustrations already familiar with his audience, by addressing a number of core Stoic and Epicurean ideas (17:23-31), and by exploiting for his own purposes two famous quotations from two of their own highly-esteemed poets, Epimenides and Aratus of Soli (17:28-29). There is even the echo of Socrates in Luke's account, as Paul is cast in the role of one who, like Socrates, comes and disputes in the marketplace and is accused of introducing strange "new deities" (17:18) and plays off an ironic theme of "ignorance" (in his reference to the altar with the inscription "to an unknown god," 17:23) over against the great learning and erudition ascribed to the Athenians.[25] Paul then elicits the attributes of the "unknown God," whom they worship in ignorance—attributes which, by natural law, on some level of their consciousness, they "can't not know." He speaks of the "God who made the world and everything in it" (17:24), in language allusive to the argument he makes in Romans, where he declares that the Gentiles "clearly perceive" God's existence and power from "the things that have been made" (Rm 1:20). After thus acknowledging the Creator's self-disclosure through the cosmos, Paul then proceeds to give credence to the Resurrection, nudging his audience in the direction of repentance with rhetorically amplified moral compulsion.

Luke records that some sneered at Paul's reference to the Resurrection, but that others, including Dionysius the Areopagite[26] and Damaris, believed and joined him. Paul *connected* with these latter members of his audience. After the compelling clarity of his illuminating speech, they were brought by God's grace to epistemic self-awareness about what they already tacitly knew to be true. The fact that they already possessed this latent knowledge anterior to Paul's speech did not make Paul's speech dispensable. Rather, it explains why Paul's speech was believable and compelling.

Here we have in a nutshell exactly the approach Paul would prescribe and exactly the result we should expect. Despite themselves, when push came to shove, both Holmes and Frank acknowledged "what we can't not know" about natural law and the transcendent sources of law. In light of this, no Christian should have the slightest hesitation about confidently asserting the facts about natural law. These facts are tacitly known, even where they are repressed, whether by individuals or by cultures. The fact that some will predictably respond with dismissive skepticism should not dampen in the least the Christian's confidence. Despite the errant drift of contemporary culture, despite the crisis of law, despite the rapidly disappearing beliefs about the objectivity and transcendence of law from the minds of philosophers, lawmakers, judges, lawyers, law teachers, and from the consciousness of the vast majority of the people as a whole, there is still a massive common ground in the very fabric of our nature and in the objective record of our history and traditions, that has not been, and indeed cannot be, utterly eradicated.

Notes

1. Delivered as the Address at the Dedication of the James Warren Smith Memorial Wing of Stuart Hall, Boston College Law School, April 28, 1984, and reprinted from *Boston College Law Review* 26 (1985): 347-352, in Harold J. Berman, *Faith and Order: The Reconciliation of Law and Religion,* Emory University Studies in Law and Religion, ed., John Witte, Jr. (Atlanta, Georgia: Scholars Press, 1993), 333-340.

2. As quoted in Berman, "Crisis of Legal Education," 335. There is a rich tradition of literature on the relation of law and religion in which the classic sources include the works of Friedrich Karl von Savigny, Otto von Gierke, Frederick Maitland, and Henry S. Maine, as well as a number of scholars whom Berman himself would have counted among his mentors, such as Eugen Rosenstock-Huessy, Hajo Holborn, Theodore F. Plucknett, R.H. Tawney and Lon Fuller. See John Witte, Jr., "A New Concordance of Discordant Canons: Harold Berman on Law and Religion," *Emory Law Journal* Vol. 42 (Spring 1993): 525.

3. Berman, "Crisis," 335.

4. *Ibid.*, 336.

5. *Ibid.*

6. *Ibid.*

7. *Ibid.*, 337.

8. *Ibid.*

9. *Ibid.*

10. Harold Berman, *Law and Revolution: The Formation of the Western Legal Tradition* (Cambridge, Massachusetts and London, England: Harvard University Press, 1983), 39.

11. Berman, *Law and Revolution*, 40.

12. St. Thomas Aquinas, "The Treatise on Law," *Summa Theologiae*, I-II, QQ. 91-95.

13. Max M. Laserson, "Positive and Natural Law and Their Correlation," in *Interpretations of Modern Legal Philosophies: Essays in Honor of Roscoe Pound* (New York: Oxford University Press, 1947), is quoted with approval by Jacques Maritain in his *Man and the State* (Washington, DC: The Catholic University of America Press, 1951), 81.

14. Sophocles, *Antigone*, II, 452-60, George Young's translation, as quoted by Maritain, *Man and the State*, 85, n. 8.

15. J. Budziszewski, *What We Can't Not Know: A Guide* (Dallas, Texas: Spence Pub-

lishing Company, 2003).

16. Ibid., 116

17. *Ibid.*, 24f.

18. Oliver Wendell Holmes, "The Path of the Law," *Harvard Law Review* 10 (1897), 458-62, cited by Robert George, *The Clash of Orthodoxies: Law, Religion, and Morality in Crisis* (Wilmington, Delaware: ISI Books, 2001), ch. 11, "What Is Law? A Century of Arguments," 212.

19. Holmes, "Path," 462; Robert George, *Clash of Orthodoxies*, 217f., cf. 361, n. 32.

20. See generally Jerome Frank, *Law and the Modern Mind* (New York: Brentano's, 1931); cited by Robert George, *Clash of Orthodoxies*, 361, n. 34; cf. 219.

21. Jerome Frank, *Law and the Modern Mind*, 6th ed. (New York: Coward-McCann, 1949); cited by George, *Ibid.*, 220; cf. 361, n. 35.

22. J. Daryl Charles argues, in *Retrieving the Natural Law: A Return to Moral First Things* (Grand Rapids, Michigan: Eerdmans, 2008), 46; cf. n. 69.

23. *Ibid.*, 48, where Charles adds, citing Luke Timothy Johnson, *The Acts of the Apostles* (Collegeville, MN: Liturgical Press, 1992), p. 218: "The point is *not*, however, lost on Luke Timothy Johnson, who writes: 'What impresses every reader with even the slightest knowledge of Hellenistic culture is how cunningly Luke has . . . everything right.'"

24. See the comment by Luke Timothy Johnson in our previous note.

25. Charles, *Retrieving the Natural Law*, 46, 50. In Plato's *Apology*, it will be recalled, Socrates was accused of introducing new, deities foreign to Athens (26b); and when the Oracle at Delphi reported that no one was wiser than he, Socrates notoriously went about Athens trying to find someone wiser than himself, proclaiming that he was better off than the next fellow who claimed to be wise but knew nothing, because he, at least, knew that he knew nothing (21d).

26. Not to be confused with *Pseudo-Dionysius the Areopagite*, the anonymous theologian and philosopher of the early sixth century whose writings were pseudonymously ascribed to Dionysius the Areopagite, the Athenian convert of St. Paul mentioned in Acts 17:34, and cited over 1700 times by St. Thomas Aquinas, who was apparently unaware of pseudonymous ascription.

Response to Philip Blosser

Rev. Joseph Isanga
Associate Professor,
Ave Maria School of Law, Naples, Florida

Introduction

Jurisprudential theories provide frameworks for understanding the nature of law and justice. Generally exclusivist, each portrays itself as the only valid explanation of law. Thus, legal positivism[1] portrays itself as antithetical to natural law theory. Legal positivism developed in different directions and inspired a variety of kindred theories, such as legalism/formalism, legal realism, and legal process.[2] In turn, these ideas attempted to monopolize legal theory, usually at the expense of natural law theory. To an extent, this is understandable because every generation confronts unique challenges, and in crafting solutions, prior theories seem outdated as they relate to different times and problems.

In fact, however, each theory contributes to the understanding of only a specific dimension of law. Therefore, it is important for each school of theorists to ultimately recognize that diverse theories can, and do, complement each other.[3] Natural law theory stands for the proposition that there are some unchanging and fundamental rules written in nature, society and the world, accessible by reason, even as society marches forward and meets new challenges. That proposition is common ground for religious and non-religious proponents of the theory.[4]

Yet, natural law has been repressed throughout history by individual nations and the international community, only to receive renewed attention again and again in the wake of horrendous atrocities—during World War II[5] and those committed in Kosovo, Bosnia[6] and Rwanda, but even now as nations try to counter violent extremism. The repression of natural law is usually done in self-interest, when adherence to it seems inconvenient or inexpedient. Reverting to the natural law for improvement in times of crisis only underscores its enduring and timeless significance. In an increasingly pluralistic and globalized world, natural law theory is a valid basis for coming together to uphold universal values.

This article explores the extent to which Pauline literature and the extant non-religious legal philosophies were accommodative and complementary of each other on the subject of natural law, how they were all better for it, and how contemporary society too—confronted as it is by challenges posed by pluralism and globalization—could benefit from similar accommodation. The article first establishes that Paul understood legal philosophy and used it appropriately to solve societal problems. Secondly, it appraises and then critiques a plethora of modern and contemporary philosophies of law to indicate why a complementary approach is imperative. Lastly, it evaluates select legal theories in light of what can be described as Paul's preferred legal theory—natural law.

Earlier Philosophies: Antecedents to Pauline Natural Law Teaching

It is important to note that there were varying contemporaneous theories of law that had an impact on Pauline thinking and literature. Paul drew upon and accommodated his teaching to a variety of Greek philosophical methodologies in a manner subsidiary or tangential to the immediate concerns he addressed.[7] He was part of Hellenistic culture and his letters were primarily addressed to Gentiles living in the Greek philosophical and cultural milieu.[8] Although Paul had an immediate religious agenda, Greek society regarded philosophy as an indispensable component of training for public life.[9] In fact, second century apologists indeed label Christianity as "philosophy." For instance, the account of the arranged debate on the Areopagus between Paul and "certain of the Epicurean and Stoic philosophers" suggests that there is no distinction.[10] Paul's mission was assimilated into these operational patterns of Hellenistic teachers.[11] While fundamentally religious, his mission had a public dimension. Paul was trying to fashion local adherents of the new teaching into a new *politeia*, with its own code of political conduct[12] and its own *metropolis* or mother-city.[13] The 'school of Christ' was not inward looking or enclosed. Continued propagation of the teaching of Christ could then take place within the 'public space' of this new community.[14]

Paul's accommodation of his teaching to the contemporaneous teachings also demonstrates that he appreciated the importance of assembling diverse worldviews to solve society's common problems. Today, "interdisciplinarity has helped law understand what, at any point, is its content and its self-conception: law as politics, culture, [or] economics."[15] Although Paul had a religious mission and philosophy, he embraced an essentially secular natural law theory where there were overlapping convergences.

The two most popular Hellenistic philosophies antecedent to Pauline teaching were the third and second century B.C.E Stoicism and Epicureanism. Both understood the person as a microcosm of the universe.[16] Paul embraced Stoic and Epicurean universalism by stating that Gentiles do not need to be circumcised, indicating that Christianity is not confined to the Jewish people. Paul was so appreciative of Greek philosophy—which he indeed lived—that Acts 17:16-34 portrays him as a second Socrates who engaged the Epicurean and Stoic philosophers of Agora.[17]

Socrates reacted to those movements within ancient Greek society, which maintained that "good" and "true" were matters of personal and democratic preference, thus denying the existence of enduring universal truths valid for all time and places. Socrates, instead, insisted on an objective definition of virtue and maintained that virtuous living was to live according to reason.[18] Aristotle reiterated and advanced Socrates' teaching, arguing, "[o]f political justice part is natural, part legal,—natural that which everywhere has the same force and does not exist by people's thinking this or that."[19] The Stoics, too, especially the philosopher Chrysippus of Soli, constructed a systematic natural law theory. According to Stoicism, the whole cosmos is rationally ordered by an active principle. The world, frequently compared to a city, is governed by divine wisdom and providence, and one's participation in that wisdom is limited by universal law.[20] The Stoics maintained that to live virtuously was to live in accord with one's nature—to live according to right reason. While rational beings are free, the Stoics postulated, there is only one natural law, which absolutely orders and preserves this natural order.[21] The Stoics sought to solve the problem of distinguishing clearly between what is in our power and what is not.[22]

Paul makes use of certain ideas derived from these philosophers, particularly Stoic ethics, as part of his own thinking.[23] He found the natural law doctrine of the Stoics relatively compatible with Christian belief. Thus, while addressing gentile Romans who were ignorant of Mosaic law, Paul argued that they were nevertheless capable of doing "by nature what the law requires,"[24] because some of the content of the natural moral law was specified in the Law of Moses. In proposing that non-Jews are subject to God's law, because "[w]hat the law requires is written in their hearts, to which their own conscience also bears witness," Paul embraced and accommodated natural law.[25] It would be reasonable to suggest that if God were to consign most of humanity to destruction, this punishment would not be without warrant, since the non-Jews failed to decipher his law, which was accessible to them through reason.[26]

Paul's appreciation and use of Greek philosophy is reflected in some of his letters. For example, the letter to the Philippians contains elements of Stoic ethics, especially the central notion in Stoic ethics—the *telos*, the 'end' of activity, that which is 'brought about' by activity.[27] The Stoics held the 'end of action' to be 'the good.' In addition, Paul's exposure to and critique of law as such is at the center of his Letter to the Romans. In that letter, Paul subscribes to the notion of an inner dialectic in law—the idea of a tension between what it is now and what it is not (but is capable of becoming). Paul makes use of the Greek opposition between potentiality and act. Romans 7:5-6 states, "[f]or when we were in the flesh, the passions of sin were enacted through the law in our members to bring forth fruit unto death. But now we are de-activated [made inoperative] from the law."[28] The inner and outer boundaries of the law appear indiscernible to Paul as he discusses the distinction between Jews and non-Jews—those within the Law of Moses and those outside the law.[29] Aristotelian ontology of privation is implicit in this. Aristotle makes a point to distinguish privation from mere absence inasmuch as privation still implies a reference to the being or form deprived, which manifests itself through its lack.[30] Law, as such, must be open to development and accommodation.

Beyond Greek influence, reference should also be made to Roman philsophical expositions of the time. The Roman, Cicero, took up the Stoic ideas and defined natural law:

> [T]rue law is right reason in agreement with Nature; it is of universal application, unchanging and everlasting; it summons to duty by its commands, and averts from wrongdoing by its prohibitions. There will not be different laws at Rome and at Athens, or different laws now and in the future, but one eternal and unchangeable law will be valid for all nations and for all times.[31]

This is a succinct statement of natural law. Cicero's ideas are in keeping with the fact that Roman law came to be identified with *jus gentium* and even *jus naturale* as the Roman Empire embraced diverse peoples and Roman citizenship came to be extended to all free inhabitants of the Roman Empire. Paul was familiar with Roman law and appreciated its characteristics—its claim to rootedness in a universal and natural ethic. The Acts of the Apostles documents that when arrested and brought before the Roman Tribunal, Paul claimed his rights as a Roman citizen[32] by appealing to Caesar to avoid being handed over to the Jewish authorities.[33]

Modern and Contemporary De-Emphasis of Natural Law

The natural law ethic to which Paul subscribed was subsequently embraced and elaborated upon at various times, but also repressed at other times by key theorists. The relationship between positive law and natural law has been a subject of much contention. According to Thomas Aquinas, "every human law has just so much of the nature of law, as it is derived from the law of nature"[34] and there is necessary participation of natural law in the divine and eternal laws.[35] Hugo Grotius argued, however, that the same relationship between positive law and natural law could be established without subscribing to religious criteria, because natural law is the body of rules which can be discovered through reason.[36] John Finnis would argue, however, that unless God is included in this analysis, it is not possible to understand why nature is normative or possesses obligatory force of law for anyone.[37]

The following critical analysis shows that none of the theories that try to displace or repress the natural law can perfectly explain the nature of law or account for its obligatory character or legitimacy, even if they remain useful for explaining certain other aspects of law.

The theory that portrays itself as most directly in opposition to natural law is legal positivism. This theory, which appears in various forms, flourished in the seventeenth and eighteenth centuries, thanks to English philosophers such as Thomas Hobbes and John Locke. By origin and definition, legal positivism—the view that the legitimacy of law depends on its being posited and obeyed and that its moral worth is a separate inquiry—was aimed at promoting the immediate interests of emerging nation-states,[38] and not global or universal values which were perceived as being stumbling blocks. Thus, John Austin would say "[n]ow, to say that human laws which conflict with the divine law are not binding, that is not laws, is . . . stark nonsense. The most pernicious laws . . . opposed to the divine will of God, have been and are continually enforced as [binding] laws by judicial tribunals."[39] With regard to the moral worth of positive law, Austin argued for a hard separability thesis, insisting that the existence of the law is one thing, its merits or demerits is another, and a law which actually exists is law, even if one dislikes it. More contemporary exponents of legal positivism, like Hans Kelsen[40] and H.L.A. Hart, tried to strike a nuanced and moderate position, without going as far as accepting the necessity of substantive moral criteria for the validation of positive law. Thus, Hart's Rule of Recognition (rules provided in a Constitution, for example, for determining which rules are and which are not part of the legal system) can include moral criteria, as a conventional matter, for the validity of laws in a particular legal system.[41]

Natural Law theory was subsequently repressed or excluded by kindred theories—utilitarianism, pragmatism, law and economics, legalism/formalism, legal realism, historical school,[42] sociological jurisprudence[43] and postmodernism, among others. Legal positivists, like Austin, were also Utilitarians. The principle of utility, based on balancing pleasure and pain (the felicific calculus), provides that in making law or judicial decisions, the guiding principle should be "the greatest happiness of the greatest number," because a law is a good law only if it makes people happy and a bad law if it makes people miserable.[44] As Robin West notes, utilitarianism is consequentialist rather than "deontic" because it rejects the notion that a law should be evaluated by determining whether or not it can be universalized or whether or not it is in accord with God's command or natural law.[45] Thus, utilitarianism rejects deontology—the idea that a thing or action is inherently right or wrong. This utilitarian ideal is present in contemporary secular democracies, which contest the existence of objective truth and reduce the qualification of an act as right or wrong to consensus.[46] Some have argued, for instance, that,

> [w]e should select our economic and political systems on the basis of what seems to produce the greatest material good for the greatest number, and leave theology out it . . . in a democracy . . . *bonos mores* are going to be the *mores* of the society [and] [u]ltimately . . . what the majority decides shall be the rights of minori-

ties is what their rights are, under that legal system.[47]

But this amounts to tyranny of the majority.[48] Contemporary societies are fascinated by the idea of democracy to the point of a total, uncompromising submission to the system. But positive law, even if it is the product of democratic consensus, must have definite limits that it shall not overstep. These limits are determined by the law of nature-otherwise democracy degenerates into 'ochlocracy' (domination by the populace).[49]

Pragmatism, which is closely linked to utilitarianism, argues that legislators and judicial officials should be guided by expediency and effectiveness—they should do whatever works.[50] As William James said, the truth of an idea is not a stagnant property inherent in it; truth happens to an idea, or an idea becomes true. Truth is "the expedient in our way of thinking just as the right is only the expedient in our way of behaving."[51] Pragmatic adjudication was highly influential throughout the 1920s and 1930s, but fell in disfavor during World War II. However, its appeal has not entirely disappeared. In moments of crisis and national calamity, it has been reverted to as a compelling justification theory in place of established legal and moral standards.

A modern and operational form of utilitarianism and pragmatism is the law and economics theory arguing that law should be guided by efficiency (wealth-maximization) on the basis of a cost-benefit analysis.[52] Economic analysis has guided modern market-based systems. Deontologists argue that judicial, policy and legal decisions are good only if they are principled, and not just because they make economic sense. Wealth is not the only end judges and legislators should pursue. Instead, or in addition, they should be guided by humanitarian and equitable principles.

Legalism argues that law consists of a set of discoverable rules laid down at some time in the past and that legal justice is the fair application of those preexisting rules in similar situations.[53] Legalism and formalism—the latter an extreme version of the former[54]—are characteristically positivistic. A more contemporary version of formalism is textualism, which, in the words of Justice Scalia, argues that "[w]ords do have a limited range of meaning, and no interpretation that goes beyond that range is permissible."[55]

For all their merits, critical jurisprudence—which consists of critical legal studies, feminist legal jurisprudence,[56] critical race theory,[57] and postmodernism, to name a few—would argue that legalism and formalism are moderate propositions because their criteria for legal justice lack legitimacy to the extent they fail to render substantive justice in concrete situations. Critical jurisprudence, in turn, does not capture all aspects of reality or the entirety of some fundamental aspects of the human person, because it stresses some dimensions of social life at the expense of others. For example, the view of postmodernism that there is a surplus of meaning and that truth is contextual, or contingent, borders on relativism and makes it impossible to speak of universal values.

Critical Legal Studies and Legal Realism target legalism. Legal realism argues that law is a matter of prophecy or prediction of what judges will do, as opposed to what they say, because reasons for judicial decision are mere *post hoc* rationalizations.[58] The real reasons may be comprised of the judge's own biases and sense of fairness based on non-legal considerations, such as prevailing social or economic policy. In insisting on the centrality of the power of the judge, Legal Realism made him/her a sovereign, unanswerable to superseding principles and to that extent this theory is characteristically positivist. Critical Legal Studies maintains that law is an instrument of political power and an expression of the interests of the privileged who relied on legalism to create a complacent and uncritical attitude in the unprivileged in order to protect the status quo.[59]

The Resilience and Enduring Significance of Natural Law

Jurisprudential theories can be further critiqued through the lens of Paul's preferred theory—natural law—and applications made to select contemporary challenges. Paul critiqued aspects of legal positivism and its "look-alikes" or derivatives, such as legalism or formalism and legal realism. He rejected the oppression implied by slavish, literal fulfillment of the Mosaic Law and the way the Jews interpreted that law based on his conviction that the content of the natural moral law is specified in, but not exhausted by, the Law of Moses.[60] Paul lived in Roman society in which the aristocracy controlled the legal system, and he challenged the complacency or helplessness created by the positivist legal system. He taught that there could be no distinctions based on gender, race or class, or as he put it: between Greek and Jew, male and female, slave or free.[61] Paul's opponents scourged him, and before Roman courts his teaching was used to prove that he was a threat to the social order.[62] He did not give in, on the contrary, he claimed his civil rights as a Roman citizen, and was brought before a Roman tribunal. In the Letter to Philemon he undermines the institution of slavery by making it clear that all men are "radically equal," which was extremely innovative at the time.

Natural law, which Paul argues is written on the heart of man (and is, consequently, even today accessible), informs all natural rights and justice discourses. Natural Law brings forth more particular ideas of justice regarding the legal rights and duties of mankind.[63] But in today's legal discourse, legal positivism is widespread. Legislation is often decided by striking a balance between competing interests,[64] and important lessons of history are thus forgotten. After World War II, the international community rejected the notion of absolute state sovereignty and recognized the universal and fundamental equality and dignity of all human beings, nationality notwithstanding. Thus, the United Nations Charter declared the respect for human rights,[65] the Universal Declaration of Human Rights (1948) recognized the "inherent dignity" of all human beings and declared that "[a]ll human beings are born free and equal in dignity and rights. They are endowed with reason and conscience . . ."[66] and a plethora of substantive international human rights instruments fleshed out or elaborated that recognition.[67] At the national level, such developments were replicated.[68]

Yet, in spite of some authentic advancements through the globalization of human rights, challenges remain in the form of racial discrimination and xenophobia, with negative consequences for governance, sustainable development, social justice, democracy and peace in the world. The genocides in Rwanda, Kosovo, and the ongoing conflict in Darfur (Sudan) are examples, as are the persistence of human trafficking, harassment of irregular immigrants, social, economic and political exclusion, and stereotyping.[69] In this latter regard, there is a persistent and dichotomous conception of international human rights, which has relegated economic, social and cultural rights to secondary status, only to reveal a prioritization of civil and political criteria and an insufficient recognition of universal solidarity for the less privileged. This problem recently prompted a representative of the Holy See to the United Nations to argue that the current global economic crisis has demonstrated "how too often racism and poverty are inter-related in a destructive combination"[70] and how too often international relations are characterized by the "paradox of a multilateral consensus…subordinated to the decisions of a few."[71]

But it does not have to be that way. The G20[72] recently put aside ideological differences and demonstrated unprecedented cooperation in committing member-states to inject a $1.1 trillion global package[73] into the international financial institutions in order to prevent a colossal collapse of the world economy.

In specific regard to civil and political rights, the universalist natural law to which Paul subscribed has been adhered to through the spread of freedom, democracy, and human rights throughout the world. Many regional, political, human rights and intergovernmental organizations have increasingly conditioned membership on rule of law and democracy and condemn extra-constitutional usurpation of political power. States have recognized that international law is based on "good faith" and the doctrine of *pacta sunt servanda* ("agreements must be kept"),[74] suggesting that it is subject to natural law. In its origin, international law was seen as an outgrowth of universal values and norms, largely derived from Roman law (*the ius gentium*, which applied to all peoples) and religious institutions (the law of the Roman Catholic Church, or canon law).[75] Unfortunately, the doctrine of state sovereignty continues to dominate, as if states owe no allegiance to a superseding moral order,[76] and to that extent international human rights have suffered a great deal. Classical writers, such as Hugo de Groot ("Grotius") (1583-1645), warned of the dangers of the excesses of sovereignty, democratic ethos, and legal positivism in international law, and emphasized that moral imperatives between nations were part of law.[77] But in response to current crises and challenges, some nations have expressed doubt in those notions. After the terrorist attacks of September 11, 2001, for example, there were disturbing developments in many countries trying to adopt anti-terrorism laws and policies that threaten to reverse longstanding international human rights conceptions. Positivist or kindred theories were often invoked for justification. With time, however, many have understood that the challenges of terrorism can best be met by more, not less, international cooperation and greater respect for human rights.[78]

Conclusion

In a world that is becoming increasingly globalized, appreciation and adherence to the natural law as articulated by St. Paul is the best road to developing a comprehensive legal theory or jurisprudence. Every strategy must ratify the fundamental principles of right and wrong, which remain vital to any sustainable effort to solve the most daunting global and national challenges, if mistakes are to be avoided.

Notes

1. See Harold J. Berman, "Toward an Integrative Jurisprudence: Politics, Morality, History" *California Law Review* 76 (1988), 779-780). Legal positivism treats law as a body of rules "posited" by the state. These rules have a separate and independent character from morality. Natural law theory provides that reason shapes legal rules and moral principles. As moral purposes are implicitly found in legal norms, the latter must be interpreted and applied in light of the former.

2. See generally Anthony J. Sebok, "Legal Positivism in American Jurisprudence," in *Cambridge Studies in Philosophy and Law*, (1998) (arguing that legal process is an instantiation of legal positivism).

3. Berman, 779 (arguing the case for an integrative jurisprudence which is "premised on the belief that each of these three competing schools has isolated a single important dimension of law, and that it is both possible and important to bring the several dimensions together into a common focus").

4. See Pope Benedict XVI, Address To Participants in The International Congress in Natural Moral Law (12 Feb. 2007), *available at* http://www.vatican.va/holy_father/benedict_xvi/speeches/2007/february/documents/hf_ben-xvi_spe_20070212_pul_en.html (last visited May 29, 2009) (arguing that "[o]n this basis it is possible to develop a fruitful dialogue between believers and non-believers; between theologians, philosophers, jurists[,] and scientists").

5. See *Trial of the Major War Criminals Before the International Military Tribunal*, Nuremberg, 14 Nov. 1945-1 Oct. 1946 (1947) Vol. 1., reprinted in American Journal of International Law 41 (1947), 172. In response to the positivist defense *nullum crimen sine lege* (no punishment of crime without a pre-existing, posited law), the Tribunal responded, "in such circumstances the attacker must know what he is doing is wrong, and so far from it being unjust to punish him, it would be unjust if his wrong were allowed to go unpunished."

6. *Case Concerning the Application of the Convention on the Prevention and Punishment of the Crime of Genocide* (Bosnia and Herzegovina v. Serbia and Montenegro), Judgment, 2007 I.C.J. General List No. 91 (Feb. 26). The ICJ stated,"[t]he origins of the

Convention [on genocide] show that it was the intention of the United Nations to condemn and punish genocide as a 'crime under international law' involving a denial of the right of existence of entire human groups, a denial which shocks the conscience of mankind and results in great losses to humanity, and which is *contrary to the moral law*. . . The first consequence arising from this conception is that the principles underlying the Convention are principles which are recognized by civilized nations as binding on States, even without any conventional obligation," *ibid.* [Emphasis added].

7. David E. Aune, "Human Nature and Ethics in Hellenistic Philosophical Traditions and Paul: Some Issues and Problems," in *Paul in His Hellenistic Context* ed. Troels Engberg-Pedersen (Minneapolis: Fortress Press, 1994), 291.

8. Ibid., xvi-xxi.

9. See Alexander Loveday, "Paul and the Hellenistic Schools: The Evidence of Galen" in *Paul in his Hellenistic Context*, 60, 74.

10. Ibid., 79. See also Acts 17:18 (Catholic Revised Standard Version).

11. Loveday, 79. Like contemporary Greek philosophers, Paul traveled with a 'disciple circle' or 'retinue' from place to place, created new disciple circles, and left behind a number of supporters in the local communities.

12. See Philippians 1:27.

13. Philippians 3:20; Ephesians 2.19; Hebrews 12:22-23.

14. Loveday, 79.

15. Tawia Ansah, "Reinterpretations of St. Paul's Concept of Law" (2008); available at: http://works.bepress.com/cgi/viewcontent.cgi?article=1000&context=tawia_ansah (last visited May 27,
2009).

16. Aune, 303.

17. See generally 1 Corinthians 8:1-13. Another example of Greek philosophy influencing Paul's views is with regard to the problem of idol food. Stoics expressed uneasiness with the declaration that the person who has the power to do whatever he wishes is free, and he corrects it by arguing that it is not permissible to do mean and unprofitable things.

18. See generally *Plato, The Trial and Death of Socrates* 2nd ed. trans. G.M.A. Grube (Indianapolis: Hackett Publishing, 1975), 22-44. Plato's *Apologia* describes Socrates' fruitless attempts to convince the Greek citizenry that truth is paramount to understanding the law.

19. Stephen E. Gottlieb et al., *Jurisprudence Cases and Materials: An Introduction to the Philosophy of Law and Its Applications* 2nd ed. (Albany, N.Y.: Lexis Nexis/Matthew Bender, 2006), 61; citing Aristotle, Nicomachean Ethics, Book V, reprinted in *The Complete Works of Aristotle* ed. Jonathan Barnes (Princeton: Princeton University Press, 1984).

20. Abraham J. Malherbe, "Determinism and Free Will in Paul: The Argument of 1 Corinthians 8 and 9" in *Paul in his Hellenistic Context,* 231, 244-45.

21. *Ibid.* at 245.

22. Troels Engberg-Pedersen, "Stoicism in Phillipians," in *Paul in his Hellenistic Context,* 256

23. Ibid.

24. Romans 2:14.

25. Romans 2:15.

26. Alan F. Segal, "Universalism in Judaism and Christianity," in *Paul in his Hel-*

lenistic Context, 1, 11.

27. Engberg-Pedersen, 269. See also Philippians 4:10-13.

28. Romans 7:5-6.

29. Giorgio Agamben, *The Time That Remains: A Commentary on the Letter to the Romans* trans. Patricia Dailey (Palo Alto, CA: Stanford University Press, 2005), 104.

30. Aristotle, *Metaphysics* trans. W. D. Ross; available at http://classics.mit.edu//Aristotle/metaphysics.mb.txt (last visited on May 4, 2009).

31. Cicero, *On the Commonwealth*, in *On the Common Wealth and On the Laws* ed. James E.G. Zetzel (Cambridge: Cambridge University Press, 2002), 1, 63-73.

32. See John W. Mauck, *Paul on Trial: The Book of Acts as a Defense of Christianity* (Nashville: Thomas Nelson, 2001), 3. Luke wrote the Book of Acts as a legal "brief" to defend Paul and essentially all Christians, as many claimed that Christianity was an illegal religion (the charges mainly related to unlawful assembly-inciting riots by preaching a false religion).

33. Acts 25:11.

34. Thomas Aquinas, *Summa Theologica*, I-II, Q. 95, art. 2, http://www.newadvent.org/summa/2095.htm (last visited Jan. 18, 2010).

35. Ibid.

36. *See generally* Hugo Grotius, *De Jure Belli Ac Pacis* [On the Law of War and Peace] (1625) (arguing that "[t]he law of nature is a dictate of right reason, which points out that an act, according as it is or is not in conformity with rational nature, has in it a quality of moral baseness or moral necessity; and that, in consequence, such an act is either forbidden or enjoined" (I.1.10.1), adding that "[w]hat we have been saying would have a degree of validity even if we should concede [*etiamsi daremus*] that which cannot be conceded without the utmost wickedness, that there is no God." According to Grotius, instead of emerging from or being otherwise dependent on God, the fundamental principles of ethics, politics and law obtain in virtue of nature. As he says, "the mother of right — that is, of natural law — is human nature" (Prol. §16).

37. See John Finnis, "On the Incoherence of Legal Positivism," *Notre Dame Law Review* 75 (2000), 1597, 1599.

38. *See* George C. Christie and Patrick H. Martin, *Jurisprudence: Text and Readings on the Philosophy of Law* (Egan, MN: Thomson and West 3d ed. 2008), 496. Legal positivism tries to legitimize the sovereign and secular state as separate from the constraints of natural law as well as divine authority personified by ecclesiastical authorities that previously enthroned secular leaders and criticized their promulgated laws. But, as discussed earlier, *see* Grotius *supra* note 36, it is arguable that the natural law exists even in a non-religious context. Several contemporary natural law theories have argued that there exists a 'secular natural law,' and that it should be recognized. *See e.g.*, Lon L. Fuller, *The Morality of Law* (New Haven: Yale University Press, 1965), 96 (rejecting substantive moral constraints on positive law and arguing for a procedural natural law, or an internal morality of law. Fuller also believed that natural law had no relation to "any brooding omnipresence in the skies . . . [nor the] . . . higher laws").

39. John Austin, *The Province of Jurisprudence Determined* (Indianapolis: Hackett, 1995), 158.

40. See generally Hans Kelsen, "What is the Pure Theory of Law?" Tulane Law Review 34 (1960), 269 (1960) (arguing that Austin's command theory was inadequate-it ar-

gued that laws are only valid if there is a commander who is never disobeyed, but this fails to explain the continuity of law. Instead, he proposed that valid laws depend on a basic or *grund* norm-a presupposed norm that is found at the basis of every legal system, making all norms in that system valid.

41. H.L.A. Hart, *The Concept of Law* (Gloucestershire, UK: Clarendon Press 2d ed., 1994), 103. According to Hart, "to say that a given rule is valid is to recognize it as passing all the tests provided by the rule of recognition and so as a rule of the system. We can indeed simply say that the statement that a particular rule is valid means that it satisfies all the criteria provided by the rule of recognition."

42. Berman, 780-81. The Historical School finds current laws to be a combination of historically developing social attitudes of a particular society. The theorists argue that law is found in the national character, culture, and historical traditions of that society. *Ibid.*

43. See generally Roscoe Pound, *The Scope and Purpose of Sociological Jurisprudence*, *Harvard Law Review* 24 (1910-1911) 591, 595-96. Sociological Jurisprudence is a futuristic and instrumentalist view of law, arguing that law is a tool for social engineering and legal reform. Law, they argue, already exists in society and is not created by legislators. The legislators merely represent the State recognizing the need to match the law on the books with the law already present in society.

44. Jeremy Bentham, *On The Principles of Morals and Legislation*, cited in Robin West, "The Other Utilitarians," *in Analyzing Law: New Essays in Legal Theory* ed. Brian Bix (New York: Oxford University Press, 1998), 197, 199.

45. See generally Robin West, 197-222.

46. William H. Rehnquist, "The Notion of a Living Constitution," *Texas Law Review* 54 (1976) 693, 704 (arguing that democracy is the moral basis of law and that the constitutional protections of individual liberties "assume a general social acceptance neither because of any intrinsic worth nor because of any unique origins in someone's idea of natural justice but instead simply because they have been incorporated in a constitution by the people."

47. Antonin Scalia, "The Common Christian Good" in *Symposium, Left, Right, and the Common Good* (June 13, 1996), available at http://www.catholicnews.com/data/stories/cns/960613.htm (last visited Jan. 18, 2010).

48. See generally Pew Research Center, "The Religious Dimensions of the Torture Debate" (Apr. 30, 2009), available at http://pewresearch.org/pubs/1210/torture-opinion-religious-differences (last visited on May 28, 2009) (discussing the contemporary popular notions regarding the torture of suspected terrorists. A survey found that 54 percent of people who attend Church services at least once a week believe that the use of torture against suspected terrorists is "often" or "sometimes" justified, *ibid.*). But *see* Pontifical Council for the Justice and Peace, *Compendium of the Social Doctrine of the Church*, 404, (June 29, 2004), *available at* http://www.vatican.va/roman_curia/pontifical_councils/justpeace/documents/rc_pc_justpeace_doc_20060526_compendio-dott-soc_en.html (last visited Jan. 18, 2010). The Catholic Church teaches that the regulation against the use of torture, no matter how serious the allegation or crime, must be strictly observed: "Christ's disciple refuses every recourse to such methods, which nothing could justify and in which the dignity of man is as much debased in his torturer as in the torturer's victim." International juridical instruments concerning human rights indicate a prohibition against torture as a principle that cannot ever be contravened.

49. See generally Pope John Paul II, *Memory and Identity: Conversations at the Dawn*

of a Millennium (New York: Rizzoli, 2005).

50. Recently emerging views that torture is tolerable because it generates important information are basically pragmatist and instrumentalist. The proponents claim that the end justifies the means and ignore its intrinsic moral baseness.

51. *See generally* James, William, *The Meaning of Truth: A Sequel to 'Pragmatism'*(New York: Prometheus Books, 1997) [originally published, 1909].

52. See generally Richard A. Posner, "The Ethical and Political Basis of the Efficiency Norm in Common Law Adjudication," *Hofstra Law Review* 8 (1980), 487. Posner argues, for example, that judges should base their decisions on efficiency and wealth maximization. See also Bentham.

53. See generally Judith Shklar, *Legalism: Law, Morals, and Political Trials* (Cambridge, MA: Harvard University Press, 1964), 1-2, 8-16

54. See generally Anthony Kronman, "The Lost Lawyer: Failing Ideals of the Legal Profession" in Gottlieb, 366. Christopher Langdell argued, for example, that the answers to all legal questions can be derived from a limited number of preexisting principles, found in classic legal cases. This analysis would put law on a scientific basis-the idea that positivists essentially advocate.

55. See generally Antonin Scalia, *A Matter of Interpretation: Federal Courts and the Law* (Princeton: Princeton University Press, 1998), 23-25 .

56. See *e.g.*, Catherine A. Mackinnon, *Feminism Unmodified: Discourses on Life and Law* (Cambridge, MA: Harvard University Press, 1987), 48-62 (noting that feminists proclaim that women and men are equally different but not equally powerful and that men use the law to dominate women). Feminist legal jurisprudence argues that by focusing on a neutral application of legal rules, legalism does not understand that law contains biases that subordinate and dominate women, *ibid.* See also Wendy W. Williams, "Notes from a First Generation," *University of Chicago Legal Forum* (1989), 99 (arguing that although males and females are equal to the state, laws contain sex-based distinctions favoring males).

57. See, e.g., Robert Cover, *Justice Accused: Antislavery and the Judicial Process* (New Haven: Yale University Press, 1975), 1-7 (arguing that judges exonerate themselves by saying that they are not responsible for the content of law, but only for its application). In addition, critical race theorists argue that, for all its insistence on neutrality, legalism lacks legitimacy because it does not recognize racial bias in the law. *Ibid.*

58. See generally Oliver Wendell Holmes, *The Common Law* (Boston: Little, Brown and Company, 1963), 5, 31-32.

59. *See* Robert W. Gordon, *Unfreezing Legal Reality: Critical Approaches to Law*, 15 Fla. St. U. L. Rev. 195, 198-215 (1987) (arguing that the goal of Critical Legal Studies (CLS) is to transform the legal system to create a society less intensively ordered by hierarchies and class status, and to combat the resolve that society can't change, *ibid.* In particular, CLS addresses civil rights, believing that they protect both the oppressor and oppressed alike. However, beyond criticizing rights, CLS proposes no alternatives. *Ibid.*

60. Jose M. Casciaro, *The Navarre Bible 27: Romans and Galatians* trans. Michael Adams (Dublin: Four Courts Press, 1993).

61. Galatians 3:24–28.

62. Mauck, 126.

63. Pope Benedict XVI, Address To Participants in The International Congress in Natural Moral Law (12 Feb. 2007).

64. Ibid.

65. U.N. Charter, Art. 1, ¶ 3, http://www.un.org/en/documents/charter/index.shtml (last visited Jan. 18, 2010).

66. Universal Declaration of Human Rights, G.A. Res. 217A, at 71, U.N. GAOR, 3d Sess., 1st plen. mtg., U.N. Doc. A/810 (Dec. 12, 1948).

67. The recognition that all human being have "inherent dignity" and are "endowed with reason" is a natural law proposition. *Ibid.* at pmbl., Art. 1. In addition to the Universal Declaration of Human Rights, the international community adopted the International Covenant on Civil and Political Rights (G.A. Res. 2200A (XXI), ¶ 21, U.N. GAOR Supp. No. 16 at 52, U.N. Doc. A/6316 (1966), 999 U.N.T.S. 171, *entered into force* Mar. 23, 1976), the International Covenant on Economic, Social and Cultural Rights (G.A. Res. 2200A (XXI), ¶ 21, U.N. GAOR Supp. No. 16 at 49, U.N. Doc. A/6316 (1966), 993 U.N.T.S. 3, *entered into force* Jan. 3, 1976), and the International Convention on the Elimination of All Forms of Racial Discrimination (G.A. Res. 2106 (XX), Annex, 20 U.N. GAOR Supp. No. 14 at 47, U.N. Doc. A/6014 (1965), 660 U.N.T.S. 195, *entered into force* Jan. 4, 1969), among others.

68. See generally Sebok (arguing that in regards to the United States, positivism was "hijacked" during the Warren Court by conservative legal scholars, creating the idea that positivism was hostile to morality in the law).

69. Archbishop Silvano M. Tomasi, Statement by Apostolic Nuncio, Permanent Mission Of The Holy See, Permanent Observer of the Holy See to the United Nations and Other International Organizations in Geneva (April 20-24, 2009).

70. *Ibid.*

71. Pope Benedict XVI, Address of Pope Benedict XVI to the United Nations (Apr. 18, 2008), *available at* http://www.vatican.va/holy_father/benedict_xvi/speeches/2008/april/documents/hf_ben-xvi_spe_20080418_un-visit_en.html (last visited May 28, 2009).

72. The G20 includes Saudi Arabia, Argentina, Australia, Brazil, Canada, China, France, Germany, Japan, Great Britain, India, Indonesia, Italy, Mexico, Russia, South Africa, South Korea, the United States, Turkey and the European Union.

73. Patrick Wintour and Larry Elliott, "G20: Gordon Brown brokers massive financial aid deal for global economy," *The Guardian* (April 3, 2009), *available at* http://www.guardian.co.uk/world/2009/apr/03/g20-gordon-brown-global-economy (last visited May 29, 2009). The G20 pledged, among other things, the sale of gold by the IMF to raise six billion dollars to help the poorest countries by creating jobs. Calling it the beginning of a new world order, the prime minister of Britain, Gordon Brown, remarked that this consensus marked "the day the world came together," and President Nicolas Sarkozy of France mused that a page had been turned on the economic model which had dominated since Bretton Woods in 1944 created the world's institutional framework.

74. Vienna Convention on the Law of Treaties, Arts. 26, 31, 46, 69 (Jan. 27, 1980), 1155 U.N.T.S. 331, 8 I.L.M. 679.

75. See ibid., art. 53. Even principles such as *jus cogens*—the peremptory norms in international law that cannot be derogated from treaty law (genocide, slavery, torture) are subject to State consent because they must be "accepted and recognized by the international community of States as a whole."

76. See David Bederman, *International Law Frameworks* 2 (Foundation Press 2d ed., 2006), 2 (arguing that legal positivism justifies sovereignty).

77. Ibid. at 3.

78. See International Commission of Jurists, *Protection of Human Rights and Fundamental Freedoms While Countering Terrorism* (Apr. 18, 2005), available at http://www.icj.org/IMG/pdf/ctos.pdf (last visited May 28, 2009). A number of resolutions adopted by the United Nations General Assembly, Security Council, and Commission on Human Rights stress that States must ensure that any measures taken to combat terrorism comply with international law. *See, e.g.*, S.C. Res. 1456, ¶ 6, U.N. Doc. S/RES/1456 (Jan. 20, 2003). The International Commission of Jurists (ICJ) noted that counter-terrorism measures must not "undermine the human rights law that member states have themselves painstakingly built up over fifty years." International Commission of Jurists, *Protection of Human Rights and Fundamental Freedoms While Countering Terrorism*, available at http://www.icj.org/IMG/pdf/ctos.pdf (last visited May 29, 2009). In July 2004, the ICJ noted that the 'war against terrorism' had given greater legitimacy to long-standing human rights violations carried out in the name of national security. Even as he dissented from the majority opinion, Judge Buergenthal wrote, "I agree that the means used to defend against terrorism must conform to all applicable rules of international law." *Legal Consequences of the Construction of a Wall in the Occupied Palestinian Territory*, Advisory Opinion, 2004 I.C.J. 136 (July 9). See also *The Digest of Jurisprudence of the UN and Regional Organizations on the Protection of Human Rights while Countering Terrorism* (OHCHR 2003) (clarifying the concept of non-derogable rights. Its main task was to establish a framework in which terrorism can be effectively countered without negatively affecting fundamental freedoms, and to address the core principles of necessity and proportionality, fundamental to valid counter-terrorism measures).

CHAPTER SIX

St. Paul, Ephesians 5, and Same-Sex Marriage[1]

Mary Healy
Associate Professor of Sacred Scripture,
Sacred Heart Major Seminary, Detroit, Michigan

Introduction

In Western society today we are faced with the increasingly aggressive demand that same-sex relationships be granted the legal status of marriage. Advocates of same-sex marriage typically appeal to principles of equality and inclusivity, arguing that it is unjust to deny the social, financial and legal benefits of marriage to some couples merely because their sexual orientation happens to be different from that of others. Marriage, we are told, is a social construct that has exhibited a wide diversity of forms among different cultures and time periods, and even within the Bible itself. Therefore marriage can and should be re-envisioned in contemporary society to accommodate people of diverse sexual orientations.

Such arguments are steadily gaining ground in the courts, in legislatures, in the educational system, and in popular culture. This situation presents defenders of the traditional Judeo-Christian understanding of marriage with a new and unprecedented challenge. Although forms of homosexual practice have existed in nearly all societies known to history, never before have homosexual relationships been viewed as equal to or even analogous to marriage, or deserving of the same rights and privileges as marriage. The radical difference between the two has been assumed as something obvious, requiring no justification. Thus our present situation forces us to formulate reasons for something that has always been taken for granted, and to do so in a way that will gain a hearing in the contemporary post-modern generation.[2] We are truly treading on new ground.

The question I would like to pose in this article is: What might the Bible, and St. Paul in particular, have to contribute to the contemporary discussion of same-sex marriage? Since Scripture is a document of faith whose authority is not accepted by all parties, obviously we cannot derive formal legal arguments from it. However, this is not the only role that Scripture can play in reasoning in the public square. Indeed, a recent *Newsweek* cover story on same-sex marriage,[3] which went to great lengths to demonstrate biblical support for gay marriage despite the author's evident disdain for the Bible, shows the continuing importance of Scripture in the contemporary marriage debate. I would like to illustrate how Scripture can clarify, deepen and enrich our public defense of marriage by examining St. Paul's famous exhortation to husbands and wives in Ephesians 5:21-33. (A literal translation is provided at the end of this chapter). In this richly theological passage, Paul refers specifically to *Christian* marriage as a sacrament of the New Covenant and an image of the union of Christ and the Church. Nevertheless, there are principles that can be gleaned from Ephesians 5 to shed light on the natural law and on society's responsibility to protect marriage as traditionally understood. I will first present a brief exegesis of the passage, and will then show how this text, supplemented by other Pauline texts, can help ground a natural law defense of marriage.

Exegesis of Ephesians 5:21-33

The first thing to note about Ephesians 5:21-33, an exhortation to husbands and wives, is that grammatically, its first part continues a single long sentence that actually begins in 5:18.[4] The sentence consists of a series of subordinate clauses governed by the main clause "Do not get drunk with wine… but be filled with the Spirit." Everything Paul says about proper relationships in the family is thus within the context of life in the Spirit—the wholly new way of life made possible by baptism into Christ and the outpouring of the Holy Spirit. He is speaking of Christian marriage and family life. To abstract what he says about marriage from this context would only result in distortion.

Our passage is also closely connected with the two following sections, in which Paul addresses relationships between parents and children (6:1-4) and between masters and slaves (6:5-9). The three units form a whole that belongs to a genre of New Testament passages known as household codes.[5] As scholars have long pointed out, these texts have certain features in common with ancient Greco-Roman and Jewish household codes, but some even more significant differences. Most non-Christian household codes took for granted that the *pater familias* (father of the family) had absolute authority over the members of the household. They described how wives, children and slaves should behave toward him, but not how he should treat them. The New Testament texts, in contrast, do not give unlimited power to men, but instead call for a high degree of responsibility and mutual respect among all members of the family. Moreover, they make no mention of an obligation for wives to obey their husbands, nor of a man's natural superiority and greater capacity to make decisions—features that were ubiquitous in pagan household codes.[6] It is important not to misread Paul's teaching as merely a baptized version of ancient domestic codes sanctioning patriarchal and oppressive family structures.

Ephesians 5:21 begins, significantly, with an injunction to *mutual subordination* within the Christian community: "subordinating yourselves to one another in reverence for Christ." The Greek verb for "subordinate," *hypotassō*, means literally to "place under." Here it is in the middle (reflexive) voice, with the meaning "subordinate oneself" or defer to. This is significant, because it indicates that Paul is referring to a voluntary self-subordination, not something imposed from without. The governing principle that must shape all relationships within the household is an attitude of humility and deference toward one another, motivated by reverence for Christ.[7] Thus the subsequent injunction to wives to subordinate themselves to their husbands[8] has to be understood within the context of the *mutual* subordination of husband and wife.[9] This is consistent with other passages in the New Testament that proclaim the fundamental equality of men and women. In the Synoptic Gospels, Jesus' teaching on divorce recognizes the equal dignity of husband and wife (Matt 5:32). Paul similarly teaches the equal rights of spouses (1 Cor 7:3-4), and asserts that in Christ all distinctions of status have been set aside: "There is neither Jew nor Greek, there is neither slave nor free, there is neither male nor female; for you are all one in Christ Jesus" (Gal 3:28). Again note that, in contrast to his instructions to children and slaves (Eph 6:1, 5), Paul does not enjoin wives to "obey." Rather, he exhorts them to defer willingly to their husbands as an expression of their devotion to Christ.

Paul then begins to draw an analogy between the wife's relation to her husband and the Church's relationship to Christ: "for a husband is head of his wife as Christ is head of the church" (v. 23). In using the metaphor of head and body, Paul is not accenting the notion of authority but rather of profound union and mutual belonging. As Pope John Paul II noted in his reflections on this passage, the precedence suggested by "head" is an order of precedence in the giving and receiving of love. The "*husband* is above all *the one who loves* and the wife, by contrast, is *the one who is loved*. One might even venture the idea that the wife's 'submission' to the husband, understood in the context of the whole of Ephesians 5:22-23, means above all 'the experiencing of love.'"[10] The husband takes the initiative in self-donation, the wife receives and responds to his gift. Thus the spousal relation Paul describes "is not command/obedience but generosity/receptivity."[11]

The model for their interaction is that of Christ and the Church; like the Church's relation to Christ, a wife's relation to her husband is meant to be a free and gracious response to his love. Like all analogies, this one has points of correspondence and points of disparity. Paul indicates his awareness of the far more comprehensive role of Christ by adding "and is himself the Savior of the body."[12] He concludes the part of his exhortation addressed to wives by reiterating the call to defer "in everything," which is not meant to express an exceptionless norm (cf. 1 Cor 7:4), but rather a general principle motivated by the generosity of the husband's self-gift.

The part of Paul's instruction addressed to husbands (vv. 25-30) is far more extensive, and perhaps more challenging, than that addressed to wives. It has absolutely no precedent in Greco-Roman or rabbinic literature.[13] Here the verb that governs the conduct of husbands is "love" (*agapaō*), which signifies not romantic passion (*eros*) but a decision of the will, a selfless desire for the good of the other.[14] It is the love so powerfully eulogized by Paul in the hymn of 1 Corinthians 13, and its primary exemplar is God himself, who "loved us" (*agapaō*) with "great love" (*agapē*) by giving up his Son for us even when we were dead in our sins (Eph 2:4; cf. 5:1-2). The paschal mystery is, in fact, the model Paul holds up for the conduct of husbands: "Husbands, love your wives, just as Christ loved the church and gave himself for her." As Christ demonstrated his limitless, unconditional love by dying for us on the cross, so husbands are to lay down their lives for their wives by seeking their good, regardless of the cost to themselves (cf. 1 Cor 10:24; 13:5; Phil 2:4).[15] Paul could not have set a more demanding standard. Indeed, as his writings elsewhere make clear (Eph 5:2; Rom 8:3-4; 2 Cor 5:14-15), it is a standard that is impossible to meet except by experiencing Christ's paschal mystery as a power at work in one's own life. A person is able to *imitate* Christ only by *participating* through grace in the act of love in which he died for us.

Paul continues the spousal imagery as he elaborates on the purpose of Christ's self-gift for the Church (vv. 26-27). The goal, mentioned twice, is that the Church be "holy," that is, set apart from what is profane, and presented to Christ as a resplendent bride. With the "washing of water" Paul alludes to the sacrament of baptism, envisioning it as a prenuptial bath—only in this case the Bridegroom shows his humility by himself bathing the bride, rather than female servants or family members as was customary. Paul may also be alluding to Jesus' act of humility in washing his disciples' feet before his passion (John 13:1–17). This image serves to further illustrate the quality of Christ's love as the model for husbands.

A different but related analogy is presented in vv. 27-28, where Paul compares a husband's love for his wife to a person's care for his own body: "for no one ever hates his own flesh but nourishes it and cares for it." The Hebrew notion of "flesh" signifies not merely the physical body but the bond of kinship, which extends to the members of one's family (Gen 29:14; Isa 58:7) or tribe (2 Sam 5:1), and ultimately to all humanity (Gen 6:12; Luke 3:6). A husband is to seek his wife's well-being as much as his own because of the intimacy of their kinship bond. It is a specific application of the second great commandment, "Love your neighbor as yourself" (Lev 19:18; Mt 19:19). The body analogy is conditioned by the Christ–Church analogy: a husband is to do good to his wife not merely out of pragmatic self-interest, but *as Christ cares for his body the Church*, his physical presence in the world.[16] With the word "nourishes" (or "feeds"), Paul alludes to the Eucharist, by which Christ nourishes the Church with his own flesh (John 6:51–58). By this point it becomes evident to what degree Paul is defying rather than accommodating ancient social conventions. His whole exhortation is premised on the fact that the gospel has power to radically transform the dynamics of family relationships and the social structures marred by sin.

At the climax of his exposition Paul cites Genesis 2:24: "For this reason a man shall leave his father and mother and be joined to his wife, and the two shall become one flesh." He then adds: "This is a great mystery, for I am speaking of Christ and the church." With this statement, Paul brings the institution of marriage to a completely new level of significance. Marriage is not only part of God's original design for humanity, it is a mystery[17] that already from the beginning of time pointed in a veiled way to the fullness of God's plan of salvation. The prophets of Israel had described God's love for his people as that of a bridegroom for his bride,[18] but Paul invests the nuptial imagery with a deeper import. "Creation itself is a prophecy of redemption. This means that in the corporate reality of man and woman, as Genesis describes it, is already present in a proleptic symbol the unity of Christ and the Church."[19] All marriages, whether between Christians or not, are an earthly image of, and in some way participate in, the ineffable mystery of Christ's love for his people.

Genesis 2 and the 'Spousal Attribute' of the Body

The quotation from Genesis 2:24 plays a crucial role in Paul's exposition, rooting the "great mystery" of which he speaks in the human reality of marriage as part of the natural order. It is worth briefly examining this text in its original context. The quotation is from the end of the second creation account (Genesis 2), which presents in narrative form a concise but profound reflection on humanity created by God, male and female. Whereas the first creation account (Genesis 1) offers a sweeping vision of the creation of the whole cosmos in order of increasing complexity, the second creation account "zooms in," so to speak, to describe from a more concrete and existential perspective the origin of humanity, the crown of God's works. Here God first creates the male alone, and breathes into him the breath of life (Gen 2:7). The divine remark, "It is *not good* that the man should be alone; I will make him a helper fit for him" (Gen 2:18), is in striking contrast to the repeated refrain affirming the goodness of creation in chapter 1: "God saw that it was *good*." It is an emphatic assertion that human beings are not made for solitude; essential to human nature is interpersonal communion.

Following this comment, there ensues a mini-drama in which God presents the animals to Adam one by one. Narrative suspense is created, as none of the animals is found capable of the communion for which the man longs. Through this process Adam learns how unique he is among animate beings. At the culmination of the narrative, God finally acts to resolve the crisis by putting Adam into a deep sleep, taking flesh from his rib and fashioning it into a woman. In a scene with strong nuptial overtones, God presents her to him like the father of the bride, and Adam responds with an expression of unrestrained joy: "This at last is bone of my bones, flesh of my flesh!" (Gen 2:23). As John Paul II observes in his reflections on this text, the scene is portrayed as a moment of existential self-discovery. The man recognizes that the woman—unlike the animals—is his equal, a *person* like himself, to whom he can give himself in love and who can freely receive and reciprocate this gift. He suddenly has a new understanding of the meaning of his existence: he is made for communion, an exchange of love in which the gift of self is freely given and received. In this perspective the meaning of the title used to describe Eve, "helper," becomes clear. Unfortunately, commentators throughout the centuries have often mangled the meaning of "helper" by reading it as evidence for the wife's role as servant or maid to her husband. But in the Old Testament "helper" (*'ezer*) is most often applied to God himself.[20]

The woman is helper, fundamentally, in that she helps the man recognize and fulfill the deepest purpose of his life, namely, to love. The sacred author is affirming that man needs woman in order to discover the full meaning of his existence, and likewise, she needs him. They help one another realize and fulfill their call to communion through a reciprocal gift of self. In the memorable statement of *Gaudium et spes* 24, "Man, who is the only creature on earth which God willed for itself, cannot fully find himself except through a sincere gift of himself."

At this point a question may arise: But what significance is there to the fact that it is a woman and not another man who is presented to Adam? Is it not often claimed today that the male-female distinction is "a purely contingent fact about human beings, a mechanism devised by nature for propagating the species,"[21]ranking in significance with racial distinctions or differences of physique or talent? Would it not have equally served the purpose to depict the second human being as a male, with whom Adam could have enjoyed deep friendship, or even sexual intimacy, and thus experienced the primary meaning of *communio* even as it exists within marriage, which is love?

But close attention to the Genesis narrative shows that, by accenting the male-female distinction (1:27; 2:22-24), the text conveys that it is precisely through *the complementarity of their bodies*—their sexual differences that render union possible—that Adam and Eve intuit their vocation to become a communion of persons. The male and female bodies are designed to be perfectly complementary—to come together in a union so potent that it becomes the means by which new human life enters the world. "The helper is someone who matches *'ādām* but is not a replica. . . . Communion is between likes who are yet unlike."[22] The gendered body, in its masculinity or femininity, has an intrinsically "nuptial" quality; it is apt for spousal union. It possesses a unity-in-difference that renders it capable of becoming the vehicle and expression of a total and mutual gift of self. John Paul II calls this aptness the "spousal attribute" of the body: "The human body, with its sex—its masculinity and femininity . . . contains, 'from the beginning,' the 'spousal' attribute, that is, *the power to express love: precisely that love in which the human person becomes a gift* and—through this gift—fulfills the very meaning of his being and existence."[23] Through their bodies, a man and woman each recognize the other as *equal* and yet irreducibly *other*. There is an "asymmetrical reciprocity" to their self-giving through the body, in which the gift is given and received differently in accord with their sexual differences.[24] It is this reciprocity that Paul later invests with a profound theological significance, as the earthly image of the spousal love between God and his people.

Genesis goes on, in the verse quoted by Paul, to show the relevance of this defining moment of self-discovery for all future marital relations: "Therefore a man leaves his father and his mother and cleaves to his wife, and they become one flesh" (Gen 2:24). Here the author depicts marriage in covenantal terms, that is, in terms of a kinship bond created by solemn commitment.[25] Marriage, the covenant by which a man and a woman commit themselves to one another wholly and irrevocably as a mutual gift of self, is enacted in their sexual union. That which is interior and personal—a communion of persons—becomes outwardly expressed, or enfleshed, in the body.

The crucial point to note for our purposes is that, through narrative, Genesis is giving symbolic expression to the truth that is inscribed in our bodies and is *therefore in principle accessible to every human being*, at least on a basic level: that the intrinsic meaning of sexual union is to embody a spousal covenant, and that therefore marriage is the uniquely appropriate context for sexual expression. Or, to put it another way, sexual union is in its essence not a meaningless bodily activity, on the level of eating or sleeping—a view that Paul refutes in 1 Cor 6:13-20—but is essentially the outward sign of a union that takes place on the deepest level of the person, in the mutual self-donation of husband and wife. Sexual union is also uniquely capable of generating life and thus giving rise to the primordial human community, the family. This is why gender is not an accidental human quality like height, eye color or ethnic origin. Every human being is specified as either male or female and thus imprinted with a visible sign of our capacity for, and vocation to, life-giving spousal communion (which can be lived out either in marriage or in consecrated celibacy). Sexuality, the body's "spousal attribute," "reaches to the core of the person, the heart of our identity, and situates it in relationality, aptness for love."[26] It is no coincidence that human society, despite all its distortions and injustices, has always recognized marriage as having an inherent and unchangeable structure that corresponds to the nature of the human person, embodied as male or female.

The Invention of Homosexuality

To return to our contemporary debate, what light do Ephesians 5:21-33 and Genesis 2:24 shed on the issue of same-sex marriage? Let us first note that for Paul, as for Genesis and for human society in general until very recently, homosexuality is a behavior, not an "orientation," much less an identity. The concept of "homosexual" as a category of persons is, in fact, a modern construct, invented by those who sought to overturn sodomy laws in nineteenth-century Germany. We must admit that this movement has been enormously successful in transforming societal perceptions. More recently, a new step has been taken in the use of "homosexuality" and "heterosexuality" as apparently symmetrical terms, implying that sexuality is an abstract, neutral concept to which homo- or hetero- are added as equally valid specifications.[27] Paul's teaching helps us recognize and resist such ideological manipulation of language. More significantly, it confirms and elucidates what is already knowable by reflection on the human body, and is thus part of the natural law: the obvious though politically incorrect truth that *no one is homosexual*; no one is intrinsically oriented to the same sex.[28] Sexual union, properly speaking, is in fact physically impossible with a person of the same sex. All that is possible is erotic activity that contravenes the purpose of, and sometimes does violence to, the reproductive organs of the human body.

But here we can anticipate an objection: Then why do some people have homosexual inclinations, even an apparently deep-seated, long-term "orientation" to the same sex (documented from as early as age two)?[29] According to Paul, this disjuncture between one's sexual desire and the sexual orientation of one's body is attributable to the same cause by which we *all* have disorder in our desires: the cataclysmic decision at the dawn of history (narrated in Genesis 3) by which sin, disorder and corruption entered the world. Note that he frequently lists homosexual activity along with other sexual sins and other forms of sin (Rom 1:26-31; 1 Cor 6:9; 1 Tim 1:10).[30]

Even among those who do not accept the Judeo-Christian doctrine of original sin, who would deny that sexuality as it is practiced is often selfish, disordered, and exploitative? It follows that the existence of a strong, overwhelming or persistent sexual desire is no argument for the rightness of satisfying the desire. Otherwise there would be no moral grounds to judge adultery, incest, bestiality, polyamory, pedophilia or other forms of sexual disorder as wrong.

Secondly, the teaching of Ephesians 5 and Genesis 2 helps us appreciate why any sexual activity that is detached from the context of marital union and its inherently procreative potential is intrinsically depersonalizing.[31] Such activity ignores the body's "spousal attribute"—its innate aptness, as male or female, to embody a spousal gift of self—and in the absence of this meaning, inevitably turns the body into an instrument of physical or emotional self-gratification. No matter how well-intentioned the partners or how sincere their affection for each other, in such acts they are using one another as means to an end and thereby undermining one another's dignity. An act whose intrinsic meaning is to express a total *gift of self* becomes instead a means of *grasping for self.* In the case of homosexual activity,

> The action is understood apart from the meaning communicated by the structure of the body, subverting the physical dynamism in order that, so it is claimed, a communion might become possible. . . . Consequently, the bodily encounter lacks its original meaning and is used simply as a means for satisfaction. This is how the acting subject becomes fragmented, which leads to an absorption in cultivating the search for pleasure, and in developing the erotic techniques necessary for producing it. The physical gesture ceases to be a means of revealing the persons to each other and becomes centered instead in the quest for mutual satisfaction.[32]

Finally, the unique capacity of marriage to mediate the reality of God's love for his people helps explain the close connection Paul frequently draws, so alien to modern sensibilities, between sexuality and religious truth. In Romans 1, Paul describes the negative side of this equation: the refusal to acknowledge the truth about God revealed in creation—or worse, the suppression of that truth—leads by a direct path to sexual conduct that degrades human dignity. Conversely, sexual sin leads to a darkened mind, and the inability to recognize truth about God.

> For the wrath of God is revealed from heaven against all ungodliness and wickedness of men who by their wickedness suppress the truth. For what can be known about God is plain to them, because God has shown it to them. Ever since the creation of the world his invisible nature, namely, his eternal power and deity, has been clearly perceived in the things that have been made. So they are without excuse; for although they knew God they did not honor him as God or give thanks to him, but they became futile in their thinking and their senseless minds were darkened. Claiming to be wise, they became fools, and exchanged the glory of the immortal God for images resembling mortal man or birds or animals or reptiles. Therefore God gave them up in the lusts of their hearts to impurity, to the dishonoring of their bodies among themselves, because they exchanged the truth about God for a lie and worshiped and served the creature rather than the Creator, who is blessed for ever! Amen. For this reason God gave them up to dishonorable passions. Their women exchanged natural relations for unnatural, and the men likewise gave up natural relations with women and were consumed with passion for one another, men committing shameless acts with men and receiving in their own persons the due penalty for their error. And since they did not see fit to acknowledge God, God gave them up to a base mind and to improper conduct (Rom 1:18-28; cf. Eph 4:17-20).

If the call to communion inscribed in our bodies, male and female, is a revelation of God in the created world, then as Livio Melina points out, "it is normal to expect the disorder of homosexuality to have a paradigmatic theological significance in the history of salvation."[33] And we have reason for concern that the wholesale denial of the privileged status of marriage in society will have long-term and gravely damaging human consequences.[34]

Conclusion

The above considerations help demonstrate why it is imperative for Christians and all people of good will to oppose legislation that grants to same-sex unions a status similar or equal to that of marriage, as recent Church teaching has frequently emphasized.[35] I would like to conclude by briefly summarizing two ways in which deeper reflection on biblical teaching can strengthen our response to the same-sex marriage challenge. First, Scripture illuminates the natural law by articulating truths about human nature and the human vocation to communion that are inscribed in our bodies and thus intrinsically knowable. It uncovers the deep logic by which we recognize marriage as a good to be upheld and homosexuality as intrinsically detrimental to the dignity of the person. Secondly, Scripture offers a vision for marriage and the family that is compelling and attractive in its own right because it corresponds to the deepest longings of the human heart, and thus can speak on some level even to those who do not accept the authority of biblical revelation. If Christians are to gain a hearing in the contemporary debate, it will only be by both articulating and modeling in our own lives an authentic vision for human sexuality—one that is so joyful and life-giving that it exposes unrestrained sexual license for the cheap counterfeit it is.

A Literal Translation of Eph 5:18-33

18 And do not get drunk with wine, which is debauchery,
but be filled with the Spirit,
19 speaking to one another in psalms and hymns and spiritual songs,
singing and making melody to the Lord in your heart,
20 giving thanks always and for everything
in the name of our Lord Jesus Christ to God the Father,
21 subordinating yourselves to one another in reverence for Christ,
22 wives to their husbands, as to the Lord,
23 for a husband is head of his wife as Christ is head of the church
and is himself the Savior of the body,
24 but as the church subordinates herself to Christ,
so also wives to their husbands in everything.
25 Husbands, love your wives, just as Christ loved the church
and gave himself for her,
26 in order to make her holy,

purifying her by the washing of water through the word,
27 in order to present to himself the church in splendor,
without stain or wrinkle or any such thing,
but that she might be holy and unblemished.
28 In this way husbands ought to love their wives as their own bodies.
Whoever loves his wife loves himself.
29 For no one ever hates his own flesh but nourishes it and cares for it,
just as Christ does for the church,
30 for we are members of his body.
31 "For this reason a man shall leave his father and mother and be
joined to his wife, and the two shall be one flesh."[36]
32 This is a great mystery:[37]
for I am speaking of Christ and the church.
33 However, let each one of you love his wife as himself in this way,
and let the wife reverence her husband.

Notes

1. This chapter was previously published in *Homiletic & Pastoral Review* (May, 2011). It is reprinted here with permission.

2. John Crosby draws an apt comparison with Chesterton's description of what it is like to be asked to explain why civilization is better than barbarism. "Our first reaction… is to stammer something about the benefits of having policemen, an observation that we know misses the mark; but we are at first too disoriented by the radicality of the challenge to say anything that really meets it." Crosby, "John Paul II on the Complementarity of Man and Woman," in Kenneth Whitehead (ed.), *The Church, Marriage, and the Family*, Proceedings from the 27th Annual Convention of the Fellowship of Catholic Scholars (South Bend, Ind.: St. Augustine's Press, 2007), 41-52; here p. 41.

3. Lisa Miller, "Our Mutual Joy," *Newsweek* (Dec. 6, 2008).

4. Verse 21 serves as a hinge joining the preceding section with what follows. Because it governs the subsequent injunctions to members of the household, nearly all modern translations and commentaries read 5:21 as beginning a new paragraph even though it is also grammatically linked with what precedes. Such intricate literary constructions are not uncommon in Paul.

5. The other instances are Colossians 3:18–4:1; Titus 2:1-10; and 1 Peter 2:18–3:7.

6. See Francis Martin, *Sacred Scripture: The Disclosure of the Word*, (Naples, FL.: Sapientia Press, 2006), 207.

7. See Phil 2:1-4 for similar Pauline teaching on attitudes within the Christian community; and Mark 10:42-45 for the dominical teaching which underlies it.

8. Verse 22 actually contains no verb; the participle "subordinating" has to be carried over from v. 21.

9. Pope John Paul II makes this point in *Mulieris dignitatem* (1988), 24.

10. See John Paul II, audience of Sept. 1, 1982, in *Man and Woman He Created Them: A Theology of the Body*, trans. Michael Waldstein (Boston: Pauline, 2006), 485. Italics in the original.

11. Martin, *Sacred Scripture*, 212.

12. See Peter Williamson, *Ephesians*, Catholic Commentary on Sacred Scripture (Grand Rapids: Baker Academic, 2009), 160.

13. Harold W. Hoehner, *Ephesians: An Exegetical Commentary* (Grand Rapids: Baker Academic, 2002), 748.

14. In his encyclical *Deus Caritas Est*, Pope Benedict XVI describes how *eros*, which is itself a gift of God, finds its fulfillment by maturing into the *agapē* of spousal love.

15. Williamson, *Ephesians*, 166.

16. Ibid.

17. The Greek term for mystery, *mysterion*, is translated *sacramentum* in Latin; thus this text provides the basis for the Church's understanding of marriage as a sacrament.

18. See, for instance, Jer 3:20; Isa 54:5-7, 10; 62:4-5; Hos 2:16-20.

19. Martin, *Sacred Scripture*, 218.

20. Nineteen of the twenty-one Old Testament instances of the noun refer to God. See, for instance, Job 29:12; Ps 10:14; 30:10; 54:4; Is 63:5.

21. Crosby, "Complementarity," 43.

22. Martin, *Sacred Scripture*, 201.

23. John Paul II, *Man and Woman*, 185-86.

24. Cardinal Angelo Scola discusses this in "The Dignity and Mission of Women: The Anthropological and Theological Foundations," *Communio* 25 (Spring 1998), 46-47; and "The Nuptial Mystery at the Heart of the Church," *Communio* 25 (Winter 1998), 634- 636, 643-647.

25. The terms "bone" and "flesh" in Gen 2:23 allude to the kinship bond formed by covenant; cf. 2 Sam 5:1; 19:13. For the essential meaning of covenant as a kinship bond, see Scott Hahn, *Kinship by Covenant: A Canonical Approach to the Fulfillment of God's Saving Promises*, Anchor Yale Bible Reference Library (New Haven / London: Yale University Press, 2009), 3-4.

26. David Schindler, "John Paul II and the 'Nuptial Attribute' of the Body: The Family and the Future of Humanity," in *The Church, Marriage, and the Family*, 363-77; here p. 365.

27. Livio Melina, "Homosexual Inclination as an 'Objective Disorder': Reflections on Theological Anthropology," *Communio* 25 (Spring 1998), 57-68; here p. 60.

28. When speaking to youth groups I tell teens who are skeptical of this point, If you don't believe me, just go home and look at your body in a full-length mirror. You'll see that I'm right! Your body, and everyone's body, is designed for spousal union with the opposite sex.

29. The empirical evidence, despite frequent media claims to the contrary, confirms that same-sex attraction results from a complex combination of factors rather than being a genetically predetermined condition. In spite of numerous attempts, no "gay gene" has been found. Even those researchers most frequently invoked in support of a "gay gene" actually refuse to claim it for their own research. Simon LeVay, who studied the differences between the brains of homosexual and heterosexual men, writes: "It's important to stress what I didn't find. I did not prove that homosexuality is genetic, or find a genetic cause for being gay. I didn't show that gay men are born that way, the most common mistake people make in interpreting my work. Nor did I locate a gay center in the brain" (D. Nimmons, "Sexual brain," *Discover* 5 [1994], 64-67. Researcher Dean Hamer said of his studies attempting to link

male homosexuality to DNA, "We knew that genes were only part of the answer. We assumed the environment also played a role in sexual orientation, as it does in most, if not all behaviors...." (D. Hamer and P. Copeland, *The Science of Desire* [New York: Simon and Schuster, 1994], 82). Hamer and Copeland further write, "The pedigree failed to produce what we originally hoped to find: simple Mendelian inheritance. In fact, we never found a single family in which homosexuality was distributed in the obvious pattern that Mendel observed in his pea plants" (p. 104). The 2000 American Psychiatric Association Fact Sheet on Sexual Orientation states: "Some people believe that sexual orientation is innate and fixed; however, sexual orientation develops across a person's lifetime... to date there are no replicated scientific studies supporting any specific biological etiology for homosexuality. Similarly, no specific psychosocial or family dynamic cause for homosexuality has been identified." Same-sex attraction has, rather, been linked to a complex combination of factors, including childhood traumas, social and parental influences, peer labeling, and indirect genetic influences, interwoven with a multitude of acts of will and the habits that result. See the statement by the Catholic Medical Assocation, "Homosexuality and Hope," available at www.cathmed.org/publications/homosexualityarticle.htm.

30. In the latter two texts Paul coins the term *arsenokoitēs* (a man who lies with a male), combining two terms found together in the Septuagint: "You shall not lie (*koimēthēsē koitēn*) with a male (*arsenos*) as with a woman; such a thing is an abomination" (Lev 18:22).

31. This also holds for practices that were widespread in the ancient world and were not recognized as immoral until later stages of biblical revelation, including polygamy and remarriage after divorce.

32. José Noriega, "Homosexuality: The Semblance of Intimacy," *Communio* 35 (Fall 2008), 451-64; here p. 460.

33. "Homosexual Inclination," 66.

34. See the compelling arguments made by Christopher Wolfe in "Homosexuality and American Political Life," in C. Wolfe (ed.), *Same-Sex Matters. The Challenge of Homosexuality* (Dallas: Spence: 2000), 3-25.

35. See especially Congregation for the Doctrine of the Faith (CDF), *Considerations Regarding Proposals to Give Legal Recognition to Unions between Homosexual Persons* (2003). See also CDF, *Some Considerations Concerning the Response to Legislative Proposals on the Non-Discrimination of Homosexual Persons* (1992); *Letter on the Pastoral Care of Homosexual Persons* (1986); and Pontifical Council for the Family, *Family, Marriage and 'De Facto' Unions* (2000).

36. Gen 2:24.

37. Greek *mysterion*; Latin *sacramentum*.

Response to Mary Healy

Jane F. Adolphe
Associate Professor,
Ave Maria School of Law, Naples, Florida

Introduction

Mary Healy has shown how St. Paul's understanding of marital love in Ephesians 5 stands in sharp contrast to the growing phenomenon of same-sex marriage. As of April 30, 2009,[1] six countries out of about 194 States have created the legal fiction of same-sex marriage (Belgium,[2] Canada,[3] Netherlands,[4] Norway,[5] South Africa,[6] and Spain[7]). Fourteen other countries have recognized some form of domestic partnership or civil marriage.[8] In the United States, although same-sex marriage is prohibited under U.S. federal legislation[9] and thirty states have approved amendments to their State Constitutions banning marriage of same-sex couples,[10] other states have recognized same-sex marriage[11] (e.g. Connecticut,[12] Vermont,[13] Massachusetts,[14] Iowa[15]), and bills are pending before legislative assemblies[16] and cases before state courts.[17]

In responding to Mary Healy's chapter, this essay will explore the deleterious effects of same-sex marriage in three parts: 1) The uncivil nature of some discussions about "same-sex marriage;" 2) how "same-sex marriage" undermines the human person's call to love according to the plan of the Creator[18] and how it threatens the social order; 3) the great disconnect between the vision of love and interpersonal communion articulated by St. Paul and the Catholic tradition and the view of the love promoted by advocates of same-sex marriage. After examining these three aspects of same-sex marriage, the fourth part of this response seeks a possible meeting point for dialogue.

Uncivil Verbal Skirmishes Over Same-Sex Marriage

In the summer of 2005, I delivered a paper at the Twelfth World Conference of the

International Society of Family Law. A total of 237 persons from thirty-four nations attended the conference including 206 family law scholars, professionals and academics in related disciplines. Among the 164 scholarly papers presented over a five-day period, only a few papers promoted the natural family, based on marriage between one man and one woman. Prior to giving my paper, a session had been held where a friend and colleague argued that marriage between one man and one woman was an important "social institution" in the United States. During the question period, a scholar who had been sitting calmly in the front seat raised his hand and commented: "Given that marriage is a social institution, it therefore can be changed."

Shortly thereafter, this same academic was seated directly in front of me while I took my place on a panel of four. Two of us were arguing against same-sex marriage, two other scholars were arguing in favor of it. To heighten the tension, the Canadian government had fully endorsed "same-sex marriage" the day before. My argument was the following: during the Canadian parliamentary debates over same-sex marriage just prior to its legalization in Canada, regardless of whether you accept or reject same-sex marriage, one should be dismayed at the fact that consideration of the best interests of the child was absent from the discussion. The title of my presentation was "Same-Sex Marriage in Canada and the Missing Debate about the Best Interests of the Child."

When the presentation ended, the room exploded into an uproar. The scholar, who had engaged in rational discourse with my colleague in the previous session, now jumped to his feet shouting: "You're a homophobic." The questions and comments from the audience that followed were fast and furious. A lawyer who introduced himself as a fellow Canadian expressed outrage that I "claimed to be a Canadian." Another scholar challenged the empirical data that had been cited showing the negative effects of same-sex parenting on children; she was directed to speak with Dr. Byrd, who was the author of one of the studies, and a presenter at the Conference.

Noting that speakers on previous panels had advanced arguments for polygamous marriages, and multiple parenthood,[19] I argued that the Canadian government's justification of same-sex marriage presented a slippery slope to a vast array of disordered relationships, including bestiality. Canadian Prime Minister, Brian Mulroney, had justified "same-sex marriage" on the basis of protecting rights of minority groups, and certainly animal rights activists, could be classified as a minority group in Canadian society.[20] The angry Canadian took the floor again stating that he was personally insulted by the argument. In response, he was directed to the work of Professor Peter Singer, who held a prestigious chair at Princeton University, and took the position that animals were persons, arguably the groundwork for person-animal marriage. In my mind, there appeared to be very little left of the institution of marriage.[21]

Another woman, contending that she had testified as an expert in the same-sex marriage case in Ontario, argued that the courts had indeed considered the best interests of the child. When asked to identify the exact paragraphs in the case, she did not respond. Exasperated, my fellow Canadian stood up abruptly shouting: "It is somewhere in the case." In point of fact, there is no best interest analysis because the Ontario case like the same-sex marriage cases in British Columbia and Quebec were argued under the Canadian Charter of Rights and Freedoms.[22] In other words, an adult living out same-sex tendencies claimed that his or her constitutional right to marry had been denied, and so according to law, the court was compelled to apply the standard of review proper to constitutional cases not that applied in family law custody cases.

Following the panel discussion, while pushing my way through the crowd and pondering the accusations that I was a liar, a homophobe, and a complete embarrassment to the Canadian people, a women turned to me and stated: "You know, the world is not going to come crashing down with the legalization of same-sex marriage." At the time, I understood her statement to be a hyperbole.[23] Today, I consider her comment less as an exaggeration and more as an opportunity to consider the depth of the disorder introduced into the world through the legalization of same-sex marriage. What is truly at stake?

Same-Sex Marriage and its Effect on the Social Order

Same-sex marriage removes the very possibility for the human person to live the love given him by his Creator that has been revealed in marriage in a particular way.[24] Such same-sex unions will undoubtedly have tragic effects. Mary Healy makes a similar point when she quotes Livio Melina: "it is normal to expect the disorder of homosexuality to have a paradigmatic theological significance in the history of salvation."[25]

Following in the footsteps of St. Paul, Pope Benedict XVI has weighed in on the topic. He points to marriage as "the very epitome of love."[26] In the Encyclical Letter *Deus Caritas Est*, he highlights how love between man and woman, wherein body and soul are inseparably joined, gives human beings a glimpse of an "apparently irresistible promise of happiness."[27] He calls it "the most complete form of love," engaging each of the dimensions of the human person.[28] Pope Benedict tells us that love between man and woman was traditionally, in Greek culture, referred to as *eros*, something neither planned nor willed, but somehow imposed upon the couple.[29] Similarly, Mary Healy has described it as romantic or passionate. In the face of modern day culture, which commonly depicts passion as raw carnal pleasure without restraints, connecting *eros* with the divine seems like a stretch of the imagination. Yet, the Greeks did think *eros* to be linked to the divine in that it promised infinity, or eternity, a reality far greater than everyday existence.[30] In so far as *eros* leads us beyond ourselves, Pope Benedict XVI contends that *eros* needs to be "disciplined and purified" if it is to protect the human person from exploitation and degradation, and ultimately provide more than just momentary pleasure.[31] This calls for love expressed as *agape:* love understood in the distinctively Christian sense as a real discovery of the other, a moving beyond the self-seeking character of *eros* into authentic care and concern for the other, a love that is ready and willing for sacrifice, even death.[32]

Pope Benedict XVI presents authentic marriage as the authentic fulfillment of both *eros* and *agape.* Man and woman are said to be ready for marriage, the foundation of the family, when "love's growth towards higher levels and inward purification" seeks to become definitive by way of exclusivity (this particular person) and permanence (forever).[33] This is hardly surprising since love's promise of happiness[34] responds to the deepest yearnings of the human heart, to mutually receive and reciprocate that which is expressed as, "I will love you forever." And so, by necessary implication, "love looks to the eternal."[35] Indeed, man is unable to perceive how love can occur in time, this fact is captured in the famous final line of narrations—"and they lived happily every after."[36]

Father John M. McDermott, S.J. has explored this tension between the infinite and finite, asking: "How can finite intelligence grasp God's infinity?"[37] He ultimately reconciles this tension with reference to the family: "God can be known by human reason" because "primordially" one has been loved by his parents:

> Without love babies die. Their parents' love mediates a meaning which harsh experience and rational conundrums later put into question. Love is the basis of morality because the love bestowed creates the obligation of a response. As one does not choose one's parents but is called to love in return, so obligation precedes right.[38]

Man's existence, then, has meaning not because he has been persuaded by philosophy but rather because he has experienced love,[39] what Mary Healy has described as a "self-less desire for the good of the other." The moral experience, Father McDermott contends, is characterized by the response to the obligation of love demanded by God who Himself is love, and who created man, in His likeness and image.[40] It follows that love is man's only appropriate response. McDermott describes this love as: *absolute* and *supra-rational* (committing to doing what is right even unto the total self-sacrifice of death, which commitment cannot be grounded merely in reason); *personal* (responding to another moral subject, by nature endowed with intelligence and free will); *free* (choosing to what is right without coercion); and *liberating* (understanding that nothing matters save fidelity to what is right).[41] The very structure of reason reflects this reality of love,[42] and the correspondence of reason to this reality of love is truth.[43] Father McDermott explains:

> Men reflect the love of God to each other and in their love God is present. Thus is established the sacramental structure of reality, i.e., in and through a finite figure the infinite God makes Himself present, calling men to the total dedication of

love, and upon man's response depends his eternal salvation and damnation.[44]

This is why marriage between one man and one woman is the "sacrament of creation."[45] It has an inherent structure that perpetuates not only openness to children as the self-sacrificial fruitfulness of love but also to eternal life.[46]

Monogamous marriage, then, corresponds to the monotheistic God.[47] As Mary Healy has shown, the spousal metaphors have frequently been used to describe the relationship between God and his people the Church, but prior to this, also between God and his people Israel. Whereas the Holy Temple of Israel had "represented the apex of all human longing: the ability of man to engage in a direct relationship with God,"[48] Jesus Christ Himself is the new and living Temple, in whom God's love descends upon humanity; He is the "promise of the kingdom of reconciliation and love."[49] In the Person of Christ, God unites himself with man and goes in search of the "stray sheep" the suffering and lost members of the human family, even to the point of death on the cross.[50] For this reason, Pope Benedict XVI describes God's love as both *eros* and *agape*, both passionate and forgiving,[51] and both within a familial context: "God is Love which saves, a loving Father who wants to see his children look upon one another as brothers and sisters, working responsibly to place their various talents at the service of the common good of the human family."[52]

Following in this line of thought, God's marriage with humanity has important consequences for the social order, especially when one considers the universal order: "God wished humanity to live in harmony and peace and laid the foundations for this in the very nature of the human being, created 'in his image.'"[53] The Church has often spoken about the natural family as the important vehicle for this peace in society. The Second Vatican Council spoke of the family as "the primary vital cell of society."[54] John Paul II taught that it is within the family, rooted in the love of the husband and the wife, that children learn to love; and that this love is the foundation for peace, which in turn, "creates the peace of the human family."[55] He further observed: "Thus, the fostering of authentic and mature communion between persons within the family is the first and irreplaceable school of social life ... the family is thus ... the place and origin and the most effective means for humanizing and personalizing society."[56] When family life declines, love and communion decline, and thus the social order and peace are threatened.

How do same-sex marriages threaten the social order? The Congregation for the Doctrine of the Faith [CDF] dealt with this question in its document entitled, *Considerations regarding Proposals to Give Legal Recognition to Unions between Homosexual Persons*. The Congregation stressed the importance of marriage and the family for the peace and stability of society. With regard to granting legal recognition to homosexual unions, it noted that:

> Society owes its continued survival to the family, founded on marriage. The inevitable consequence of legal recognition of homosexual unions would be the re-

> definition of marriage, which would become, in its legal status, an institution devoid of essential reference to factors linked to heterosexuality; for example, procreation and raising children. If, from the legal standpoint, marriage between a man and a woman were to be considered just one possible form of marriage, *the concept of marriage would undergo a radical transformation, with grave detriment to the common good.* By putting homosexual unions on a legal plane analogous to that of marriage and the family, the State acts arbitrarily and in contradiction with its duties.[57]

The "grave detriment to the common good" introduced by same-sex marriages might not be apparent to all. But this is because people fail to see the underlying importance of monogamous marriage and male-female complimentarity to the well-being of society. Once society begins to rebel against the natural order of the Creator, which includes the natural law, the common good invariably suffers. This is why the social order ultimately depends on adherence to the moral law of God. John XXIII articulated this so powerfully in his encyclical, *Pacem in Terris*:

> Now the order which prevails in human society is wholly incorporeal in nature. Its foundation is truth, and it must be brought into effect by justice. It needs to be animated and perfected by men's love for one another, and, while preserving freedom intact, it must make for an equilibrium in society which is increasingly more human in character.
>
> But such an order—universal, absolute and immutable in its principles—finds its source in the true, personal and transcendent God. He is the first truth, the sovereign good, and as such the deepest source from which human society, if it is to be properly constituted, creative, and worthy of man's dignity, draws its *genuine vitality.*[58]

Same-sex marriage violates the four pillars of peace: the authentic meaning of truth (conformity of reason with reality), justice (to give to the other what is his due), freedom (to seek and act in accordance with truth and good), and charity (to selflessly seek the good of the other, body and soul, and be ready and willing for sacrifice).[59] All of this follows because same-sex marriage stands in opposition to the divine and natural law, which is the ultimate source for "the genuine vitality" of human society.

The Disconnect in Public Debates

Mary Healy has asked whether there are "any natural law principles that can be gleaned from Eph. 5 to shed light on society's responsibility to protect the institution of marriage as traditionally understood?" In other words, can the thought of St. Paul on the topic of "sacramental marriage as a supernaturally graced way of life in Christ" assist us in grounding a natural law defense of marriage?

Dr. Healy aptly notes that scripture confirms what is already knowable by reflection on the complimentarity of the female and male bodies: sexual difference renders union possible—one might say there is unity in diversity. In her words, "Every human being is specified as either male or female and thus imprinted with a visible sign of [his or her] vocation to, and capacity for, spousal communion," which in turn, gives rise to the "primordial human community, the family." Human sexuality, then, is constitutive. She makes this point most eloquently: sexuality gives the body its nuptial meaning that "'reaches to the core of the person, the heart of [his or her] identity, and situates it in relationality, aptness for love.'" She argues that our efforts in the public square must focus on dialogue and modeling of behavior based on "an authentic vision for human sexuality—in a way that is so joyful and life-giving that it exposes unrestrained sexual license for the cheap counterfeit it is." I could not agree with her more.

However, there is a complete disconnect between the meaning of love as unfolded by Mary Healy and others, on the one hand, and the position of many academics, politicians, lawyers, and judges, on the other hand.

The arguments for and against same-sex marriage have been greatly debated in the United States as well as in Canada. It is common in such debates about "same-sex marriage" to highlight the love between homosexual or lesbian partners usually in reference to the length of their respective relationship and the fact that they are raising children, some of whom are their own biological offspring from a previous heterosexual relationship. Many emphasize the complementarity of their respective relationships, especially as regards emotional support as well as day-to-day management of the home and duties of child care. Others point to the fact that such couples have adopted children many other families would not have adopted, and in cases where adoption is not possible, artificial reproduction technology is available as an important resource. A few even justify the manipulation of the law to adopt a child from another country as an act of compassion for the child, who they claim would have otherwise remained in an orphanage. Consequently, couples in same-sex relationships argue that their respective relationships are equivalent to heterosexual relationships, including parenting based on the fundamental argument that procreation is not central to marriage. In support, they point to the legal requirements for entering into marriage, which does not oblige spouses to demonstrate the intent to have children. They look to the vast numbers of intentionally childless marriages of heterosexual couples and access to contraceptive and abortion services, employed by these same couples.

Most will admit that one is born either male or female, but will contend that this fact is irrelevant. Many argue that how one lives out masculinity and femininity has largely been controlled by socially constructed sex roles in a male dominated society. In this regard, they often point to the State's past denial of a woman's right to vote, right to own property, and right to be protected from an abusive husband. Certainly, hormonal treatments coupled with sex change operations further prove, as the argument goes, that one's sex has little meaning. Finally, some might maintain that they felt a same-sex attraction from a very young age, and suggest that it may be the result of an immutable or genetic condition. Lastly, since children are available by way of adoption and through artificial reproduction technology, the relevance of one's sex is, once again, further undermined.

In addition, many would likely agree with the propositions that a person is relational; that it is not good for a person to be alone; and that selflessness and commitment are positive things; indeed, all these considerations would be used to further justify the need for "same-sex marriage." This type of marriage, as other forms of marriages, would certainly not be permanent or indissoluble, an obvious fact based on the existence of divorce laws. Hence, they claim that preventing a person from marrying a same-sex partner is akin to that form of discrimination, which once prevented the marrying of persons with different skin colors, namely black and white.

I have responded to the aforementioned arguments elsewhere and will not repeat them here.[60] What is important to emphasize, for our purposes, is that redefining marriage to include same-sex relationships offends basic biological and psychological facts, authentic notions of equality, and the dignity of the child, and will ultimately lead to a serious and grave subversion of the social order.[61]

A Meeting Point for Dialogue

Roderick Macdonald, Professor of Law at McGill University, argues that both supporters of institutionalized expert law reform bodies and even some of its skeptics share at least one basic misconception about the nature of law, namely, that the "highest type of law" is that made by legislatures.[62] He laments that this assumption "rest[s] on an impoverished view of the law and normativity."[63] I agree. Such a perspective ignores or denies a more capacious view of the human person upon which it must be founded: a view that does not reduce the complexity and the profundity of the human being to an autonomous chooser.

There are a number of deleterious effects that flow from a strictly legal positivist view; consequences which Professor Viladrich refers to as the "agony of matrimonial legality."[64] First, the legal positivist paradigm is founded on a flawed anthropology that inextricably links human flourishing to marriage. Then marriage is embedded in a divorce system, which is supported and promoted by a culturally accepted divorce mentality. This, in turn, feeds into a legal system that favors the emptying of the "I do"—words that mean very little when they can be revoked at any moment. This then supports the false idea that marriage "is an act of social conformity" to obtain permission to have sexual relations or to bear children with "social honorability."[65] It also presents the distorted picture that the State is free completely to ignore the essential reality of marriage and call any type of union a marriage.[66] The end result is that marriage is stripped of its content to mean nothing more than the attainment of a legal document.

In order to judge whether a law is just or unjust, one must make reference to a higher norm, which acts as a principle of unity in a world where man differs according to race, time, locality, beliefs, and language. Any positive law ought to be founded on "the common nature of man and the course of action it indicates."[67] It is the foundation and primary measure of the positive laws and all rights.[68] Indeed, this has been the starting point for many discussions about human rights at the international level; as one scholar puts it: "At the basis of the discourse on Human Rights there is the assumption of a *universal human nature* common to all peoples. . . ."[69]

In what does this universal human nature consist? One might reasonably speak about the universal essence of man—that which transcends the limits of culture and history, and rests in the fact that all human beings are inherently social, male and female, endowed with reason and free will.[70] These essential characteristics have been recognized in the 1948 Universal Declaration of Human Rights [UDHR],[71] when State representatives, despite cultural and religious differences, responded to the call of reason in the face of "barbarous acts which . . . outraged the conscience of mankind."[72] Article 1 provides: "All human beings are born free and equal in dignity and rights. They are endowed with reason and conscience and should act towards one another in a spirit of brotherhood." It is noteworthy that one of the key drafters of the UDHR, Charles Malik, had pushed to ensure that this particular language be included because it was founded on Christian natural law principles.[73] From the very beginning Charles Malik had passionately claimed that prior to any talk of rights, one had to pose and answer the essential question: Who is man?[74]

As the first modern statement of human rights, which has come to be generally understood as binding customary international law, the UDHR recognizes and proclaims universal rights that flow from the inherent dignity of the human person. With regard to marriage and the family, Article 16 states:

> 1. Men and women of full age, without any limitation due to race, nationality or religion, have the right to marry and to found a family. They are entitled to equal rights as to marriage, during marriage and at its dissolution.
>
> 2. Marriage shall be entered into only with the free and full consent of the intending spouses.
>
> 3. The family is the natural and fundamental group unit of society and is entitled to protection by society and the State.

Many Americans, especially Catholics, might find reference to the UDHR surprising, and perhaps even disappointing. However, they should consider the following. John XXIII referred to the UDHR as "an act of highest importance" in which "the recognition and respect of those rights and respective liberties [of the human person] is proclaimed as a goal to be achieved by all peoples and all countries."[75] John Paul II contended that the UDHR "remains one of the highest expressions of human conscience in our times."[76] Benedict XVI noted that it has "enabled different cultures, juridical expressions and institutional models to converge around a fundamental nucleus of values, and hence of rights."[77] Similarly, the Pontifical Council for the Family in "The Family and Human Rights" contended that the UDHR is consistent with a Christian anthropological perspective of the human person.[78] And finally, Harvard Professor Mary Ann Glendon, who headed the Holy See delegation to the controversial Beijing conference on women,[79] described the UDHR as "the single most important reference point for cross-cultural discussion of human freedom and dignity in the world today."[80]

The aforementioned, at the same time, do not ignore the problems associated with the UDHR, in particular, and human rights language in general. It is well known that certain groups and States challenge the universality of human rights in favor of cultural relativism.[81] Others seek to multiply rights according to disordered desires and disturbing ideologies which deny a universal human nature.[82] Some pick and choose rights from the UDHR without consideration of the interpretative principles embedded therein.[83] But the response of the Catholic Church has not been to reject this important meeting point for dialogue. Rather, Benedict XVI urges all persons of good will to redouble their efforts to oppose "pressures to reinterpret the foundations of the *Declaration*" in a way that "compromises its inner unity . . . moves away from the protection of human dignity towards the satisfaction of simple interests, often particular interests."[84]

Conclusion

The legal fiction of same-sex marriage introduces a new type of chaos into the human family, which is based on the marriage between God and humanity. One possible converging point, from a perspective of international law, is the inherent dignity of the human person with reference to the essential characteristics of a universal human nature, known by reason and largely recognized in the first article of the Universal Declaration of Human Rights. Obviously, divine revelation will continue to assist the faithful in illuminating the truths about the human person, especially in the world community, where "[h]uman rights are increasingly being presented as the common language and the ethical substratum of international relations."[85]

Notes

1. Sweden's same-sex civil marriages will be legally effective May 1, 2009; *see also* The Official Website of SR International—Radio Sweden, Gays Win Marriage Rights,

http://www.sr.se/cgi-bin/International/nyhetssidor/artikel.asp?ProgramID=2054&Format=1&artikel=2739765 (last visited on April 20, 2009).

2. Loi du 13 février 2003 ouvrant le mariage à des personnes de même sexe et modifiant certaines dispositions du Code civil (Feb. 28, 2003) (Belg.) http://www.disced.unisa.it/lemur/ITALIANO/Belgio/LEMUR_B%C3%A9lgica_Matrim_Hol.htm (last visited April 27, 2009).

3. Civil Marriage Act, S.C., ch. 33 (July 20, 2005) (Can.). In Canada the road to nationalization of same sex marriage started with the trilogy of cases: Halpern v. Can., [2003] 65 O.R.3d. 161; EGALE Can. v. Can. (A.G.), [[2003]13 B.C.L.R.2d 1; Hendricks v. Québec, [2002] R.J.Q. 2506. See Jane Adolphe, "The Case Against Same-Sex Marriage in Canada: Law and Policy Considerations," *BYU Journal of Public Law* 18 (2004) 479. Then, in December 2004, the Supreme Court opinion in Re: Same-Sex Marriage was followed by the enactment of the Civil Marriage Act, which was introduced by Prime Minister Paul Martin in the Canadian House of Commons in early 2005, later passed by the House of Commons and Senate that June and July, and finally enacted on July 20, 2005.

4. Stb. 2001, nr. 9 (Dec. 21, 2000) (effective 2001) (Neth.).

5. Ot.prp. nr. 33 No. 33 (2007-2008)(effective Jan. 01, 2009) (Norway) On June 11, 2008 the Norwegian parliament adopted new gender-neutral marriage legislation that permits same-sex couples to marry and adopt children, as well as artificial insemination for lesbians. The text of the law was adopted by a vote of 84 to 41. This new legislation replaces the 1993 partnership law allowing same-sex registered partnerships. The new law came into force on January 1, 2009. *See* text of new law (only available in Norwegian) http://www.regjeringen.no/nb/dep/bld/dok/regpubl/otprp/2007-2008/otprp-nr-33-2007-2008-/16.html?id=502804 (last visited April 27, 2009).

6. Civil Union Bill, 2006, Bill 26B-2006, (S.Afr.), http://www.info.gov.za/view/DownloadFileAction?id=65493 (last visited April 27, 2009), succeeded by Civil Union Act 17 of 2006, No. 29441 (GG) (S. Afr.). South Africa adopted a Civil Union bill and did not amend or alter the existing marriage provisions of the law; however, the bill grants the same legal rights of marriage to civil unions, and allows same-sex couples to choose to have their union solemnized using the term "marriage." It is noteworthy that change was introduced through the ruling of the South African Constitutional Court on December 1, 2005 (Minister of Home Affairs and Another v Fourie and Another 2006 (1) SA 524 (CC) (S. Afr.) (holding that marriage-equivalence is required by the South African Constitution and imposing a deadline of December 1, 2006 to make same-sex marriage legal), *see also* http://www.southafrica.to/people/Marriage/Gay-Marriage/Civil-Union-Act-2006.pdf (last visited April 27, 2009).

7. Proyecto de Ley: Por la que se modifica el Código Civil en materia de derecho a contraer matrimonio, 121/000018 (June 30, 2005) (Spain).

8. As of April 27, 2009, Andorra, Czech Republic, Denmark, Finland, France, Germany, Greenland, Iceland, Luxembourg, New Zealand, Slovenia, Switzerland, United Kingdom, and Uruguay all allow civil unions and registered partnerships; *see* the website of European Laboratory on Marriage and Registered Partnership, http://www.disced.unisa.it/lemur/ENGLISH/LEMUR_3_ENG.htm (last visited April 27, 2009); *see also* Reuters Online, Uruguay Ok's Gay Unions in Latin American First, http://www.reuters.com/article/worldNews/idUSN1854039020071219 (last visited April 22, 2009).

9. Defense of Marriage Act," Pub. L. 104-199, 110 Stat. 2419 (approved Sept. 21, 1996) (to be codified at 1 U.S.C. §7, 28 U.S.C. §1738c) *available at* http://www.senate.gov/legislative/LIS/roll_call_lists/roll_call_vote_cfm.cfm?congress=104&session=2&vote=00280 (last visited April 27, 2009); It was passed by Congress by a vote of 85-14 in the Senate and a vote of 342-67 in the House of Representatives, and signed into law by President Bill Clinton on September 21, 1996. According to the DOMA, no state is forced to recognize other state's same-sex marriages. *See also* The Official Website of the National Conference of State Legislatures, Same Sex Marriage, Civil Unions and Domestic Partnerships, http://www.ncsl.org/programs/
cyf/samesex.htm#DOMA (last visited April 20, 2009).

10. See the Official Website of the National Conference of State Legislatures, Same Sex Marriage, Civil Unions and Domestic Partnerships, http://www.ncsl.org/programs/cyf/samesex.htm#DOMA (last visited April 20, 2009).

11. See Human Rights Campaign, Statewide Marriage Prohibitions, http://www.hrc.org/documents/marriage_prohibitions_2009.pdf (last visited April 20, 2009).

12. Connecticut, SB 899 (November 12, 2008), text *available at* www.cga.ct.gov/2009/TOB/s/pdf/2009SB-00899-R00-SB.pdf (last visited April 27, 2009)

13 Vermont, S.115 (eff. September 1, 2009) text *available at* http://www.leg.state.vt.us/database/status/textonly.cfm?Bill=S.0115 (last visited April 27, 2009). In regard to the legal recognition of same-sex marriage, it is noteworthy that only Vermont was initiated by legislative enactment rather than judicial decision. On April 7, 2009, Vermont became the first state in the nation to legalize same-sex marriage through legislative action without a judicial order to do so. S.115, "An Act to Protect Religious Freedom and Recognize Equality in Civil Marriage," was initially passed by the Senate on a vote of 26-4 on March 24, 2009, and then by the House on a vote of 95-52 on April 3, 2009. As promised, Governor Douglas promptly vetoed the bill on Tuesday, April 7, 2009. The Senate and House immediately convened to vote to override the bill and did so by a vote of 23-5 and 100-49 respectively, giving the legislature the necessary 2/3 majority to successfully override the governor's veto. The Act takes effect as of September 1, 2009. *See* text of bill, http://hrc.vermont.gov/sites/hrc/files/pdfs/ss%20marriage/S-115.pdf (last visited Jan. 5, 2010).

14. Mass. General Laws c. 207 (May 17, 2004). The same laws and procedures that govern traditional marriage also apply to same-sex marriages. There are no special procedures for a same-sex marriage. *See* law's text http://www.mass.gov/legis/laws/mgl/gl-207-toc.htm (last visited April 27, 2009).

15. As a result of the recent Supreme Court's decision on April 3, 2009 in Varnum v. Brien decision, the Court ordered that the unconstitutional language of this statute — Iowa Code section 595.2(1) — must be stricken and the remaining statutory language interpreted and applied in a manner which allows gay and lesbian people "full access to the institution of civil marriage"(eff. April 27, 2009), *see* http://www.state.ia.us/government/ag/latest_news/releases/apr_2009/AG_Statement_ISC_ruling.html (last visited April 27, 2009).

16. On April 16, 2009, New York Governor Paterson officially introduced same-sex marriage legislation and promised to push for its passage; *see* New York Times, Paterson Introduces a Same-Sex Bill, http://www.nytimes.com/2009/04/17/nyregion/17marriage.html?_r=2&ref=nyregion (last visited April 20, 2009).

17. Proposition 8 was a constitutional amendment passed in the 2008 California gen-

eral election ballot in November 2008 by 52% majority that ban gay marriage Since its passage, it has been challenged in the California Courts. *See* Human Rights Campaign, Marriage & Relationship Recognition, http://www.hrc.org/issues/marriage/marriage_laws.asp (last visited April 20, 2009).

18. Livio Melina, Carl A. Anderson, eds. *The Way of Love* (San Francisco: Ignatius Press, 2006), 269.

19. An American lawyer who worked in California discussed one of her cases where, in order to produce a child, body fluids had privately been exchanged between a lesbian couple, on the one hand, and a homosexual couple, on the other hand. All four persons were claiming to be parents of the child, but California law had limited parenthood to two persons.

20. For many at the conference bestiality was still repugnant from a public morality point of view even though animal farms exist, where people can pay to be intimate with animals. Obviously, the pedophilia movement, which has long lobbied for reducing the age of consent for children and the right of children to have "inter-generational" sex, also presents concern. For example, an article entitled "A Meta-analytic Examination of Assumed Properties of Child Sexual Abuse Using College Samples" was recently published in the *American Psychological Association's Psychological Bulletin*, which concluded that, "negative effects [of sexual abuse] were neither pervasive nor typically intense." For a discussion of this study see: Joseph Nicolosi, Dale O'Leary, "On the Pedophilia Issue: What the APA Should Have Known," at http://www.narth.com. Furthermore, in May 2003, the American Psychiatric Association hosted a symposium in San Francisco that discussed whether pedophilia should be removed from the upcoming categories of mental illness. For a discussion of this event see: Linda Ames Nicolosi, "Should These Conditions Be Normalized: American Psychiatric Association Symposium Debates Whether Pedophilia, Gender Identity Disorder, Sexual Sadism Should Remain Mental Illnesses" at http://www.narth.com. On the same website also see: Linda Ames Nicolosi, "The Pedophilia Debate Continues and DSM is Changed Again;" Linda Ames, Nicolosi, "International Academy of Sex Research Joins the Debate: Is Pedophilia a Mental Disorder?" and finally see the paper on "The Problem of Pedophilia." See also a recent article discussing the battle of pedophiles to gain acceptance in society, Russ Flanagan, "I'm Tired of Being Forced into the Shadows by Society," *the Express-Times*, February 22, 2004, http://www.nj.com/specialprojects/expresstimes/index.ssf? /news/expresstimes/stories/moleters1_otherside.html.

21. He is the Ira W. DeCamp Professor of Bioethics at Princeton University, and laureate professor at the Centre for Applied Philosophy and Public Ethics (CAPPE), University of Melbourne, where he specializes in applied ethics. *See* his website at http://www.princeton.edu/~psinger (last accessed April 28, 2009) as well as the compilation of his writings at http://www.utilitarian.net/singer/ (last accessed April 28, 2009).

22. See *supra*, note 3.

23. The irony was that by the aggression of the crowd one would have thought that the world would come to an end without legalization of same-sex marriage.

24. Melina and Anderson, 269.

25. Livio Melina, "Homosexual Inclination as an 'Objective Disorder': Reflections on Theological Anthropology," *Communio* 25 (Spring 1998), 66.

26. *Deus Caritas Est*, 2.

27. Ibid., 2.

28. Melina and Anderson, 268.

29. *Deus Caritas Est*, 3.

30. Ibid., 5 ("The Greeks—not unlike other cultures—considered *eros* principally as a kind of intoxication, the overpowering of reason by a "divine madness" which tears man away from his finite existence and enables him, in the very process of being overwhelmed by divine power, to experience supreme happiness." *Ibid.*, 4).

31. Ibid., 4.

32. Ibid.

33. Ibid., 6.

34. Melina and Anderson, 269.

35. *Deus Caritas Est*, 6.

36. Melina, and Anderson, 272.

37. John M McDermott, S.J. "Faith, Reason and Freedom," *Irish Theological Quarterly* 67 [2002], 323.

38. Ibid., 328.

39. Ibid., 328; see also John M McDermott, S.J. "The Mystery of Freedom," *Lateranum* 74 [2008], 493-542.

40. See McDermott, "The Mystery of Freedom," 539-542.

41. McDermott, "Faith, Reason and Freedom," 328-329.

42. Ibid., 329.

43. Ibid., 329-330.

44. Ibid., 330.

45. Ibid.

46. Ibid., 330-331; see also McDermott, "The Mystery of Freedom," 537.

47. *Deus Caritas Est*, 11.

48. Israel Ariel and Chaim Richman, eds. *Carta's Illustrated Encyclopedia of the Holy Temple of Jerusalem*, (Jerusalem: The Temple Institute and Carta, 2005), 39

49. Homily of Benedict XVI on Palm Sunday, March 16, 2008 ("He who passed through the Cross and was raised is the living space of spirit and life in which the correct form of worship is made. Thus, the purification of the temple, as the culmination of Jesus' solemn entry into Jerusalem, is at the same time the sign of the impending ruin of the edifice and the promise of the new Temple; a promise of the kingdom of reconciliation and love which, in communion with Christ, is established beyond any boundary.")

50. See Lk 15:4-7 and Jn 10:15.

51. See *Deus Caritas Est*, 10: "God's passionate love for his people—for humanity—is at the same time a forgiving love. It is so great that it turns God against himself, his love against his justice."

52. Benedict XVI, World Day of Peace Message, January 1, 2006, 11

53. John Paul II, World Day of Peace Message, January 1, 1994, 1.

54. *Apostolicam Actuositatem*, 11.

55. John Paul II, World Day of Peace Message, January 1, 1994, 1.

56. John Paul II, *Familiaris Consortio*, 43.

57. Congregation for the Doctrine of the Faith, *Considerations regarding Proposals to Give Legal Recognition to Unions between Homosexual Persons*, June 3, 2003, 8 (emphasis added).

58. John XXIII, *Pacem in Terris* (April 11, 1963), 37-38 (emphasis added).

59. *Ibid.; See also* John Paul II, *Message for the World Day of Peace 2003* (January 1, 2003), 3 (The topic was devoted to *Pacem in Terris* wherein the following was stated: "Truth will build peace if every individual sincerely acknowledges not only his rights, but also his own duties toward others. Justice will build peace if in practice everyone respects the rights of others and actually fulfills his duties towards them. Love will build peace if people feel the needs of others as their own and share what they have with others, especially the values of mind and spirit which they possess. Freedom will build peace and make it thrive if, in the choice of means to that end, people act according to reason and assume responsibility for their own actions.").

60. See Jane Adolphe, "The Case Against Same-Sex Marriage in Canada: Law and Policy Considerations," 519-528.

61. Ibid., 528-541.

62. Roderick A. Macdonald, "Recommissioning Law Reform," *Alberta Law Review* 35 (1997), 851.

63. Ibid.

64. Pedro Juan Viladrich, *The Agony of Legal Marriage* (Navarra, Spain: University of Navarra, 1990), 147

65. Ibid.

66. Ibid., 141-47. Viladrich explains that marriage does not come into being simply because the couple carried out a wedding ceremony in accordance with State laws. For example, two persons of the same sex may possess a marriage certificate but such a "marriage" as a natural law reality does not exist nor could it ever exist. If marriage were constituted by the mere legal formality, then there would be little difference between a man and woman who live in a *de facto* union and a man and a woman who marry in accordance with positive law requirements. The difference would be superficial. It would be a matter of social conformity based solely on the legal ceremony. As a result, this would render marriage nothing more than the legislature's view on how sexual relations should be conducted.

67. Raymond F. Begin, *Natural Law and Positive Law* (Washington, D.C. Catholic University of America Press, 1959), 42.

68. Ibid.,50.

69. Raimundo Panikkar, "Is the Notion of Human Rights a Western Concept," in *International Human Rights in Context* ed. Henry J. Steiner & Philip Alston (Oxford: Oxford University Press, 2000), 384. (Having cited Panikkar, I do not accept every aspect of his analysis nor the conclusions reached in his paper).

70. See Thomas Aquinas, *Summa Theologica*, (Allen, TX: Christian Classics, 1981), Part I, Q. 76, art. 3 & Q. 79; Q. 83.

71. Universal Declaration of Human Rights, G.A. Res. 271A (III), U.N. GAOR, 3rd Sess., U.N. Doc A/810 (1948)) [hereinafter UDHR].

72. Ibid, preamble, para. 2.

73. Jane Adolphe, "The Holy See and the UDHR: Towards a Legal Anthropology of Human Rights and the Family," *Ave Maria Law Review* 4 (2006), 354.

74. Ibid., 352.

75. John XXIII, *Pacem in Terris*, 143.

76. John Paul II, Address to the General Assembly of the United Nations, October 5, 1995, 2.

77. Benedict XVI, Address to the General Assembly of the United Nations, April 18,

2008 ("It is evident that the rights recognized and expounded in the *Declaration* apply to everyone by virtue of the common origin of the person, who remains the high-point of God's creative design for the world and for history. They are based in natural law inscribed on human hearts and present in different cultures and civilization.").

78. Pontifical Council for the Family, *The Family and Human Rights*, December 9, 1999; For further discussion of this document see: Jane Adolphe, "The Holy See and the UDHR: Towards a Legal Anthropology of Human Rights and the Family," 343.

79. Mary Ann Glendon, "What Happened at Beijing," *First Things*, 59 (January 1996), 30-36.

80. Mary Ann Glendon, "Knowing the Universal Declaration of Human Rights," *Notre Dame Law Review*. 73 (1998), 1153; For a more detailed study of the Declaration and its drafting process, see Mary Ann Glendon, *A World Made New: Eleanor Roosevelt and the Universal Declaration of Human Rights* (New York: Random House, 2002); Johannes Morsink, *The Universal Declaration of Human Rights: Origins, Drafting and Intent* (Philadelphia: The University of Pennsylvania Press, 1999).

81. Benedict XVI, Address to the General Assembly of the United Nations, April 18, 2008 ("This great variety of view points must not be allowed to obscure the fact that not only rights are universal, but so too is the human person, the subject of these rights.").

82. Congregation for the Doctrine of the Faith, *Letter to the Bishops of the Catholic Church on the Collaboration of Men and Women in the Church and in the World*, May 31, 2004, 2-3.

83. Mary Ann Glendon, "*Knowing the Universal Declaration of Human Rights*," 1153.

84. Benedict XVI, Address to the General Assembly of the United Nations, April 18, 2008.

85. Ibid.

CHAPTER SEVEN

The International Theological Commission and the Natural Law

Rev. John M. McDermott, S.J.
Professor of Theology,
Sacred Heart Major Seminary, Detroit, Michigan
Member of the International Theological Commission, 2004-2009, and Advisor to the Committee on Doctrine of the U.S. Conference of Catholic Bishops

The study on the natural law recently published by the International Theological Commission "*A la Récherche d'une Èthique universelle: Nouveau Régard sur la Loi naturelle*," is primarily intended to assist bishops speaking up in civic debate on moral issues. Naturally, when the foundations of society are being shaken world-wide, it can provide a good resource for other Catholics engaged in the public forum. Biological science and a virulent secularist *Weltanschauung* have provided the manipulative tools and the ideology for remaking man in the image of the man chosen by the scientific-political elite and promulgated by the mass media. Secularists would disqualify all contrary voices in the public forum based upon religious conviction because religion is dismissed as a purely private and subjective matter.[1] Paradoxically, while the secularists on the whole adopt an agnostic or atheistic position grounded in a postmodern stance denying objective, universal standards of morality, the Catholic Church argues from a natural law morality which implies an objective standard for human conduct accessible to human reason. In other words, secularists are intent upon imposing their views upon the rest of us because they acknowledge no standard which they might appeal to in a rationally persuasive argument. They are egalitarians only so long as they decide to recognize certain people or groups of people as belonging to their notion of humanity. The most obvious case of such destructive selection concerns laws permitting and encouraging a right to abortion and death as a choice. In a world without objective standards their campaign initiates an attack upon humanity in the allegedly humane desire to abolish suffering from the planet. But, as Flannery O'Connor noted, such "tenderness" leads to the gas chambers.[2] Already some self-proclaimed liberals are mounting a campaign that would override conscientious objections for the killing of infants. Such "liberals" only support their limited version of "liberty."[3] This presentation intends to indicate the origin of natural law in Western culture, its historical difficulties, and the grounds for its reinstatement. It also considers the current debate about natural law in the Church and proposes a solution whereby freedom grounds the natural moral law. This final step goes beyond the ITC document while, it is hoped, remaining faithful to its trajectory.

The Natural Law: History

In this time of intellectual and moral conflict how does the Catholic Church understand the natural moral law? *In nuce,* "natural law" refers to objective standards of conduct recognizable by reason and applying to all human beings insofar as they possess the same human nature. It provides a secure foundation for peace, society's common good, and the recognition of human rights. It should lay the basis for common law in its various forms. This natural law theory develops in Western culture over the ages. The Sophists first make appeal to the distinction between nature and custom when their travels bring them into contact with diverse laws and customs among different nations. What one nation might regard as barbaric and detestable another might regard as pious and obligatory. In his *Histories* (III, 38) Herodotus tells the story of Darius, the Persian king, who asked some Greeks for what reward they would eat their parents; they rejected the suggestion entirely. Then Darius summoned some Indians who consumed their dead fathers and asked what they thought of cremating the dead, a Greek custom. They were horrified at the thought. So, Herodotus concludes by citing Pindar, "custom (*nomos*) is the king of all."[4] As opposed to custom the Sophists appeal to nature to provide the moral underpinnings of human society. Naturally there are diverse interpretations of "nature" and its laws. While some, like Thrasymachos in Plato's *Republic* (I, 336A-341A), discover in nature the law of the stronger determining what is right and wrong, Sophocles's Antigone appeals to "unwritten and immovable laws of the gods" (*Antigone*, 454-55) to override the statutory laws of the Theban city-state, and willingly suffers the supreme penalty for burying her brother.

While Plato seeks to forefend moral relativism by grounding human law in the universe's structure and divine judgment, Aristotle develops a more complete theory of natural law. For him a nature is a principle of inherent motion (Meta. V, 4, 1015a 13-15). While everything is what it is by its form embodied in matter, the form orients it dynamically to its fulfillment, the goal of its striving (ibid. 10-11;

Phy. II, 1, 193b 8-16; 8, 199a 31-32). All things move and develop according to their inherent forms. A planted acorn produces not a cow, but an oak tree; an egg laid by a chicken produces not a horse, but another chicken. Even to inanimate things a motion is attributed: light things, like air and fire, naturally rise; heavy things, like earth and water, fall to their natural positions of rest (De Cael. I, 3-5, 311a 1-8.20-312b 19; 8, 276b 22-277b 25; II 13; III, 2, 295b 20-296a 21, 300a 20-301b 32; De Gen. et Cor. II, 3, 230b 31-34). Clearly in such a world the solid, immobile, spherical earth occupied the lowest point, providing an absolute point of reference for motion (De Cael. II, 14, 296a 24; IV, 1, 307b 29-308a 33). Around the earth the various planets moved in thirty-three visible spheres and twenty-two invisible spheres. Under the moon all things are mutable and corruptible, but beyond the moon the heavenly bodies move in eternal motion. Since a circle represents perfect motion, remaining the same throughout uninterrupted motions, their motions approximate ever more perfectly the perfect, circular motion of the outmost sphere to whose perfection they are attracted (much as a chicken tends by inherent teleology to become the best chicken possible). The twenty-two invisible spheres are postulated (somewhat like anti-matter in modern physics) to explain why the visible planets are not wrenched irresistibly out of their own spheres to the outmost, perfect sphere. Beyond that outmost sphere in the empyrean is the Prime Mover, pure formal actuality, who moves all by being loved, by final causality. As Thought Thinking Thought, He does not concern Himself with mobile beings advancing from potency to actuality. He could not think their motion without being Himself moved. He rests in His own perfection, moving all, moved by none (De Cael. I, 2-3, 269a 3- 270b 32; Meta. XII, 7-9, 1072a18-1075a 11).

Now to go against nature means to go against the inherent laws of one's own being which seeks to fulfill itself. Consequently acting against nature brings frustration and pain, whereas acting in accord with nature brings fulfillment, pleasure, and happiness. Happiness is consequent upon the unimpeded operation of any natural faculty (Nic. Eth. VIII, 12, 1153a 8-16; X, 4, 1174b 15-34; 1175a 19-22; Rhet. I, 11, 1369b 33; cf. also Aquinas, S.T. I-II, 31, 1; 32, 1). When your belly is full, but not overfull, after a good meal, its functions happily and renders you content. Similarly your mind, which by nature seeks to know, finds pleasure in resolving intellectual puzzles. The ethical theory of the *Nicomachean Ethics* accords perfectly with Aristotle's understanding of man as a hylomorphic composition of matter and form, body and spirit. Since man is midway between beast and pure form (what Thomists recognize as an angel), virtue is understood as the mean between two extremes. Just as a full belly is the mean between an empty belly and a bloated belly, both of which bring pain, so courage is neither foolhardiness nor timidity, sobriety is neither teetotalism nor drunkenness (II, 6-7, 1106b 36-1107b 8; cf. also Aquinas, S.T., I-II, 66, 3, 3). Prudence oversees the virtues, adapting them properly to life's circumstances, ordering the means to their end (VI, 5, 1140b 20-30; 13, 1144b 26-1145a 10; cf. also Aquinas, S.T., II-II, 47, 6-8). Nonetheless this perfect equilibrium is thrown slightly out of kilter by Aristotle's insight that man desires to be like God, and he is most like God in contemplation, where knowledge is sought and possessed for its own sake (X, 7, 1177a12-1178a 8). Nature is good, but it is not sufficient for man.

The Stoics also develop a strong notion of the natural law. For them the world order is established by God, indeed the world itself is identified with God. If Plato sees the universe as a living organism (*Timaeus* 31A-33A) and Aristotle comes close to seeing it as animated (Phy. VIII, 1, 250b 14; 2, 252b 17-28 and 253a 7-20)—all this is long before the Gaia hypothesis and environmental movement—then the Stoics actually postulate pantheism. Nature, or the world order, is God. Consequently the wise man, who is governed by reason, adapts himself to nature. Thereby he avoids excess and does not let himself be upset by passions that disturb the universe's rational order, bring pain, and obfuscate rational clarity. He masters himself and achieves concomitantly rational joy. He even concurs without perturbation in the loss not only of possessions and life but also of people close to him, parents, wife, and children. He recognizes that God determines all according to wisdom and justice, and it is useless to trouble oneself about what cannot be changed.[5] Though the Epicureans differ widely from the Stoics on many points, certainly not identifying the world with reason, they agree that nature should be followed. But their analysis of nature concentrates on the pleasure which nature brings when it is followed. Seek pleasure, therefore, as all the animals do, but realize that pleasure is retained in moderation. Pleasure is more an absence of pain and serenity of soul than positive titillation. So they counsel withdrawing from the world of politics and business as much as possible and retreating into an enclosed garden to enjoy friendship and life's moderate pleasures. That is what nature teaches the Epicurean wise man. The gods do not concern themselves with mankind, and nature itself is determined by the play of atoms with an inbuilt "swerve" to allow for contingency and freedom.[6]

Other philosophers are more intent upon pleasure as the highest good and end of life. Aristippus holds that everything, fame, friendship, and virtue, is to be sacrificed for pleasure, which should be enjoyed with good taste and mental freedom; philosophy's purpose consists in regulating the senses so as to produce the greatest pleasure. Aristippus's school flourishs only briefly since Hegesias, one of its most famous members, concludes from the presupposition of pleasure as life's sole good that life's uncertainty renders pure pleasure impossible of attainment; hence the true philosopher seeks to end his life by suicide. Dubbed *Peisithanatos* (Lethal Persuader), he is banished from Alexandria.[7]

Christianity and the Natural Law

When Christianity arrives on the scene, its proponents borrow the common notion of nature and the natural law to support their arguments. Given the flexibility in the

Greek and Roman understanding of the natural law, not surprisingly its use among Christians is not completely systematized. St. Paul states, "When the Gentiles, who do not have the Law do by nature the deeds of the Law, those who do not have the Law are to themselves a Law; they manifest the Law's work written on their hearts, as their conscience bears witness in the midst of reasonings which condemn or even defend them" (Rom. 2:14-15). Though this text supplies the Scriptural foundation for the Church's adoption of the natural law, St. Paul's applications of the natural law are varied: he appeals to it to condemn homosexuality (Rom. 1:26-28) and to command women to veil their heads while praying (1 Cor. 11:14). Later Tertullian argues, among other reasons, protesting against forced participation in pagan ceremonies, that Christian soldiers ought not to be compelled to wear crowns of flowers on their heads because it is contrary to nature: nature intends flowers to be seen and smelt; hence anyone placing flowers on his head contradicts the purpose of nature (*De Corona* 5-7). Most Church Fathers are content to hand on moral norms in Scripture commentaries and in addresses to particular problems without expounding a whole moral system. Augustine gives the first impulse toward a developed natural law theory. He distinguishes temporal laws enacted by men for particular transient purposes from God's eternal, immutable law, to whose justice men are bound by knowledge mediated in conscience, even when they disobey (*De libero Arbitrio* I, 6, 14-15; *Confessiones* II, 2, 4; III, 7, 13; *De civ. Dei* XIX, 12, 19-15). "The eternal law is the reason or will of God which orders the preservation of the natural order and forbids its disturbance." The universe is subject to that law: beasts must obey it, angels, participating in the divine law, willingly obey it, and men are called to obey it. For those believing and obeying, it effects peace, the harmonious balancing of all elements in man's God-given nature, whereas sin disrupts order and causes pain (*Contra Faustum Manichaeum* XXII, 27-30; *De civ. Dei* XXII, 12-14). Faced by the difficulty arising from Rom. 2:14-15 that the Gentiles apparently enjoy an advantage over the Jews whose law is written on external tablets and over Christians who only lately receive the law written on their hearts (2 Cor. 3:3), Augustine responds that the Gentiles intended are those to whom the gospel came. The Holy Spirit renews the image of God, which was not entirely destroyed in the human soul by sin, in order that in "nature repaired through grace" faith may work through charity. Thus will be reestablished a proper hierarchical ordering of love of God, self, and neighbor (*De spiritu et littera* 26, 43-28, 48).[8] In his time the distinction between natural and supernatural orders has not been elaborated. Thus at the beginning of Gratian's *Decretum*, the basis of medieval canon law, is found the simple identification of natural law with the gospel: "The natural law is what is contained in the Law and the gospel" (*Concord discor. can.* I, 1).

The medieval distinction of nature from grace encourages the systematization of natural law argumentation by the great Scholastics, especially Thomas Aquinas. Building on Augustine, they deepen its foundations. Since God, identical with the eternal law, creates natures for an end, or purpose, His will is expressed in natures, whose natural inclinations aim at fulfillment or happiness. To follow nature is not just a matter of prudence but of obedience to God. To act contrary to nature is not just stupid; it is also sinful. Christianity also explains why those following the moral law are not always happy; indeed, they often suffer because of their moral convictions and actions. Due to original sin and personal sin, the world's order has been skewed; things are not as they should be, but heaven will recompense the just and the evil will undergo the torments of hell. The natural law, whose basic commands are expressed in the Decalogue and are thus fortified by revelation, provides standards for all human beings since a common nature is possessed by all. Insofar as man's spiritual powers, by which he knows and loves God, are superior to his carnal appetites, a hierarchy is established in natural desires which manifest the promptings of nature: the carnal appetites are to be subordinated to spiritual desires. Consequently all men need not be equal since all do not equally fulfill the moral law. The law's standards are not arbitrary since they are grounded in man's rational nature and supply a common goal for mankind. In this world they supply the state with its *raison d'être*: it exists to contribute to the fulfillment of man's nature and God's will. Men are social by nature and are obliged to help each other attain their common goal, which may demand sacrifices performed by individuals for the common good.[9]

The notion of nature is also essential for understanding faith, a supernatural gift. As the natural is distinct from the supernatural order, so reason is distinguished from faith. Faith comes from beyond reason, but it is not unreasonable. For grace heals and elevates nature in order that men may cooperate with grace. A good natural order is required as the presupposition for free choices. Unless man possesses a reason for his choices, he is, like the beasts, subject to irrational desires. The natural order, created by God as good, witnesses to supernatural revelation through miracles performed to motivate faith. For Thomists, freedom is located in the will, which should follow the intellect's lead. Then just as man is by nature social and corporeal as well as rational, so also the Church has to be a corporate, visible body of salvation.

The Breakdown of the Christian Order

This *Weltanschauung* is placed into question by four related elements:[10]

First, in philosophy, late medieval nominalism stresses the primacy of existing individuals, who are known directly by God. By contrast, the human intellect only abstracts ideas from the hylomorphic compositions which it encounters through its body. Hence our abstract knowledge of natures is a merely mental fabrication that fails to bring us to reality; at best concepts allow us to organize it for practical purposes. Unknowable natures no longer serve as the norm for human conduct; for that there is always revelation, which can be trusted as God's word.

Furthermore, insofar as natural forms remain unknown, the link between formal and final causality is broken. Efficient causality comes to the fore to explain physical movement. Things are moved from without by the application of force. Thinkers like J. Buridan and N. Oresme think that efficient causality explains better why thrown objects continue in motion and need not immediately go down or up to their natural place in the universe as soon as the hand or instrument impeding their natural movement is removed.[11]

Second, Protestantism undoes the earlier trust in nature and reason. Since faith alone saves, nature must be corrupt. There is no freedom vis-à-vis God because original sin disorients man's will from its original orientation to Him. The perversion of the will is indicated in concupiscence, fallen man's natural resistance to fulfilling God's moral law. As inherently perverse, the will cannot turn itself back to God. Only God can redirect it by the attraction of His grace. Hence all glory is His, and no man can boast of good works.

For Luther, reason can operate effectively in dealing with mundane matters, but when it comes to knowledge of God and His will, fallen reason is considered the devil's whore, turning itself in all directions to justify disordered passions, until it is wed to faith in God's word. Although he allows nature a type of abstract, non-experiential "general" knowledge of God's existence and judgment, only the Holy Spirit brings "proper," evangelical knowledge of the true God. He alone gives certitude of God. Analogously, although a notion of the natural law remains as God's law, fallen natures draw conclusions from it only with difficulty for application in the civil sphere; like the Mosaic Law, it serves basically to maintain civic discipline and convict man of his sin. Given nature's corruption, a natural common good no longer serves as society's goal. Government is established to restrain evil with the sword lest sinners destroy each other. Salvation cannot be mediated through social structures. Individuals are saved directly by God's omnipotent grace removing them from original sin's perdition through the bestowal of faith in Christ and His word. Although Christians are expected to join a church to help each other, the true Church is the spiritual *congregatio fidelium*, the assembly of believers, in the official, external church. Even if visible churches come together, the elect are known to God alone and the assemblies are judged by their fidelity to God's Word, which teaches the proper administration of sacraments.

Calvin lays more stress on natural knowledge of the moral law and of God's existence. But God is known only as Creator until in faith, which alone saves, He is recognized as Father. Knowledge of the natural law does not help man since he is inherently incapable of fulfilling it. God's grace alone saves and men are predestined to heaven or hell. Despite his adaptation of Augustinian language, Calvin primarily understands God as infinite efficient Cause effecting men's choices from without. In this he disagrees with Luther, who in the Augustinian tradition understands God's causality primarily as final causality, working by attraction upon a disoriented will. In accord with St. Paul, Luther only acknowledges a "predestination" to heaven, even if God is responsible for those going to hell insofar as He does not bestow His grace on them.[12]

Third, the new science of Copernicus and Galileo contributes mightily to overthrowing the Aristotelian-Scholastic view of nature. As we saw, Aristotle's cosmos is almost alive, each reality in it moving itself to its proper place (but cf. Phys. VIII, 4, 255a 1-19). It is hard for post-Newtonians to recreate that world, but it is just as rational or irrational as Newton's physics. To the question why material objects, e.g., a piece of chalk, fall to earth, we normally respond, "Because of the law of gravity; the earth attracts material objects to itself." How then do we recognize the law of gravity? "Because things fall." In other words, a circular argument justifies itself: things fall because of the law of gravity, and there is a law of gravity because things fall; this reduces to the tautology: things fall because things fall. The law of gravity explains nothing unless it is placed within wider parameters, which in turn have certain presuppositions that cannot be demonstrated. Certainly the Aristotelian stable earth at the universe's bottom-center makes initially more sense than the Newtonian view which has the world revolving on its axis at the amazing velocity of 465.1 meters per second while also orbiting around the sun at the even more ridiculous speed of 29.783 kilometers per second. Why is no one blown off the earth or how can there be days of calm, utterly devoid of wind? But there are problems with Aristotelian explanations of "motion at a distance" (Phys. VIII, 10, 266b 28- 127a 22; De Cael. III, 2 301b 17-32) i.e., the continuation of motion after contact with the propelling instrument is broken off. Nominalism prefers efficient causality. So, though most at first dismiss Copernicus's insight that the motion of the spheres can be simplified into circular orbits without the need of epicycles, if the sun, not the earth, is placed at the universe's center, some are attentive to his new vision. One of those is Galileo Galilei, who develops laws of motion in terms of efficient causality that apply to all material realities. For him matter is essentially dead; it follows necessary laws which can be calculated in mathematical terms and applied to all visible reality. A pound of feathers falls at the same velocity as a pound of lead; only the air resistance to the heap of feathers makes its descent slower. What matters in physics is not a reality's form or nature, but only mass, shape, and mobility. Newton's genius is required to expand the basic insights of Galileo and extend his laws of motion to cover both celestial and terrestrial motion. Yet even Newton fails to explain how a dead mass exercises an attraction upon another dead mass, and the analogy of a magnet remains a mystery. Later, of course, Einstein explains gravity in terms of indentations in the space-time continuum. But we need not go into that now.[13]

What happens to natural law with the "new physics" of the sixteenth and seventeenth centuries? There are still laws in nature, but nature is dead, and man stands outside nature. His freedom can manipulate those physical laws to attain chosen ends. Dead nature can be forced to satisfy human needs. But which needs are to be satisfied? What purpose serves man's manipulation of nature? What are the norms for moral action and how are they grounded? Is human action arbitrary? Or is it determined to the fulfillment of needs? Or, if man is subject to the same laws as all material reality, are not all his actions similarly physically determined? Inversely, with man's freedom now liberated from nature, is he also not simultaneously alienated from nature, even from his own nature? It takes a long while for the full force of these questions to become apparent. For one thing, Newton is a believing, if somewhat unorthodox, Anglican, and he needs God for his physics. God not only gave the original shove to start things in motion but He also keeps the universe's irregularities within bounds so that order is not destroyed. To explain space's infinity He postulates it as God's *sensorium*. Here he faces an impossible difficulty. Newton imagines three-dimensional space as the distance between material objects. Thus he escapes the opposite notion of space as the pre-existent receptacle in which material bodies are located. This latter view (Plato's) labors under the difficult of describing space before it can be related to anything; an empty infinity is unintelligible. But Newton's option involves a similar difficulty: if space is the distance between bodies, how can it be limited? What can limit it? So he allows for infinite extension grounded in God. This option leads to conundrums, like Olber's paradox: in an infinite universe an infinite number of stars should make the night sky as bright as the sun at noon. Similarly, since all bodies exercise an attraction on each other, in an infinite universe with infinite bodies an infinite force should pull the earth to smithereens from all sides. It is no wonder that Einstein has space curve back upon itself like a möbius strip. But in rendering space finite and self-reflexive he evokes another conundrum: what is outside space? The question is not illegitimate since it can be imagined along with his four-dimensional space-time continuum.[14]

While the new physics is being developed, the natural law has a real efflorescence at the hands of Catholic and Calvinist thinkers. The strong Catholic distinction between a fundamentally good nature and grace leads Catholics to flesh out the natural order presupposed by grace, and New World discoveries encourage theologians and jurists to debate the status of natives living in a state of nature. In northern Europe after the wars of religion leave the theological struggle undecided and the nations exhausted, jurists and philosophers seek a basis for international peace and find it in natural law, which is valid, in Grotius's phrase, "even if God did not exist."[15]

Fourth, the political breakdown of Christendom results from and contributes to the other three elements undermining natural law. The Holy Roman Empire, which expressed the desire of Christians to live in political harmony, is splintered by the Protestant Reformation as never before. Although previously personal and dynastic rivalries led to wars and disunity, the breakdown in religious unity destroys the ideological basis for political unity. There need be no pretense to follow the prescribed norms of Christian morality. Natural loyalties and natural hierarchies are also placed in question not only on religious grounds by the Anabaptists and Levelers but also theoretically. Machiavelli might well describe the hypocrisy of a prince intent upon gaining power, but no one openly supports the principles of *The Prince* until T. Hobbes (without mentioning his source). Calvinist theology and mechanistic physics contribute to *Leviathan*, whereby power justifies itself. Hobbes starts with a state of nature in which selfish individuals wish to enjoy possessions without restriction. Aware that others with unlimited desires and claims desire to enjoy their property and pleasures, but fearful of expropriation and death, they resolve upon a mutual contract in order to secure the peaceful enjoyment of possessions. They surrender all their rights to the sovereign, a mortal god, who assumes all power over them; they are obliged to follow the will of the sovereign since on earth nothing higher than the state exists; only defense against death, wounds, imprisonment, and self-accusation limits the contract. The sovereign has no duty to subjects, and no law, depending of the sovereign's will, can be unjust. The state can even impose religion. All citizens are obliged to obey insofar as they do not have a direct commission from God, and in such a case they must accept the consequences meted out by the state.[16] Thus Hobbes proposes a radical egalitarianism for fallen, selfish men who explicitly accept the civil contract or implicitly agree to it by living in conformity to laws and enjoying its benefits of established peace.

John Locke builds upon that foundation. Besides gentrifying Hobbes's savages he adds an essential novelty to contract theory: natural law guarantees property rights. Even though individuals might surrender their rights to the state in a contract for mutual benefit, the state can no longer expropriate private property. Property belongs to man as much as his life since it assures him of the means to perpetuate life.[17] Perhaps Locke is thus defending his patron Shaftesbury, whose property the charge of treason renders subject to expropriation.

While Locke argues on the basis of a rational natural law whereby the basic needs of men in society are to be fulfilled through a mutually agreed social contract, others appeal to moral sentiments permitting one to feel the agreeableness of altruism. Ultimately in Mill's utilitarianism, the "Greatest Happiness Principle," a sophisticated version of Bentham's procurement of the greatest happiness for the greatest number, serves as the stated norm of morality and justice. But the specification of happiness is seemingly left to the desires of the greatest number.[18]

During the Enlightenment government is rationalized. Whereas in feudal society the main image employed in describing the state was of a living plant or animal whose many diverse members' rights, privileges, and obligations have to be balanced in an harmonious whole, the Enlightenment introduces the dominant image of a bureaucratic machine. Already in the Middle Ages kings extended their effective power through courts to which aggrieved persons, dissatisfied with the justice of a noble's court, might appeal. In this project kings were assisted by trained lawyers. This process of centralization is accelerated during the early Enlightenment, despite the nobility's opposition at key moments, as the lawyers blaze the way to absolute monarchy. It is better that one intelligent, responsible person rule the divided, bickering, oft uneducated nobility who are concerned more with maintaining their own status than the common good. After the noble's power is reduced to that of satellites revolving around the Sun King or, outside France, around his epigones, the bourgeois bureaucracy begins to realize that they are at least as smart as the king. Thus the movement toward participatory, egalitarian democracy is set into motion. Not only is everyone to be treated as equal before the law—such a view facilitates the work of bureaucracy—but also all intelligent, educated people ought to have a voice in the establishment of public policy. Differences of birth do not count. At most intelligence and property qualifications should be taken into account since educated property owners have a personal stake in the continued well-being of the state whose purpose, after all, is to ensure property. They are educated enough to come to a reasoned, mature judgment about public policy. Ultimately these preconditions for voting are dropped and the vote is extended to women; some even propose giving it to children.[19]

Locke greatly influences the Declaration of Independence and the U.S. Constitution, both of which presuppose the contract theory and government's role as protector of property rights. Although Hobbes and Locke appeal to natural law, they interpret it from the perspective of individuals with inborn rights or claims. In the Protestant tradition individuals are selfish, and human nature is explained reductively in terms of basic desires and need-fulfillment. "Rights language" at the basis of morality and law easily leads to confusion and conflict. On the one hand, each aggrieved party claims "inalienable rights" without respect to a wider field of obligations, thus absolutizing the claim of the individual. And there is no objectively grounded list of rights beyond the loud claiming of them. On the other hand, "rights" can be understood as what government grants its citizens. In the 1980s the word "entitlement" threatens to replace "right" in political jargon, as social assistance programs are extended and politicians seek votes by expanding the claims of recipients. But entitlements depend upon the legislator's arbitrary will and the individual soon finds himself enslaved to the state.

Despite these dangers and inconsistencies such views have persuasive power because they describe man as he is. He does desire power, pleasure, and possessions, and a good part of modern education is dedicated to understanding him in terms of the fulfillment of basic needs. Every modern university boasts departments of economics, psychology, and political science because these "sciences" describe and predict the results of man's fundamental determining needs. Marx, Freud, and Nietzsche become the prophets of the modern age when they detail the basic presuppositions of Hobbes and Locke. Yet their view of man is not particularly new. The Bible long ago recognized that man is dominated by the world (possessions), the flesh (pleasures), and the devil (power for power's sake) and summoned believers to struggle against them for their salvation.

The Hobbesian-Lockean interpretation of natural law differs greatly from the

Catholic understanding which begins with a common human nature imposing responsibilities not only to the common good of citizens but also to an objective order of values, spiritual as well as material. Rights are based upon obligations to the natural law. Only with Vatican II and John Paul II does the Church begin to "talk rights language." Even then the perspective is quite different from Locke's rights. John Paul II identifies religious freedom as the "cornerstone of the structure of human rights" (*Christifideles Laici* 39). Treating basic human rights, he clarifies, "The source and synthesis of these rights is religious freedom, understood as the right to live in the truth of one's faith and in conformity with one's transcendent dignity as a person" (*Centesimus Annus* 47).[20] This is not understood as a right to satisfy arbitrarily one's religious needs; rather one's conscience is obliged to follow God's will. John Paul quotes *Dignitatis Humanae* 2, "All are impelled by their own nature and are bound by a moral obligation to seek truth, above all religious truth. They are further bound to hold to the truth once it is known and to regulate their whole lives by its demands" (*Redemptoris Missio* 8). Obligation still precedes right. Furthermore among fallen human being "rights" serve as a legal barrier to protect free persons from the state's totalitarian claims.

The Foundation of the Natural Law

The International Theological Committee's document attempts to lay out the objective bases for human society and law. After calling attention to the need of objective, universal moral norms for a world becoming ever more closely and complexly joined and tracing the development of natural law theory in Western civilization and the Church, the document points out a common basis recognized by various cultures in all parts of the world, the various formulations of the Golden Rule. Deeper than that expression is the basic human sense of ethical obligation expressed in the primary natural law: good should be done and evil avoided. This corresponds to man's profound desire for full realization, happiness. Natural law is rooted, therefore, in man's nature, which is dynamically oriented to a goal. In the Thomistic analysis offered by the document, the natural dynamism expresses itself in three basic desires of the complete person: first, the tendency to preserve and develop one's own existence; second, the inclination to reproduce and perpetuate the species; third, the inclination to know the truth about God and to live in society (S.T. I-II, 94, 2).[21] Although the natural law is grounded in natural desires, it is not reduced to instinctual determinisms. Certainly the desire to preserve and develop one's own existence is basic to all beings. Thomists agree with Hobbes and Locke on that point. But the subsequent inclinations distinguish man ever more. Along with other animals he naturally desires to perpetuate his species by procreation. The individual is fundamentally related to others in his species. The last inclination corresponds to desires specifically human: to know the truth about God, the final ground of his being and the final goal of his action, and thereby to live morally with others. From this higher perspective devolves the moral responsibility to respect the demands contained in the first two inclinations.

On such a broad basis the natural law's secondary precepts can be developed. They too correspond to fundamental human needs and obligations but are more flexibly formulated in regard to specific situations. The document handles this flexibility under the rubric "historicity of the natural law." Because the natural law has been variously interpreted in the past, some arguments employed justified practices and institutions which today are recognized as immoral. For example, slavery, dueling, and the death penalty have been justified by past theorists, while usury, taking interest for the loan of money, a practice basic to modern economic life, has been condemned. The reversal of position by natural law thinkers and the Church has lent weight to the contestations of moral relativists that no universal moral norms can be discovered. Admittedly the brunt of the relativists' attack can be substantially diminished by careful distinctions. For example, "slavery" can be applied to any type of dependence whereby one person is compelled to do another's will. But there are great, even substantial differences among a child forced to obey his parents, a wage-earner forced to work to feed his family, a serf bound to the soil, but free to marry and earn money by labor, an indentured servant, a prisoner from a just war forced to labor for his captors, a criminal condemned to hard labor, and a slave entirely subservient to his master's will.[22] Similarly "dueling" may apply indiscriminately to legitimate self-defense of life and honor (in societies based on honor one cannot live in society without honor), the deliberate, humiliating provocation of others, and intentional killing. And today the legitimate application of the death penalty is much debated. But the document chooses another approach, contending that with time the human race grows in insight into the requirements of the natural law. Many things might always have been wrong, but sin, limited intelligence, and the state of society prevented others in the past and prevent us in the present from recognizing the full implications of the natural law. How can moralists justify abortion which seems so abhorrently immoral? The reality of current abortion legislation makes us realize that progress in moral insight is not unilinear. Furthermore we can be wrong in condemning some practices as immoral.[23] Certainly there is also much flexibility in the application of principles and laws to concrete cases. That is why casuistry is a necessary and noble art applying reason and experience to dilemmas of moral conduct. Prudence is still a central virtue, and sanctity helps tremendously in preventing a concupiscent will from distorting the intellect's perception of complex situations. Indeed, a well-ordered love of justice and one's neighbor strengthens the intellect's power of perception. The entire person is engaged in moral conduct.

Current Conflicting Interpretations

The present debate among Catholic natural law theorists concerns the formulation and validity of universal norms regarding human nature. One's understanding of human nature depends upon one's understanding of human understanding: how does it arrive at truth? Is truth found in a form as the con-*form*-ity of mind and reality, or in judgment? St. Thomas allows for both. First, he writes, "since every reality is true insofar as it possesses the proper form of its own nature, the intellect, insofar as it knows, must be true insofar as it possesses the likeness of the reality known, which is its form insofar as it is knowing. Hence truth is defined by the conformity of intellect and reality." Then he continues: when the intellect knows the conformity it knows truth. "But it does not apprehend [the conformity] insofar as it knows any thing's essence (*quod quid est*), but when it judges the reality to be such as is the form which it apprehends about the reality; then it first knows and says the truth. This it does by combining and separating." This judgment attains truth in its proper sense as the intellect's perfection, although Thomas allows for a certain truth in the senses and in the intellect's knowledge of an essence (S.T. I, q. 16, a. 2). Consequently the intellect is not deceived regarding essences, its proper object; falsity can occur only in judgment; errors about essences happen only when the judgment intervenes (S.T. I, 17, 3c-1). Earlier, Aristotle placed truth in judgment but also held that the intellect cannot err regarding essences (De interpr. 1, 16a 9-18; Meta. 6, 4, 1027b 17-34; 9, 10, 1051b 1-52a 2). In the Thomistic school there is diversity on this issue. Some define truth as the conformity or conformability of mind and intellect without going much further.[24] Others see an imperfect or inchoative truth in simple apprehension through the formal concept while locating formal conformity or full "adequation" of mind and reality in the judgment.[25] Still others insist upon the truth found in judgment without discussing conceptual truth, or seeing the concept as a preparation for the judgment (e.g., Gilson, Maritain, Lonergan) or produced with the judgment (Owens, Rahner).[26]

The Conceptualist View

To the tension about truth corresponds a diversity of opinions whether being is encountered and known in a concept or a judgment. The Cajetanian school concentrates on the analogous concept of being, whose content is "what is or can be."[27] The inclusion of possibility within "being" reflects the abstract nature of concepts. The fundamental concept of being is attained by a triple abstraction: from individual sensible matter, from all sensible, but not all intelligible matter, and from all matter (physical, mathematical, and metaphysical abstraction).[28] Thereby all reality can be conceptualized. If such is the case, the human mind knows primarily by means of concepts which are subsequently joined in propositions. Since by receiving abstracted forms the passive intellect is conformed to reality, its formal object is the true (*verum*); this easily distinguishes it from the will, the spiritual dynamism whose formal object is the good (*bonum*).[29] The soul's distinction from the body is clear because the intellect's operation, viz., knowing through concepts, can be exercised without a corporeal organ. But because the proper and proportionate object of the human intellect is the essence of a material reality, self-knowledge occurs only indirectly, i.e., by reflection on an already accomplished intellectual act.[30] Finally this view grounds the natural-supernatural distinction. The supernatural order surpasses all potencies and exigencies of created nature and involves a participation in God's life. Since the natural operation of the intellect consists of abstracting forms from the unified sense impression, the phantasm, the immediate vision of God promised to believers must be supernatural. It prescinds from sensation and abstraction. Likewise anything leading to the beatific vision, like grace, faith, and the Church, must also be supernatural.[31] These presuppositions prepare for the Church's understanding of morality. The natures of material realities, the intellect's proper and proportionate object, are grasped as universal forms abstracted from non-intelligible "prime matter," which renders them here and now, concrete individuals. Hence the knowledge of human nature with its dynamic tendencies applies to all cases and can be expressed in universal laws. However much individuating circumstances might mitigate or increase guilt, at least some actions can be understood to be contrary to the natural law in all cases. Despite the weakness of his fallen intellect in penetrating matter, man knows his own nature from within, and the Church is enlightened by the Holy Spirit to interpret morality. Since the Decalogue presents the natural law's core precepts, revelation confirms practical reason. In moral difficulties a Catholic Christian always has recourse to the sacraments for strength and forgiveness.[32]

The Transcendental View

In the alternate view, truth is in judgment. Natural knowing is interpreted as a dynamic process synthesizing subject and predicate, essence and existence. Hence there is no objectivity apart from subjectivity. Moreover, since judgment involves a return to the phantasm, the subject is originally aware of his knowing in this reflective act. He enjoys self-awareness concomitant with knowing the essence of a material reality. Furthermore, insofar as the conversion to the phantasm refers form to matter, a fundamental unity of matter and spirit is affirmed. Then, since the intellect actively searches for the true, its motion has a goal to which it is oriented as its good; insofar as their formal objects coincide, intellect and will merge and influence each other. As Karl Rahner writes, "The deepest truth is also the most free." Because the goal of the spiritual dynamism is God, He is implicitly affirmed in every act of knowing and willing. Finally, because man's spiritual dynamism transcends every finite abstraction or sensation, no finite representation can satisfy its quest for truth before it attains God. God in Himself, not an abstract concept of

God, must be man's final end. But the vision of God in Himself is supernatural. Hence, Thomas's paradoxical natural desire for the beatific vision dominates theology.[33] Applied to morality, this view relativizes all concepts, since they are insufficient to reach reality and are transcended in the intellect's movement to God. Thus, universal moral norms can be questioned in view of the subject's existential experience which he knows better than any other human and which only God perfectly evaluates. Given the complexity of choices and insofar as there is no objectivity apart from subjectivity, the subject's intention finally decides the moral goodness or badness of a moral act. Acts regarded in themselves are at worst only ontic evils, i.e., imperfect, finite realizations of the good; they can be weighted in the balance with other goods which the subject intends to realize by his act. When he judges that the proportionate ontic good outweighs the accompanying ontic evil he is justified in his choice, even if the act performed is designated inherently evil by traditional Catholic theology. For nothing is inherently good or evil apart from the subject's intention. Moreover, since every person is oriented to God, in every intellectual-volitive act, God is co-affirmed and co-chosen. Since each human being has a supernatural immediacy to God and is enlightened by God, the Church's role is reduced to being a moral counselor on the basis of its accumulated wisdom, but she cannot pronounce inherently evil any act, except direct sins against God, like blasphemy (provided the subject has an adequate notion of the God he is rejecting).[34]

Toward Reconciliation

Which view is correct? Each has its weaknesses: the former tends to absolutize finite intelligibility while the latter relativizes all finite intelligibility and structures. While abstractions cannot exhaust reality, no thinking is possible without valid concepts. Actually the more intelligent thinkers of each school follow Thomas in seeking to maintain a sane balance between truth in concepts and truth in judgments. Certainly the balance pertains to the Catholic sacramental view of reality whereby the infinite God makes Himself present in and through finite signs, e.g., Jesus' humanity and the Church's sacraments, in order to call men to the absolute commitment of love. Men will be judged according to their responses. This structure is also freedom's prerequisite. A free choice presupposes some knowledge of the object chosen, but the knowledge cannot compel the will; nothing finite and no finite reason or argument can force a free choice. Freedom presupposes openness to a mystery transcending finite intelligibility as well as finite intelligibility mediated by concepts.

The Theological Commission's document ultimately interprets the natural law in terms of personal freedom. Thereby it grounds natures in a deeper reality and avoids the simplistic opposition of necessary natures to freedom. But before explaining the meaning of person in respect to nature, it is profitable to examine how we might intellectual justify the sacramental structure of reality that actuates freedom. First, let us recognize that the basic problems of human thought concern balancing the infinite and the finite. The infinite cannot be comprehended by finite human intelligence. Yet the finite *qua* limited is always referred to something else limiting it; this limiting reality is itself limited and therefore referred to something else again; an endless regress, however, would be unintelligible insofar as a final answer can never be attained. We have seen that paradox with regard to the spatial extension of the universe; it also applies to its temporal extension. In addition, the paradox touches man as a hylomorphic composition. Matter, the principle of individuality, cannot be grasped in universal concepts. Classical philosophy recognized prime matter as unintelligible to the human intellect and therefore infinite. Matter is a mystery to man. This is why human beings can have identity conflicts; they cannot comprehend their own individuality. But if men cannot know themselves, who can inform them of their identity? Obviously the ultimate intelligibility of the universe depends upon an infinite intellect that penetrates matter's infinity and knows us as individuals, calling us by name. Nonetheless agnostics and atheists stress the lack of proportion between finite and infinite which prevents predicating of God qualities obtained in knowing finite realities. At issue is the question of analogy. More profoundly, atheists highlight apparent contradictions in the very notion of God. If God is infinite, how can anything finite exist alongside Him? Does not my finite being, which is not divine, prevent God from being infinite? Again, how can any human intellect, which perceives only finite realities, perceive an infinite God? Finally, how can God be omnipotent if human beings are free? Can I not sin and contradict His will? These conundrums all concern the apparent contradiction between infinite and finite in being, knowing, and acting. Of course, negating the existence of an infinite God does not render the universe more intelligible. It just throws us poor humans willy-nilly into an irrational, uncaring universe without hope of intelligibility.

Fortunately our speculative intellects do not speak the last word. We recognize that we have moral responsibilities in the world and that there is a fundamental difference between good and evil. We stand under obligation to do the good, whatever the cost. Otherwise the morally good becomes something defined by our own preferences. Yet people have given their lives for what they perceive as their moral obligation; unless they did so they would forfeit their humanity. Soldiers die for their country, spouses offer their lives for each other, and parents sacrifice themselves for their children. We praise them. Even in antiquity Achilles dies for his friend Patroclus, Alcestes offers her life for her husband Admetus, and Socrates spends his life for the moral well-being of his fellow Athenians. If such cases exemplify the fulfillment of moral obligation, morality must involve an *absolute* commitment, going even to death for duty's sake. Morality is also *suprarational* since no finite, rational argument can of itself lead to an absolute commitment; every rational argument can be turned by appealing either to the universal against the particular ("much as I am committed to you, I should leave you for the sake of the common good") or to particular circumstances against universal claims ("though all men should be willing to die for their county, it has to be in a just war"). Yet the person addressed by the moral obligation knows that he is bound to its fulfillment. Furthermore morality involves *persons*, i.e., beings possessing intelligence and freedom. One does not rightly offer his life for an animal or a tree. Though men have sacrificed themselves for an ideal, like justice, the ideal must be more than an abstraction, which is lifeless and can be manipulated insofar as it does not fully correspond to reality. Is it commutative or distributive justice, treating all equally or in view of particular circumstances? Rather "justice" must be referred to the actual conditions of human beings lest it become an ideological tool to deceive unwary innocents. Finally, moral commitment involves *liberating freedom*. Morality addresses us with a "should" instead of a "must." It binds us to the here and now. Yet once its demands are accepted, we are liberated from all other relative cares and concerns. The whole universe with all its attractions is relativized before the moral claim and the individual addressed becomes aware of a destiny transcending this world.[35]

The obvious objection to this analysis is that to finite beings all things are relative. No one can claim total dedication for himself or herself. Since a true absolute cannot be limited and therefore rendered relative, we once again confront the conundrum of the infinite and finite. But rather than reject the claim of morality because it seems irrational, we should recognize that our sense of meaning does not depend upon an encounter with a philosopher who explained to us at an early age the meaning of reality. Somehow human beings learn from their parents that they are loved. (We are not all conceived in test tubes for utilitarian purposes to fulfill the desires of others.) Indeed the basic demand of morality is ultimately the call to love: giving one's life freely for another person (cf. Jn. 15:13). I cannot more explain why I am loved than why my contingent being is. But rather than reject love as irrational and then discover that reason can neither justify itself nor discover a comprehensive meaning for reality—thereby the reason which relativized love is relativized—love can save reason from its own conundrum. For the structure of love and the structure of reason reflect each other: both manifest the tension between finite and infinite. Now if love is reality, more basic than the reason which develops later in human life, then the structure of thought reflects the structure of reality. Thought reflects a mystery greater than itself and therefore it is justified as truth; it corresponds to reality. But only the one who remains faithful to love can perceive that correspondence. Here the Hebrew and Greek notions of truth, fidelity and correspondence of mind and reason, coincide and support each other. If love is real, a personal absolute greater than man exists, for only the infinite God can ground an absolute claim for fidelity. God is known, therefore, as interior to human love; He is present as its ground. The infinite and the finite are reconciled in love since love preserves the greatest diversity within the greatest unity. It is clear why

John Paul II called marriage the primordial sacrament of creation. Husband and wife mediate God to each other. For God is love, and man, male and female, is created in His image. Indeed, if God calls any person to give his life in fidelity to love's call—and the command to accept death freely concentrates awareness of one's own free subjectivity—God in His fidelity will not destroy the self-awareness which He has created.[36] Of course sin destroyed the primordial unity between man and God and among men, thereby rendering it easy to doubt love's reality. For mankind's redemption the Incarnation not only assured us of love's reality and showed what love involves but also reestablished unity between God and man and provided the renewed unity of the human race. The visible Church, Christ's Body, is redeemed humanity in its militant condition. She is responsible for living and preaching the reality of Christ's love. Since marriage has been restored to its paradisiacal state by Christ (Mk. 10:1-12), she has a special responsibility to maintain the full symbolic reality of marriage and is concerned with all that touches family life. The family is the primordial hearth of love where, for the vast majority of mankind, love's reality is to be daily lived and transmitted.

On Person and Nature

As John Paul II notes, the person acts, actuating the gift of freedom in response to love. The relation of person to nature has to be understood from freedom. Man is a unity, body, soul, and existence. This composition corresponds to his ways of knowing: sensation, conceptual abstraction, and judgment. While the body senses and the intellect abstracts, there is no particular faculty for perceiving existence. The whole man exists and perceives existence. Maritain, following Aquinas (cf. S.T. I, 77, 4-7), identifies a central point in man where existence, abstraction, and sensation are unified. (This unity in diversity corresponds to every existential judgment joining a particular material essence to existence.) This "essence," or apex, of the soul flows hierarchically into man's various intellectual and sensible faculties, viz., intellect, will, intellectual memory, imagination, sensible memory, various senses, and these faculties flow back to the apex where they are unified in judgment and freedom. This is the ultimate point of self-awareness and freedom, where man is open to God's call and intervention. Though the abstract knowledge of natures mediate a relative intelligibility of the world, in man's personal center the ultimate free commitment is actuated in response to God's call of love. The person is one with the nature, yet transcends nature. Here the Incarnation takes place as the eternal Son freely assumes a human nature to serve as His means of self-expression and the revelation of His Father. Long before Maritain and John Paul II, during the Monotheletic controversy, St. Maximus Confessor identified this point of unity in diversity as the person.[37]

Nature is created to be assumed into personal love. God does not intend that nature should be opposed to personal freedom. That is why nature's inclinations already anticipate the self-giving of love. This is most clear in sexual attractions whereby man and woman are drawn to union with each other in corporeal as well as affective, spiritual complementarity. They learn to live each other's life on various levels and their union is open to the procreation of children because love is of itself expansive, as is manifested in God's trinitarian self-giving, in creation, and in the self-emptying and self-giving of the cross. Although God alone can judge the heart's intentions, human beings should strive to make their civilization a reflection of God's self-giving love by all means possible. Thus, all are required to respect and uphold the human institution most conducive to creating and communicating love, the family. Although civil government may permit lesser evils lest in fallen humanity insistence upon the better may result in the worse, the Church is especially committed to preserving effective signs of love. Those signs are guaranteed *ex opere operato* in the Eucharist and the other sacraments. To preserve the meaning of love, moral laws governing human behavior must be proclaimed. Especially in the sacrament of marriage, strict standards must be protected. For sexuality's power can easily distort thinking, and for the vast majority of mankind marriage is the locus of love's daily realization. If clear standards are not maintained, the power of Christian witness is enfeebled and believers are not vivified by the challenge of love. For their part, believers who accept salvation by the cross know that they are called upon to sacrifice themselves for love and should be willing to accept all the responsibilities of indissoluble, monogamous marriage with openness to children. Since other requirements of justice and the natural law may not be so closely bound to love, there is more leeway for interpreting and adapting them, e.g., usury, slavery, and the death penalty, to varying circumstances.[38]

God's answer to sin in Jesus' cross and resurrection effects a deepening of the Golden Rule. Whereas its bare statement, "do unto others as you would have others do unto you," can be understood as a precept of commutative justice or in a Kantian sense as obedience to a universal moral norm or as a reformulation of Mill's collective self-interest,[39] Jesus transforms its application just as He inverts the question "Who is my neighbor?" into "Who was neighbor to the man who fell among robbers?" (Luke 10:29, 36) The Golden Rule is now embedded in a section of the gospel that begins with "Love your enemies, do good to those who hate you" and culminates in the command, "Be merciful as your heavenly Father is merciful" (Luke 6:27-36).[40] Instead of making one's own desires for just treatment the norm of morality, the Christian, a redeemed sinner, is summoned to place fellow sinners in the center of his concern. This reflects God's unmerited, superabundant love that alone can overcome the selfish ravages of sin and enable man to recognize and interpret his true nature. As John Paul II notes, love is the pre-condition of a just society. Unless we have the eyes of love we will never interpret correctly the demands of the natural moral law. But with those eyes, nature and person are unified and the natural law is recognized as the law of personal love.

Notes

1. Perhaps none has been so consistently articulate and balanced as Richard J. Neuhaus in *First Things* about the secularist attempt to drive a wedge between religion and public policy. He identified the danger in *The Naked Public Square* (Grand Rapids: Eerdmans, 1984) and pointed our secularism's inroads into the Catholic Church in *The Catholic Moment* (San Francisco: Harper & Row, 1987), esp. 233-81.

2. F. O'Connor, *Mystery and Manners* (New York: Farrar, Straus & Giroux, 1969), 227. This insight serves as the theme of W. Percy's novel *The Thanatos Syndrome* (New York: Farrar, Straus & Giroux, 1987), cp. 360-61.

3. The vagueness attendant upon the popular notion of freedom leaves itself open to exploitation by many groups. For various historical understandings of freedom cf. John McDermott, S.J., "The Mystery of Freedom," *Lateranum* 74 2008), 493-542.

4. The original meaning of Pindar's phrase is anything but clear: cf. W.K.C. Guthrie, *A History of Greek Philosophy* (Cambridge: University Press, 1962-81), 3:131-34.

5. Epictetus, "Encheiridion," in *Epicteti dissertationes ab Arriano digestae*, editio major, ed. Heinrich Schenkl and Johannes Schweishäuser (Leipzig: Teubner, 1916), cc. 1, 3, 5-6, 8, 14, 19, 21, 26-27, 29-32, 38, 48, 52; Diogenes Laertius, "Vita Zenonis," VII, 87, 147-150, in *Vitae Philosophorum*, ed. H. S. Long, 2 vols. (Oxford: Clarendon, 1964), 2:334.; Cleanthes, "Hymn to Zeus," in *Stoici Antici Stoicorum Veterum Fragmenta*, ed. Joannis ab Arnim, 3 vols. (Leipzig: Teubner, 1903), no. 537, 2:121-23. Cf. F. Copleston, S.J., *A History of Philosophy*, I (Westminster: Newman, 1955), 388-400; cf. also J. Rist, *Stoic Philosophy* (Cambridge: Cambridge U., 1969), 23-36, 120-32; L. Edelstein, *The Meaning of Stoicism* (Cambridge: Harvard, 1966), 1-9, 31-44, 83-85.

6. Copleston, 403-11; N. DeWitt, *Epicurus and His Philosophy* (Minneapolis: U. of Minnesota, 1954), 121-132, 155-196, 216-288; G. Panichas, *Epicurus* (New York: Twayne, 1967), 39-45, 52-81, 98-109, 118-22..

7. Copleston, 121-123; Panichas, 101-02.

8. As S. Pinckaers, O.P., *The Sources of Christian Ethics*, tr. M. Noble (Washington: Catholic U., 1995), 191, admits, "Our knowledge of the history of moral theology is sketchy." Cf. his short overview of patristic morality in 191-215, and, for Augustine, A. Chroust, "The Philosophy of Law of St. Augustine," *Philosophical Review* 53 (1944), 195-202; G. Schlabach and A. Fitzgerald, O.S.A., "Ethics," *Augustine through the Ages*, ed. A. Fitzgerald et alii (Grand Rapids: Eerdmans, 1999), 320-30; R. Dougherty, "Natural Law," ibid., 582-84.

9. Cf. A. Chroust, "The Philosophy of Law from St. Augustine to St. Thomas Aquinas," *New Scholasticism* 20 (1946), 26-71. For brief overviews of St. Thomas's thought cf. Pinckaers, 220-229; H. Rommen, *The Natural Law*, tr. T. Hanley (St. Louis: Herder, 1948), 45-57; J. Maritain, *Man and the State* (Chicago: U. of Chicago, 1951), 84-94. Divergences in the interpretation of Thomas's natural law theory will be discussed below.

10. We leave aside other contributing factors such as the rise of the bourgeoisie, the black plague, and the inventions of gun powder and the printing press in order on concentrate on intellectual movements affecting the natural law. Nonetheless the political breakdown should be mentioned because of its direct impact upon political theory and,

consequently, philosophy and theology.

11. Pinckaers, 240-53; Rommen, 57-60; A.C. Crombie, *Medieval and Early Modern Science*, 2nd ed. (Garden City: Doubleday, 1959), 2:29-35, 59-98. S. Jaki, *The Savior of Science* (Washington: Regnery Gateway, 1988), 50-54, 66-69, attributes the insight into the impetus theory of motion and the moving earth to Christian faith in *creatio ex nihilo* and intelligibility; true, the Christian faith supports research for intelligibility, but nominalist presuppositions encourage interpretation in terms of efficient causality. Aquinas considered the world's beginning in time a proposition of faith, not of reason (S.T. I, 24, 1-2); so it cannot be used strictly in science. While holding that Aristotle's reasons for the world's eternity were not strictly demonstrative, he followed him in giving primacy to final, not efficient, causality (S.T. I, 5, 4).

12. B. Gerrish, *Grace and Reason* (1962; rpt. Chicago: U. of Chicago, 1979), 10-56, 107-13, 138-41, 168-71; F. Cranz, *An Essay on the Development of Luther's Thought on Justice, Law, and Society* (Cambridge: Harvard, 1959), 73-111, 161-73, esp. 105-11; P. Althaus, *The Theology of Martin Luther*, tr. R. Schultz (Philadelphia: Fortress, 1966), 15-19, 64-71, 123, 144-51, 224-33, 245-60, 304, 341-44, 386-91; B. Lohse, *Martin Luther's Theology*, tr. R. Harrisville (Minneapolis: Fortress, 1999), 154-59, 181-84, 196-205, 270-74; McDermott, "Mystery of Freedom," 496-98, 503; ——, "Faith, Reason, and Theology," *Irish Theological Quarterly* 67 (2002), 308-309; ——, M. Luther, *The Large Catechism of Martin Luther*, tr. Robert Fischer (Philadelphia: Fortress, 1959), 42, 52, 60-64; cf. also *Luther's Small Catechism with Explanation* (St. Louis: Concordia, 1986), 34-35, 48-50, 67-68, 96-97, 153-60. John Calvin, *Institutes of the Christian Religion*, ed. J. McNeill, tr. F. Battles (Philadelphia: Westminster, 1960), I, 3, 1-2; 5, 1-3; II, 6, 4; 7, 2-5; 8, 1; III, 14, 17; 20, 36-37; 21, 1.5-7. Q. Skinner, *The Foundations of Modern Political Thought: vol. II: The Age of Reformation* (Cambridge: Cambridge U., 1978) traces the development of early Lutheran and Calvinist theories of the state vis-à-vis the gospel in their historical context: cf. esp. 64-108, 189-238.

13. Cf. H. Butterfield, *The Origins of Modern Science*, rev. ed. (1957; rpt. New York: Collier, 1962), 13-48, 67-107, 151-70; E. Burtt, *The Metaphysical Foundations of Modern Science*, 2nd ed. (1932; rpt. Garden City: Doubleday, 1954); and A. R. Hall, *The Scientific Revolution 1500-1800*, 2nd ed. (Boston: Beacon, 1966), 101-128, 159-85, 244-76, for a good overview of the changes from medieval to Newtonian physics. Cf. A. Einstein, *Relativity*, tr. R. Lawson (New York: Crown, 1961), 63-78, 100-04; —— and L. Infeld, *The Evolution of Physics* (1938; rpt. New York: Simon and Schuster, 1966), 199-245, for Einstein's gravitational theory.

14. Burtt, 239-64, 283-97; S. Hawking, *A Brief History of Time* (Toronto: Bantam, 1988), 4-6.

15. For overviews of the later development of natural law theories cf. Rommen, 68-158; Pinckaers, 254-92; P. Hazard, *The European Mind 1680-1715*, tr. J. May (London: Hollis & Carter, 1953), 257-260, 268-283.

16. T. Hobbes, *Leviathan*, ed. B. Macpherson (Harmondsworth: Penguin, 1968), I, 13-14; II, 17-18, 26.30: III, 33.39.42.43; pp. 183-201, 223-39, 312-313, 388, 415-27, 496-99, 526-31, 550-552, 567-571, 575-576, 584-86.

17. J. Locke, *Two Treatises of Government*, rev. ed., ed. P. Laslett (New York: New American Library, 1963), II, 85, 138-40, 171, 183; pp. 365-366, 406-08, 428-429, 437-438.

18. J. Mill, "Utilitarianism," in *Essential Works of John Stuart Mill*, ed. M. Lerner

(1961; rpt. New York: Bantam, 1965), 195, 198-199, 204-205, 217-218, 220-221, 244-248.

19. J. Sheehan, *German History 1770-1866* (Oxford: Clarendon, 1989), 29-35; P. Hazard, *European Thought in the Eighteenth Century*, tr. J. May (Cleveland: World, 1963), 32-33, 176-181, 225-234, 262-267.

20. *Evangleium Vitae* 5 considers as fundamental the right to life and *Christifideles Laici* 38 calls it "the most basic and fundamental right and the condition for all other personal rights." There is no contradiction in the description as fundamental of both the right to religious freedom and the right to life. Life is the condition of possibility for the exercise of religious freedom and human life is so inviolable because man is made in God's image with freedom and responsibility. Indeed, "the individual's relation to God is a constitutive element of the very 'being' and 'existence' of an individual" (ibid., 39). Animals enjoy no right to life.

21. This analysis agrees with the previous presentation of Pinckaers, 405-456.

22. Cf. A. Dulles, S.J., "Development or Reversal?" *First Things* 156 (Oct., 2005), 53-61.

23. We only need consider the example of anti-vivisectionists who would impose their view on society.

24. A. Dulles, S.J., J. Demske, S.J., R. O'Connell, S.J., *Introductory Metaphysics* (New York: Sheed and Ward, 1955), 124; G. Klubertanz, S.J., *Introduction to the Philosophy of Being*, 2nd ed. (New York: Appleton-Century-Crofts, 1963), 224-25, 236; L. de Raeymaeker, *The Philosophy of Being, tr.* E. Ziegelmeyer (St. Louis: Herder, 1954), 76-77.

25. J. Gredt, O.S.B., *Elementa Philosophiae Aristotelico-thomisticae*, 10th ed. (Freiburg: Herder, 1953), 1:28; 2:45-48; E. Hugon, O.P., *Logica* (Paris: Lethielleux, 1927), 264-69; P. Dezza, S.J., *Metaphysica Generalis*, 3rd ed. (Rome: Gregorian, 1952), 83.

26. E. Gilson, *Le Thomisme*, 5th ed. (Paris: Vrin, 1948), 317-29; J. Maritain, *An Introduction to Logic*, tr. I. Choquette (New York: Sheed and Ward, 1937), 85-92; J. Owens, C.Ss.R, *An Elementary Christian Metaphysics* (Milwaukee: Bruce, 1963), 118-19, 248-58; G. Klubertanz, S.J., *The Philosophy of Human Nature* (New York: Appleton-Century-Crofts, 1953), 166, 428; F. Van Steenberghen, *Ontology*, tr. M. Flynn (New York: Wagner, 1952), 57; W. N. Clarke, S.J., *The One and the Many* (Notre Dame: University of Notre Dame, 2001), 319; Lonergan, *Insight*, 3-8, 357-58, 552, 556-57; ——, *Verbum*, ed. D. Burrell (Notre Dame: University of Notre Dame, 1967), 1-95; K. Rahner, S.J., "Die Wahrheit bei Thomas von Aquin," *Schriften zur Theologie* (Zurich: Benziger, 1954-84), 10: 24-25, 29, 35-37; ——, *Geist in Welt* (Innsbruck: Rauch, 1939), 85, 159, 191; J. McDermott, S.J., "Dialectical Analogy: The Oscillating Center of Rahner's Thought," *Gregorianum* 75 (1994), 680-86. Klubertanz's designation of truth as "conformability" (*Introduction*, 224) to the human intellect stands in tension with his emphasis on truth in judgment. A change of perspective is involved. *Introduction* considers first the ontological truth of creatures in relation to God, then their "knowability," or "conformability," to the human intellect, whereas *Philosophy* considers the human truth known in judgment.

27. J. Maritain, *Sept Leçons sur l'Être* (Paris: Tequi, 1934), 72; ——, *The Degrees of Knowledge*, tr. G. Phelan et alii (1959; rpt. Notre Dame: University of Notre Dame, 1995), 226-32; R. Garrigou-Lagrange, O.P., *Reality*, tr. Patrick Cummins (St. Louis: Herder, 1950), 31; E. Hugon, O.P., *Metaphysica* (Paris: Lethielleux, 1935), 255; Sebastian Uccello, S.S.S., *Philosophia Scholastica ad Mentem Sancti Thomae* (Turin: Marietti, 1921), 1:194-95; F.X. Maquart, *Elementa Philosophiae* (Paris: Blot, 1937-38), 3:15; 3/2:15-16; R. P. Phillips, *Modern Thomistic Philosophy* (London: Burns Oates & Washbourne, 1934-35), 2:159.

Gredt, ibid., 2:4-8, defines being (*ens*) as that whose act is to be (*esse*), but includes in it "*ens* actually existing and *ens* merely possible."

28. Maritain, *Degrees*, 145-96, 215-40; Gredt, 1:188-90; Maquart, 2:351-52; Hugon, *Logica*, 444-45; A. Pirotta, O.P., *Summa Philosophiae Aristotelico-Thomisticae* (Turin: Marietti, 1931-36), 1:262-63, but cf. 1:171-72 for metaphysical abstraction by a *separatio*.

29. Gredt, 1:396-98; Phillips, 1:254, 272-74; Maquart, 2:447-50; Garrigou-Lagrange, *Reality*, 187-88; Pirotta, 2:761-77: Pirotta first, 2:761-65, characterizes the will as passive to make sure that it is guided by the concept of the good presented by the intellect but later, 2:772, defines the will as "by nature that appetitive potency which of itself and intrinsically tends and inclines toward the object proper to itself." Though guaranteeing the will's dependence on the intellect, he fails to explain how the will, as a concrete faculty with a concrete goal, can tend toward an abstraction.

30. Gredt, 1:427-30, 435-447; Pirotta, 2:649-652, 721-730; Phillips, 1:258-263; Maquart, 2:243-244, 346-351, 361-365, 501-502; Uccello, 2:102-106, 130-131.

31. Garrigou-Lagrange, *De Revelatione*, 1:185-194, 199-201, 417-418; J. Solier, "Supernatural Order," *The Catholic Encyclopedia*, ed. C. Herbermann et al. (New York: Appleton, 1907-13), 14:336-339; E. Hugon, O.P., *Tractatus Dogmatici*, 11th and 10th ed. (Paris: Lethielleux, 1933-35), 2:57-59; A. Tanquerey, *Synopsis Theologiae Dogmaticae Fundamentalis*, 24th ed., ed. J.B. Bord (New York: Benziger, 1937), 47-48.

32. J. McDermott, S.J., "The Context of *Veritatis Splendor*," in *Prophecy and Diplomacy*, ed. J. Conley and J. Koterski (New York: Fordham, 1999), 128-40.

33. We present mainly the outline of Rahner's thought; though many others agree with him, they differ on some points: cf. J. McDermott, S.J., "Karl Rahner in Tradition: The One and the Many," *Fides Quaerens Intellectum* 3 (2004-07), 10-20 (summarizing many articles), and Patrick Burke, *Reinterpreting Rahner* (New York: Fordham, 2002), 1-72. The citation is from Rahner's *Hörer des Wortes*, 2nd ed., ed. J.-B. Metz (Munich: Kösel, 1963), 131.

34. McDermott, "Context," 140-166.

35. For more detail cf. J. McDermott, S.J., "A New Approach to God's Existence," *The Thomist* 44 (1980), 220-227; other aspects of this article have been revised and expanded in "Faith, Reason, and Freedom," 307-332, and "Mystery of Freedom," 492-542.

36. John Paul II, *The Theology of the Body* (Boston: Pauline, 1997), 333-347; *Letter to Families* 18.

37. Cf. G. Bausenhart, *"In allen uns gleich ausser der Sünde,"* (Mainz: Grünewald, 1992), 147-78, B. Ritzler, *Freiheit in der Umarmung des ewig Liebenden* (Bern: Lang, 2000), esp. 409-93; J. McDermott, S.J., "The Theology of John Paul II: A Response," in *The Thought of Pope John Paul II*, ed. J. McDermott (Rome: Gregorian, 1993), 55-68; ——, "How Did Jesus Know He Was God? The Ontological Psychology of Mark 10:17-22," *Irish Theological Quarterly*, 74 (2009), 272-297.

38. For lack of space the question of Church-State relations is omitted. The document's treatment is simplified and rather sketchy.

39. Mill, 204, 236-239; I. Kant, *Foundations of the Metaphysics of Morals*, tr. L. Beck (Indianapolis: Bobbs-Merrill, 1959), 48, n. 14, denies that the golden rule is the principle of morality; viz., treating humanity always as an end and never as a means only, for "it is only derived from the principle and is restricted by various limitations." Yet some have interpreted it as "the basis or equivalent of Kant's categorical imperative" (M. Singer, "Golden Rule," in *Encyclopedia of Philosophy*, 2nd ed., ed. D. Borchart [Detroit: Thomson-Gale,

2006], 4:144-147). Kant's rejection of the evangelical rule as basic probably results from his refusal of love as the foundation of morality. Reason never finds a reason for loving, and Kant wished to stay with reason.

40. Matthew's version of the golden rule, presented as the equivalent of "the Law and the prophets" (7:12), is presented in the Sermon on the Mount which demands love of enemies as well as forgiveness, abstention from condemning others, and abandonment of concern about money and earthly possessions.

Bibliography of Cited and Selected Sources

Adolphe, Jane. "The Case Against Same-Sex Marriage in Canada: Law and Policy Considerations." *BYU Journal of Public Law* 18 (2004): 479-541.

———. "The Holy See and the UDHR: Towards a Legal Anthropology of Human Rights and the Family." *Ave Maria Law Review* 4 (2006): 343- 354.

Agamben, Giorgio. *The Time That Remains: A Commentary on the Letter to the Romans*. Translated by Patricia Dailey. Palo Alto, CA: Stanford University Press, 2005.

Althaus, P. *The Theology of Martin Luther*. Translated by R. Schultz. Philadelphia: Fortress, 1966.

Ambrosetti, G. *Diritto naturale cristiano. Profili di metodo, di storia e di teoria*. Milano, 1985.

Amiot, François. *Les Idées Maîtresses de Saint-Paul*. Paris: Les Éditions du Cerf, 1959.

Aquinas, St. Thomas. *Commentary on Aristotle's Nichomachaen Ethics*. Translated by C.I. Litzinger. South Bend, Ind.: Dumb Ox Books, 1993.

———. *Summa Theologica*. Translated by the Fathers of the English Dominican Province. New York: Benzinger Brothers, 1948 and Allen, TX: Christian Classics, 1981.

Ariel, Israel and Chaim Richman, eds. *Carta's Illustrated Encyclopedia of the Holy Temple of Jerusalem*. Jerusalem: The Temple Institute and Carta, 2005.

Aristotle. *The Complete Works of Aristotle*. 12 Volumes, edited by Jonathan Barnes. Princeton, N.J., Princeton University Press, 1971.

Augustine, St. *The City of God*. Translated by Marcus Dods. New York: Random House, 1950.

———. *On the Spirit and the Letter*, chapter XLIV, in *The Basic Writings of St. Augustine*, Vol. 1 ed. W.J. Oates. New York: Random House, 1948.

———. *Confessions*. Translated by Henry Chadwick. New York: Oxford University Press, 1991.

Austin, John. *The Province of Jurisprudence Determined and the Uses of the Study of Jurisprudence*. Indianapolis: Hackett Publishing, 1998.

Barth, Karl. "No! Answer to Emil Brunner" in *Natural Theology*. Translated and edited by Peter Fraenkel. London: Centenary Press, 1946: 94-103.

Barrett, C.K. *A Commentary on the First Epistle to the Corinthians, Harper's New Testament Commentaries*. New York: Harper & Row, 1968.

Barton, J. "Natural Law and Poetic Justice in the Old Testament." *Journal of Theological Studies New Series* 30 (1979).

Bausenhart, G. *"In allen uns gleich ausser der Sünde."* Mainz: Grünewald, 1992.

Bederman, David. *International Law Frameworks* 2nd ed. New York. Foundation Press, 2006.

Begin, Raymond F. *Natural Law and Positive Law.* Washington, D.C. The Catholic University of America Press, 1959.

Benedict XVI, Encyclical Letter, *Deus caritas est* (December 25, 2005).

———. "Address to the Participants in the Convention at Verona Exhibition Centre." Verona, Italy (Oct. 19, 2006).

———. "Address To Participants in The International Congress in Natural Moral Law" (Feb. 12, 2007).

———. "To Members of Catholic-Inspired Non-governmental Organizations: Counter Relativism by Truth" in *L'Osservatore Romano* [English edition] (December 12, 2007).

———. Homily on Palm Sunday (March 16, 2008)

———. "Address to the General Assembly of the United Nations" (April 18, 2008).

———. "St. Paul Migrant, 'Apostle of the Peoples,'" Message for World Refugee and Migrant Day (Oct. 9, 2008).

———. "Encyclical, *Caritas in veritate* (June 29, 2009).

Berkouwer, G.C. *De Algemene Openbaring.* Kampen: J.H. Kok, 1951.

———. *De Mens Het Beeld Gods*. Kampen: J.H. Kok, 1957. English translation: *Man: The Image of God*. Translated by Dirk w. Jellema. Grand Rapids, MI: Eerdmans, 1962.

Berman, Harold J. *Faith and Order: The Reconciliation of Law and Religion,* Emory University Studies in Law and Religion, edited by John Witte, Jr. Atlanta: Scholars Press, 1993: 333-340.

———. "Toward an Integrative Jurisprudence: Politics, Morality, History." in *California Law Review* 76. (1988): 779-780.

———. *Law and Revolution: The Formation of the Western Legal Tradition.* Cambridge, MA and London, England: Harvard University Press, 1983.

Bix, Brian, ed. *Analyzing Law: New Essays in Legal Theory.* Oxford: Oxford University Press, 1998.

Bossuet,W. *Kyrios Christos*. Nashville: Abingdon, 1970.

Bradley, Gerard V. and Robert P. George. "The New Natural Law Theory: A Reply to Jean Porter." in *American Journal of Jurisprudence* 38 (1994): 303-315.

Braund, D. ed. *Augustus to Nero: A Sourcebook on Roman History 31BC-AD68.* London: Croom Helm, 1985.

Braybrooke, David. *Natural Law Modernized.* Toronto: University of Toronto Press, 2001.

Brock, Stephen Louis. *The Legal Character of Natural Law According to St.*

Thomas Aquinas. doctoral thesis. Toronto: University of Toronto, 1988.

Brooke, John Hedley. *Science and Religion: Some Historical Perspectives*. Cambridge: Cambridge University Press 1991.

Brown, Raymond E., S.S., Joseph A. Fitzmyer, S.J., Roland E. Murphy, O.Carm., eds. *The New Jerome Biblical Commentary*. Englewood Cliffs, N.J.: Prentice Hall, 1990.

Bruce, F. F. *The Curse of the Law, in Paul and Paulinism. Essays in honour of C. K. Barrett*. Oxford: Alden Press, 1982.

Brunner, Emil. "Nature and Grace" in *Natural Theology*, edited and translated by Peter Fraenkel. London: Centenary Press, 1946.

Budziszewski, J. *Written on the Heart: The Case for Natural Law*. Downer's Grove, Illinois: Intervarsity Academic, 1997.

———. *What We Can't Not Know: A Guide*. Dallas: Spence Publishing Co., 2003.

———. *The Line Through the Heart: Natural Law as Fact, Theory and Sign of Contradiction*. Wilmington, Del: Intercollegiate Studies Institute, 2009.

Burke, Patrick. *Reinterpreting Rahner*. New York: Fordham University Press, 2002.

Burtt, E. *The Metaphysical Foundations of Modern Science*, 2nd ed. Garden City: Doubleday, 1954.

Butterfield, H. *The Origins of Modern Science*. rev. ed. New York: Collier, 1962.

Buttricks, George A. General Editor. *The Interpreter's Bible*. New York: Abingdon-Cokesbury, 1952.

Calvin, John. *The Institutes of the Christian Religion*. 2 vols. John T. McNeill, ed. Trans. Ford Lewis Battles. Louisville & London: Westminster John Knox Press, 2006.

Casciaro, Jose M. *The Navarre Bible 27: Romans and Galatians*. Translated by Michael Adams. Dublin: Four Courts Press, 1993.

Cassidy, Richard J. *Paul in Chains: Roman Imprisonment and the Letters of St. Paul* (New York: Crossroad Publishing, 2001.

———. *John's Gospel in New Perspective*. Maryknoll, NY: Orbis, 1992.

Catechism of the Catholic Church. Second Edition. Washington, D.C. and Vatican City: U.S. Conference of Catholic Bishops and Libreria Editrice Vatican, 1997.

Catholic Medical Association. *Homosexuality and Hope*. 2000 and 2008, available through www.cathmed.org/publications/homosexualityarticle.htm.

Cessario, Romanus O.P. *Christian Faith & The Theological Life*. Washington, D.C.: Catholic University of American Press, 1996.

Charles, J. Daryl. *Retrieving the Natural Law: A Return to Moral First Things*. Grand Rapids, MI: Eerdmans, 2008.

Christie, George C. and Patrick H. Martin, *Jurisprudence: Text and Readings on the Philosophy of Law* 3rd ed. Eagan, MN: Thomson West, 2008.

Chroust, A. "The Philosophy of Law of St. Augustine." *Philosophical Review* 53 (1944): 195-202

———. "The Philosophy of Law from St. Augustine to St. Thomas Aquinas," *New Scholasticism* 20 (1946): 26-71.

Cicero, *On the Commonwealth and On the Laws*, edited by James E.G. Zetzel. Cambridge: Cambridge University Press 2002.

Clark, J. *The Language of Liberty, 1660-1832*. Cambridge: Cambridge University Press, 1994.

Clarke, W. N., S.J. *The One and the Many*. Notre Dame: University of Notre Dame Press, 2001.

Cleanthes, "Hymn to Zeus," in *Stoici Antici Stoicorum Veterum Fragmenta*, edited by Joannis ab Arnim, 3 vols. Leipzig: Teubner, 1903.

Collins, Raymond F. *First Corinthians*, *Sacra Pagina* 7. Collegeville, MN: The Liturgical Press/Michael Glazier, 1999.

Congar, Yves. *Laity, Church and World*, Translated by Donald Attwater. Baltimore: Helicon Press, 1960.

Congregation for the Doctrine of the Faith. *Letter to the Bishops of the World on the Pastoral Care of Homosexual Persons* (Oct. 1, 1986),

———. *Considerations Regarding Proposals to Give Legal Recognition to Unions between Homosexual Persons* (June 3,2003).

———. *Letter to the Bishops of the Catholic Church on the Collaboration of Men and Women in the Church and in the World* (May 31, 2004).

Conzelmann, Hans. *The Pastoral Epistles*. Philadelphia: Fortress Press, 1972.

——— *1 Corinthians: A Commentary on the First Epistle to the Corinthians*. Philadelphia: Fortress Press, 1975.

Copleston, F. S.J. *A History of Philosophy*, I. Westminster: Newman, 1955.

Coughlin, John M., OFM. "The Human Being, Catholic Social Teaching and the Law." *Journal of Catholic Social Thought* (2004): 313-326.

Coulanges, Fustel. *The Ancient City: A Study on The Religion, Laws And Institutions Of Greece And Rome*. Boston: Lee and Shepherd, 1877.

Covell, Charles. *The Defense of the Natural Law*. New York: St. Martin's Press, 1992.

Cover, Robert. *Justice Accused: Antislavery and the Judicial Process*. New Haven, CT: Yale University Press, 1984.

Cranz, F. *An Essay on the Development of Luther's Thought on Justice, Law, and Society*. Cambridge, MA: Harvard, 1959.

Cromartie, Michael, ed. *A Preserving Grace: Protestants, Catholics and the Natural Law*. Grand Rapids, MI: Eerdmans, 1997.

Crombie, A.C. *Medieval and Early Modern Science*, 2nd ed. Garden City: Doubleday, 1959.

Crosby, John. "John Paul II on the Complementarity of Man and Woman," in Kenneth Whitehead, ed. *The Church, Marriage, and the Family*, Proceedings from the 27th Annual Convention of the Fellowship of Catholic Scholars. South Bend, Ind.: St. Augustine's Press, 2007: 41-52.

Dawson, Christopher Henry. *The Making of Europe: An Introduction to the History of European Unity*. New York: Sheed and Ward, 2001.
Delhaye, P. *Permanence du Droit Naturel*. Louvain: Éditions Nauwelaerts, 1960.
Dezza,, P. S.J. *Metaphysica Generalis*, 3rd ed. Rome: Gregorian, 1952.
DeWitt N. *Epicurus and His Philosophy. Minneapolis*: University of Minnesota, 1954.
Derrett, J. Duncan M. *Law in the New Testament*. London: Darton, Longmann & Todd, 1970.
Deissmann, A. *Light from the Ancient East*. Translated by L. Strachan. Reprint, Grand Rapids: Baber, 1965.
de Lubac, Henri. *Theological Fragments*. San Francisco: Ignatius Press, 1989.
Denzinger, Heinrich and Peter Hünermann. *Enchiridion symbolorum definitionum et declarationum de rebus fidei et morum* 40th ed. Freiburg: Herder, 2005.
de Raeymaeker, L. *The Philosophy of Being*. Translated by E. Ziegelmeyer. St. Louis: Herder, 1954.
De Torre, Fr. Joseph M. *Contemporary Philosophical Issues in Historical Perspective*. Pasig City, Philippines: University of Asia and the Pacific Press 2001.
Di Blasi, Fulvio. *God and the Natural Law: A Rereading of Thomas Aquinas*. Translated by David Thunder. South Bend, Ind.: St. Augustine's Press, 2002.
d'Entrèves, Alessandro. *Natural Law* 2nd. ed. London: Hutchinson, 1970.
Diogenes Laertius. "Vita Zenonis," VII, 87, 147-150, in *Vitae Philosophorum*, edited by H. S. Long, 2 vols. Oxford: Clarendon, 1964.
Dougherty, Richard J. "Natural Law," in *Augustine Through the Ages: An Encyclopedia* ed. Allan D. Ftizgerald, O.S.A. et al. Grand Rapids, MI: Willaim B. Eedrmans, 1999.
Dostoevsky, Fyodor. *The Brothers Karamazov*. Translated by Richard Pevear and Larissa Volokhonsky. New York: North Point Press 1992.
Dulles, A. S.J., J. Demske, S.J., R. O'Connell, S.J. *Introductory Metaphysics*. New York: Sheed and Ward, 1955.
Dulles Avery, S.J. "Development or Reversal?" *First Things* 156 (Oct., 2005): 53-61.
Easterbrook, Frank H. *Cyberspace and the Law of the Horse*, 1996 *U Chi Legal F* (1996).
Eberstadt, Mary. "The Vindication of *Humanae Vitae*." *First Things* (July 2008),
———. "The Will to Disbelieve." *First Things* (February 2009).
Echeverria, Eduardo. *Slitting the Sycamore: Christ and Culture in the New Evangelization*. Grand Rapids, MI: Acton Institute, 2008.
Edelstein, L. *The Meaning of Stoicism*. Cambridge: Harvard University Press,1966.
Einstein, Albert. *Relativity*. Translated by R. Lawson. New York: Crown, 1961.
Engberg-Pedersen, Troels, ed. *Paul in His Hellenistic Context*. Minneapolis: Fortress, 1994.

Epictetus. "Encheiridion," in *Epicteti dissertationes ab Arriano digestae*, editio major, edited by Heinrich Schenkl and Johannes Schweishäuser. Leipzig: Teubner, 1916.

Essati, Abus Al-Fazl. *Islam and Natural Law*. London: Islamic College for Advanced Studies, 2002.

Fastiggi, Robert. "Vitoria, Francisco de." in Michael L. Coutler et al. eds. *Encyclopedia of Catholic Social Thought, Social Science and Social Policy*. Lanham, MD: Scarecrow Press, 2007: 1125-1127.

Fee, Gordon. *1 and 2 Timothy, Titus*. San Francisco: Harper & Row, 1984.

———. *The First Epistle to the Corinthians, The New International Commentary on the New Testament* Grand Rapids, MI.: William B. Eerdmans, 1987.

Finnis, John. *Natural Law and Natural Rights*. Oxford: Oxford University Press, 1983.

———. *Moral Absolutes: Tradition, Revision and Truth*. Washington, D.C.: Catholic University of America Press, 1991.

———. *Aquinas: Moral, Political and Legal Theory*. New York: Oxford University Press, 1998.

———. "On the Incoherence of Legal Positivism." *Notre Dame Law Review* 75 (2000): 1597-1599.

Finocchiaro, F. *Il matrimonio nel diritto canonico*. Bologna: Il Mulino, 1989.

Fiore, B. *The Function of Personal Example in the Socratic and Pastoral Epistles*. Rome: Biblical Institute Press, 1986.

Fitzgerald, A, O.S.A. et al. eds. *Augustine Through the Ages*. Grand Rapids: Eerdmans, 1999.

Flanagan, Russ. "I'm Tired of Being Forced into the Shadows by Society." *The Express-Times* (February 22, 2004): http://www.nj.com/specialprojects/expresstimes/index.ssf? /news/expresstimes/stories/moleters1_otherside.html.

Flannery, Austin, O.P. ed. *Vatican Council II: The Conciliar and Post Conciliar Documents* New Revised Edition. Boston, MA: St. Paul Books & Media, 1992.

Frank, Jerome. *Law and the Modern Mind*. New York: Brentano's, 1931.

Frohnen, Bruce. *The New Communitarians and the Crisis of Modern Liberalism*. Lawrence, KS: University Press of Kansas, 1996.

Fuller, Lon L. *The Morality of Law*. Revised Edition. New Haven, CT: Yale University Press, 1969.

Gahl, Robert A. *Practical Reason in the Foundation of Natural Law according to Germain Grisez, John Finnis and Joseph Boyle, Jr.* doctoral thesis. Rome: Pontifical Atheneum of the Holy Cross, 1991.

———. "From the Virtue of a Fragile Good to a Narrative Account of Natural Law." in *International Philosophical Quarterly*, 37/4 (1997).

García-Huidobro, J. *Razón práctica y dercho naturel: El iusnaturalismo de Tomás de Aquino*. Valparaíso: EDEVAL, 1993.

Garrigou-Lagrange, R., O.P., *Reality*. Translated by Patrick Cummins. St. Louis: Herder, 1950.

Gilson, Etienne. *Christianity and Philosophy*. Translated by Ralph MacDonald, C.S.B. New York/London: Sheed & Ward, 1939).

George, Robert P. and Christopher Wolfe, eds. *Natural Law and Public Reason*. Washington, D.C.: Georgetown University Press, 2000.

George, Robert P., "Recent Criticisms of Natural Law Theory" in *University of Chicago Law Review*, 55 (1988).

———. ed. *Natural Law Theory: Contemporary Essays*. Oxford. Oxford University Press, 1992.

———. ed. *The Autonomy of the Law: Essays on Legal Positivism*. Oxford: Clarendon Press, 1996.

———. "Public Reason and Political Conflict: Abortion and Homosexuality." *Yale Law Journal* (1997): 2475.

———, ed. *Natural Law and Moral Inquiry*. Washington, D.C.: Georgetown University Press, 1998.

———. *In Defense of Natural Law*. Oxford. Clarendon Press, 1999.

———. *The Clash of Orthodoxies: Law, Religion, and Morality in Crisis*. Wilmington, DE: ISI Books, 2001,

Gerrish, B. *Grace and Reason*. Chicago: University of Chicago Press, 1979.

Gilson, E. *Le Thomisme*, 5th ed. Paris: Vrin, 1948.

Glendon, Mary Ann. "What Happened at Beijing." *First Things* 59 (January 1996): 30-36.

———. "Knowing the Universal Declaration of Human Rights." *Notre Dame Law Review* 73 (1998): 1153.

———. *A World Made New: Eleanor Roosevelt and the Universal Declaration of Human Rights*. New York: Random House, 2002.

Gottlieb, Stephen E. et al. eds. *Jurisprudence Cases and Materials: An Introduction to the Philosophy of Law and Its Applications*. New York: Lexis-Nexis/ Matthew Bender, 2006.

Goyette, John, Mark S. Latkovic, and Richard S. Myers, eds. *St. Thomas Aquinas and the Natural Law Tradition: Contemporary and Philosophical Perspectives*. Washington, D.C.: Catholic University of America Press, 2004.

Gredt, J., O.S.B. *Elementa Philosphiae Aristotelico-thomisticae*, 10th ed. Freiburg: Herder, 1953.

Grisez, Germain. *Contraception and Natural Law*. Milwaukee. Bruce Publishing, 1964.

———. "The First Principle of Practical Reason." in *Natural Law Forum* 19 (1965): 168-196.

———. "Natural Law and Natural Inclinations." in *New Scholasticism* 61 (1987): 307-320.

———. "Natural Law, God, Religion and Human Fulfillment." in *American Jour-*

nal of Jurisprudence 46 (2002): 3-35.

Grocholewski, Cardinal Zenon. "La Legge naturale nella dottrina della Chiesa," in *Studia Moralia* 46/2 (2008): 383-412.

Grosheide, F. W. "Commentary on the First Epistle to the Corinthians," in Ned B. Stonehouse and F. F. Bruce, eds. *The New International Commentary of the New Testament.* Grand Rapids: Eerdmans Publishing, 1974: 132-142.

Grotius, Hugo. *De iure belli ac pacis* [1625], *Prolegomena*. Italian edition: *Prolegomenti al diritto della Guerra e della pace*. Translated by G. Fassò. Naples: Morano, 1979.

Guthrie, W.K.C. *A History of Greek Philosophy.* Cambridge: University Press, 1962-1981.

Hahn, Scott. *Kinship by Covenant: A Canonical Approach to the Fulfillment of God's Saving Promises*, Anchor Yale Bible Reference Library. New Haven/ London: Yale University Press, 2009.

Hall, A. R. *The Scientific Revolution 1500-1800*, 2nd ed. Boston: Beacon, 1966.

Hamer, D. and P. Copeland. *The Science of Desire*. New York: Simon and Schuster, 1994.

Hart, H.L.A. *The Concept of Law* 2nd ed. Gloucestershire, UK: Clarendon Press, 1994.

Hawking, S. *A Brief History of Time*. Toronto: Bantam, 1988.

Hazard, P. *The European Mind 1680-1715*. Translated by J. May. London: Hollis & Carter, 1953.

———. *European Thought in the Eighteenth Century*. Translated by. J. May. Cleveland: World, 1963

Herlihy, David. *Medieval Households*. Cambridge, MA: Harvard University Press, 1985.

Hervada, Javier. *Introducción critica al Derecho Natural*. Pamplona: Ediciones Universidad de Navarra, 1981.

———. *Introduzione critica al diritto naturale*. Milan: Giuffrè.1990.

———. *Critical Introduction to Natural Law*. Translated by Emmons Mindy. Montréal: Wilson & Lafleur [Gratianus Series]. 2006.

———. *What is Law? The Modern Response of Juridical Realism: An Introduction to Law.* Montréal: Wilson & Lafleur [Gratianus Series]. 2009.

Himmelfarb, Gertrude. *The Demoralization of Society*. New York: Random House Vintage Books, 1995.

Hittinger, Russell. *A Critique of the New Natural Law Theory*. South Bend, Ind.: University of Notre Dame Press, 1987.

———. *The First Grace: Rediscovering the Natural Law in a Post-Christian World.* Wilmington, Del: ISI Books, 2003.

Hobbes, T., *Leviathan*. edited by B. Macpherson. Harmondsworth: Penguin, 1968.

Hoehner, Harold W. *Ephesians: An Exegetical Commentary*. Grand Rapids: Baker Academic, 2002.

Hoitenga, Dewey J., Jr. *John Calvin and the Will, A Critique and Corrective*. Grand Rapids, MI: Baker Books, 1997.

Holmes, Oliver Wendell. "The Path of the Law." *Harvard Law Review* 10 (1897), 458-62.

Hugon, E. O.P. *Logica*. Paris: Lethielleux, 1927.

———. *Tractatus Dogmatici*, 11th and 10th ed. Paris: Lethielleux, 1933-35.

———. *Metaphysica*. Paris: Lethielleux, 1935.

Hultgren, A. *I-II Timothy, Titus*. Minneapolis: Augsburg, 1984.

Infeld, L. *The Evolution of Physics*. New York: Simon and Schuster, 1966.

International Commission of Jurists, *Protection of Human Rights and Fundamental Freedoms While Countering Terrorism* (Apr. 18, 2005), *available at* http://www.icj.org/IMG/pdf/ctos.pdf.

International Theological Commission, *A la Récherche d'une Ėthique universelle: Nouveau Régard sur la Loi naturelle* (In Search of a Universal Ethic: A New Look at the Natural Law). 2009.

Jaki, Stanley. *The Savior of Science*. Washington: Regnery Gateway, 1988.

James, William. *The Meaning of Truth: A Sequel to 'Pragmatism*. New York: Prometheus Books, 1997 [1909].

Janoski, Thomas. *Citizenship and Civil Society*. Cambridge: Cambridge University Press, 1998.

John XXIII, Encyclical, *Pacem in Terris* (April 11, 1963).

John Paul II. Apostolic Exhortation, *Familiaris Consortio* (November 22, 1981).

———. Post-Synodal Apostolic Exhortation, *Reconciliatio et Paenitentia*, (December 2, 1984).

———. Encyclical Letter *Dominum et Vivificantem* (May 30, 1986).

———. Apostolic Letter, *Mulieris dignitatem* (August 15, 1988)

———. Apostolic Exhortation, *Christifideles Laici* (December 30, 1988).

———. Encyclical, *Veritatis Splendor* (August 6, 1993)

———. *World Day of Peace Message* (January 1, 1994).

———. *Letter to Families* (February 2, 1994).

———. Encyclical, *Evangelium Vitae* (March 25, 1995).

———. *Address to the General Assembly of the United Nations* (October 5, 1995).

———. *The Theology of the Body*. Boston: Pauline Editions, 1997.

———. *Message for the World Day of Peace 2003* (January 1, 2003).

———. *Memory & Identity, Conversations at the Dawn of a Millennium*. New York: Rizzoli, 2005.

———. *Man and Woman He Created Them: A Theology of the Body*. Translated by Michael Waldstein. Boston: Pauline Editions. 2006.

Johnson, Alan F. "Is there a Biblical Warrant for Natural-Law Theories?" *Journal of the Evangelical Theology Society* 25 (June, 1982).

Johnson, Luke Timothy. *The Acts of the Apostles*. Collegeville, MN: Liturgical Press, 1992.

Journet, Charles. *The Meaning of Grace*. Translated by A.V. Littledale. Princeton, N.J.: Scepter Publishers, 1996.

Kaczor, Christopher. *Proportionalism and the Natural Law Tradition*. Washington, D.C.: Catholic University of America Press, 2002.

Kainz, Howard P. *Natural Law: An Introduction and Re-examination*. Chicago: Open Court, 2004.

Kant, I. *Foundations of the Metaphysics of Morals*. Translated by L. Beck. Indianapolis: Bobbs-Merrill, 1959.

Kee, H. "The Linguistic Background of 'Shame' in the New Testament," in *On Language, Culture, and Religion: In Honor of Eugene A. Nida*. The Hague: Mouton, 1974).

Kelly, Anthony J. "The Global Significance of Natural Law: A Communications Problem?" in *Studia Moralia* 47/1 (Gennaio-Giugno, 2009): 141-168.

Kelly, J. *A Commentary on the Pastoral Epistles*. New York: Harper and Row, 1963.

Kelsen, Hans. "What is the Pure Theory of Law?" *Tulane Law Review* 34 (1960): 269.

Klubertanz, G., S.J. *The Philosophy of Human Nature*. New York: Appleton-Century-Crofts, 1953.

———. *Introduction to the Philosophy of Being*, 2nd ed. New York: Appleton-Century-Crofts, 1963.

Koterski, Joseph, S.J. "Fides et Ratio and Biblical Wisdom Literature" in *The Two Wings of Catholic Thought: Essays on Fides et Ratio*, edited by David R. Foster and Joseph W. Koterski, S.J. Washington, D.C.: Catholic University of America Press 2003: 129-62.

Knight, G. *The Pastoral Epistles*. Grand Rapids: Eerdmans, 1992.

Knox, John. *Chapters in the Life of Paul*, edited by Douglas R. A. Hare. Macon, Georgia: Mercer University Press, 1987.

Knox, Wilfred A. *Saint Paul and the Church of Jerusalem*. Cambridge: University Press, 1935.

Krąpiec, M.A., O.P. *Person and Natural Law*. Translated by Maria Szymańska. New York: Peter Lang, 1993.

Kronman, Anthony. *The Lost Lawyer: Failing Ideals of the Legal Profession*. Cambridge, MA: Harvard University Press, 2001.

Küng, Hans. *Global Responsibility: In Search for a New World Ethic*. Translated by John Bowden. New York: Crossroad, 1991.

———. *A Global Ethic for Global Politics and Economics*. Translated by John Bowden. Oxford: Oxford University Press, 1997.

Ladd, George Eldon. *A Theology of the New Testament*. Grand Rapid, MI: Eerdmans, 1974.

Laserson, Max M. "Positive and Natural Law and Their Correlation," in *Interpretations of Modern Legal Philosophies: Essays in Honor of Roscoe Pound*. New York: Oxford University Press, 1947.

Lea, T. *The New American Commentary: 1, 2 Timothy*. Nashville: Broadman, 1992.

Lisska, Anthony J. *Aquinas' Theory of Natural Law*. Oxford: Clarendon Press, 1996.

———. "On the Revival of Natural Law: Several Books from the Last Half Century," in *American Catholic Philosophical Quarterly* 81:4 (Fall, 2007): 613-638.

Locke, J. *Two Treatises of Government*, rev. ed., edited by P. Laslett. New York: New American Library, 1963.

Lohse, B. *Martin Luther's Theology*. Translated by R. Harrisville. Minneapolis: Fortress, 1999.

Lonergan, Bernard, S.J. *Verbum: Word and Idea in Aquinas*, edited by D. Burrell. Notre Dame: University of Notre Dame Press, 1967.

Lugosi, Charles I. "Conforming to the Rule of Law: When Person and Human Being Finally Mean the Same Thing in Fourteenth Amendment Jurisprudence," in *Journal of Law & Public Policy* (2006): 361-364.

Luther, Martin. *The Large Catechism of Martin Luther*. Translated by Robert Fischer. Philadelphia: Fortress, 1959.

———. *Luther's Small Catechism with Explanation*. St. Louis: Concordia, 1986.

MacIntyre, Alasdair. *After Virtue. A Study in Moral Theory*. Notre Dame: University of Notre Dame Press, 1981.

———. *Three Rival Versions of Moral Enquiry: Encyclopaedia, Genealogy, and Tradition*. Notre Dame: University of Notre Dame Press, 1991.

Macdonald, Roderick A. "Recommissioning Law Reform," *Alberta Law Review* 35 (1997): 831- 851.

Mackinnon, Catherine A. *Feminism Unmodified: Discourses on Life and Law*. Cambridge, MA: Harvard University Press. 1987.

Maquart, F.X. *Elementa Philosophiae*. Paris: Blot, 1937-1938.

Maes, B. *La loi naturelle selon Ambroise de Milan*. Roma: Analecta Gregoriana, 1967.

Maritain, Jacques. *Sept Leçons sur l'Être*. Paris: Tequi, 1934.

———. *An Introduction to Logic*. Translated by I. Choquette. New York: Sheed and Ward, 1937.

———. *Man and the State*. Chicago: University of Chicago Press, 1951.

———. *On the Philosophy of History*, edited by Joseph W. Evans. New York: Charles Scribner's Sons, 1957.

———. *The Degrees of Knowledge*. Translated G. Phelan et alii (1959), reprint: Notre Dame: University of Notre Dame Press, 1995.

———. *Natural Law: Reflections on Theory and Practice*. South Bend, IN: St. Augustine's Press, 2001.

Martin, Francis. *Sacred Scripture The Disclosure of the Word*. Naples, FL.: Sapientia Press, 2006.

Mauck, John W. *Paul on Trial: The Book of Acts as a Defense of Christianity*. Nashville, TN: Thomas Nelson, 2001.

May, William E. *An Introduction to Moral Theology*. Second Edition. Huntington, IN: Our Sunday Visitor, 2003.

McDermott, S.J, John M. "A New Approach to God's Existence," *The Thomist* 44 (1980): 220-227.

———. "The Theology of John Paul II: A Response," in *The Thought of Pope John Paul II*, edited by J. McDermott (Rome: Gregorian, 1993: 55-68;

———. "Dialectical Analogy: The Oscillating Center of Rahner's Thought," *Gregorianum* 75 (1994): 680-86.

———. "The Context of *Veritatis Splendor*," in *Prophecy and Diplomacy*, edited by J. Conley and J. Koterski. New York: Fordham University Press, 1999: 128-40.

———. "Faith, Reason and Freedom." *Irish Theological Quarterly* 67 (2002): 307-332.

———. "Karl Rahner in Tradition: The One and the Many." *Fides Quaerens Intellectum* 3 (2004-07): 10-20.

———. "The Mystery of Freedom," *Lateranum* 74 (2008): 493-542.

———. "How Did Jesus Know He Was God? The Ontological Psychology of Mark 10:17-22." *Irish Theological Quarterly*, 74 (2009): 272-97.

McGrath, Alister E. *Intellectuals Don't Need God & Other Modern Myths*. Grand Rapids, MI: Zondervan, 1993.

McInerny, Ralph. "The Principles of Natural Law." in *The American Journal of Jurisprudence*, 25 (1980).

———. *Ethica Thomistica*. Notre Dame: University of Notre Dame Press, 1982.

McLoughin, William G. *Revivals, Awakenings, and Reform*. Chicago: University of Chicago Press, 1980.

Meir, John P. *A Marginal Jew, Volume IV, Law and Love*. New Haven: Yale University Press, 2009.

Melina , Livio and Carl A. Anderson, eds. *The Way of Love*. San Francisco: Ignatius Press, 2006.

Melina, Livio. "Homosexual Inclination as an 'Objective Disorder': Reflections on Theological Anthropology." *Communio* 25 (Spring 1998): 57-68.

Mill, J.S. "Utilitarianism," in *Essential Works of John Stuart Mill*, edited by M. Lerner. New York: Bantam, 1965.

Miller, Lisa. "Our Mutual Joy," *Newsweek* (Dec. 6, 2008).

Morsink, Johannes. *The Universal Declaration of Human Rights: Origins, Drafting and Intent*. Philadelphia: The University of Pennsylvania Press, 1999.

Murphy-O'Connor, J. *Paul: A Critical Life*. Oxford: Clarendon, 1996.

Nasr, Seyyed Hossein. *Religion and the Order of Nature*. Oxford: Oxford University Press, 1996.

Neuhaus, Richard J. *The Naked Public Square*. Grand Rapids: Eerdmans, 1984.

———. *The Catholic Moment*. San Francisco: Harper & Row, 1987.

Newman, John Henry. *Apologia Pro Vita Sua*. London: J.M. Dent & Sons LTD., 1912 [1864].

Nicholas, Barry. *An Introduction to Roman Law*. Oxford: Clarendon Press of Oxford University, 1962.

Nicolosi, Joseph and Dale O'Leary. "On the Pedophilia Issue: What the APA Should Have Known," at http://www.narth.com.

Nicolosi, Linda Ames. "Should These Conditions Be Normalized: American Psychiatric Association Symposium Debates Whether Pedophilia, Gender Identity Disorder, Sexual Sadism Should Remain Mental Illnesses" at http://www.narth.com.

Nimmons, D. "Sexual brain." *Discover* 5 (1994), 64-67.

Noll, Mark A. *The Old Religion in a New World: The History of North American Christianity*. Grand Rapids, MI: Eerdmans, 2001.

Noriega, José. "Homosexuality: The Semblance of Intimacy." *Communio* 35 (Fall 2008), 451-464.

Novak, David. *Natural Law in Judaism*. Cambridge: Cambridge University Press, 1998.

Nuremberg Trial, *Trial of the Major War Criminals Before the International Military Tribunal, Nuremberg, 14 Nov. 1945-1 Oct. 1946*. Reprinted in *American Journal of International Law* 41 (1947).

O'Callaghan, Nora. "Human Origins and Human Rights in the Genome Age." *Ave Maria Law Review* (2005).

O'Connor, F. *Mystery and Manners*. New York: Farrar, Straus & Giroux, 1969.

Orr, William F. and James Arthur Walthar. *I Corinthians, The Anchor Bible, vol. 32*. Garden City, New York: Doubleday, 1976.

Otto, W. "Augustus Soter." *Hermes* 45 (1910): 448-60.

Owens, J., C.Ss.R. *An Elementary Christian Metaphysics*. Milwaukee: Bruce, 1963.

Pace, Paul, S.J. "Immutable yet Inadequately Formulated: The Natural Law in Francisco Suárez (1548-1617)" in *Studia Moralia* 45/2 (Diciembre, 2007): 217-255.

Pagden, Anthony and Jeremy Lawrance, eds. *Vitoria: Political Writings*. Cambridge: Cambridge University Press, 1991.

Panchias, G. *Epicurus*. New York: Twayne, 1967.

Panikkar, Raimundo. "Is the Notion of Human Rights a Western Concept," in Henry J. Steiner & Philip Alston, eds. *International Human Rights in Context*. Oxford: Oxford University Press, 2000.

Paul VI. Apostolic Exhortation, *Evangelii Nuntiandi* (December 8, 1975).

Percy, W. *The Thanatos Syndrome* (New York: Farrar, Straus & Giroux, 1987.

Pereira, José. "The Achievement of Suárez and the Suarezianisation of Thomism," in A. Cardoso et al. eds. *Francisco Suárez (1548-1617): Tradição e Modernidade*. Lisbon: Edições Colibri, 1999.

Perry, Michael J. "Why Political Reliance on Religiously Grounded Morality Does Not Violate the Establishment Clause." *William & Mary Law Review* 42 (2001): 663

Pew Research Center, *The Religious Dimensions of the Torture Debate* (Apr. 30, 2009), available at http://pewresearch.org/pubs/1210/torture-opinion-religious-differences.

Phillips, R. P. *Modern Thomistic Philosophy.* London: Burns Oates & Washbourne, 1934-35.

Pinckaers, Servais O.P. *The Sources of Christian Ethics*. Translated by M. Noble. Washington: Catholic University Press, 1995.

Pirotta, A., O.P. *Summa Philosophiae Aristotelico-Thomisticae.* Turin: Marietti, 1931-1936.

Pizzorni, R.M. *Il diritto naturale dalle origini a S. Tommaso d'Aquino: saggio storico-critico*. Bologna: Edizioni Studio Domenicano, 2000.

Plato, *The Trial and Death of Socrates*. Translated by G.M.A. Grube. Indianapolis, IN: Hackett Publishing Company 2d ed., 1975.

Pontifical Council for the Family, *The Family and Human Rights* (December 9, 1999)

———. *Family, Marriage and "De Facto" Unions* (November 21, 2000).

Pontifical Council for the Justice and Peace, *Compendium of the Social Doctrine of the Church* Vatican City and Washington, D.C: Libreria Editrice Vaticana and United States Conference of Catholic Bishops, 2005.

Porter, Jean. *Nature as Reason: A Thomistic Theory of the Natural Law*. Grand Rapids, MI: Eerdmans, 2005.

Posner, Richard A. "The Ethical and Political Basis of the Efficiency Norm in Common Law Adjudication," in *Hofstra Law Review* 8 (1980): 487.

Pound, Roscoe. "The Scope and Purpose of Sociological Jurisprudence." *Harvard Law Review* 24 (1910-1911): 591-596.

Principe, Walter, C.S.B., "Affectivity and the Heart in Thomas Aquinas' Spirituality," in *Spiritualities of the Heart*. Edited by Annice Callahan, R.S.C.J. New York: Paulist Press, 1990: 45-63.

Prior, M. *Paul the Letter- Writer and the Second Letter to Timothy.* Sheffield: Sheffield Academic Press, 1989.

Rahner, Karl, S.J. *Geist in Welt*. Innsbruck: Rauch, 1939.

———. "Die Wahrheit bei Thomas von Aquin." *Schriften zur Theologie* (Zurich: Benziger, 1954-84): 24-37.

———. *Hörer des Wortes*, 2nd ed., edited by J.-B. Metz. Munich: Kösel, 1963.

Ratzinger, Joseph [see also Benedict XVI]. *Behold the Pierced One: An Approach to a Spiritual Christology*, Translated by Graham Harrison. San Francisco: Ignatius Press, 1986.

———. *A New Song for the Lord: Faith in Christ and Liturgy Today*, Translated by Martha M. Matesich. New York: Crossroad, 1996.

Rawls, John. "*The Idea of Public Reason Revisited,*" 64 *U. of Chi. L Rev*. 765, 781 (1997).

———. *Political Liberalism*. New York: Columbia University Press, 1996.

Rehnquist, William H. "The Notion of a Living Constitution." *Texas Law Review*

54 (1976): 693-704.

Rice, Charles. *50 Questions on the Natural Law*. San Francisco: Ignatius Press, 1993.

Ridderbos, Herman. *Paul: An Outline of His Theology*, Translated by John Richard De Witt. Grand Rapids, MI: Eerdmans, 1975.

Rist, J. *Stoic Philosophy*. Cambridge: Cambridge University Press, 1969.

Ritzler, B., *Freiheit in der Umarmung des ewig Liebenden*. Bern: Lang, 2000.

Robinson, John A.T. *The Body: A Study in Pauline Theology*. London: SCM Press LTD, 1952.

Robinson, Daniel N. *A Student's Guide to Psychology, ISI Guides to the Major Disciplines*. Wilmington, DE: ISI Books, 2002.

Rommen, H. *The Natural Law*. Translated by T. Hanley. St. Louis: Herder, 1948.

Sanders, E. P. *Saint Paul, the Law, and the Jewish People*. Minneapolis: Fortress Press, 1983.

Scalia, Antonin. *A Matter of Interpretation: Federal Courts and the Law*. Princeton, N.J.: Princeton University Press, 1998.

Scarnecchia, Brian. "The Tension Between Faith and Culture." in Federation of Asian Bishops Conference and the Pontifical Council for Culture, *Dialogue Between Faith and Culture: Towards Integral Human and Social Development*. Manila: Lucky Press 1998.

Schockenhoff, Eberhard. *Natural Law and Human Dignity: Universal Ethics in an Historical World*. Translated by Brian McNeil. Washington, D.C.: Catholic University of America Press, 2003.

Schönborn, Cardinal Christoph, O.P. *Chance or Purpose? Creation, Evolution, and a Rational Faith*. San Francisco, Ignatius Press: 2007.

Scheeben, Matthias Joseph. *Natur und Gnade. Versuch einer systematischen, wissenschaftlichen Darstellung der natürlichen und übernatürlichen Lebensordnung im Menschen* (Mainz 1861). English Translation: *Nature and Grace*, Translated by Cyril Vollert, S.J. St. Louis/London: B. Herder Book Co., 1954

Schindler, David. "John Paul II and the 'Nuptial Attribute' of the Body: The Family and the Future of Humanity." in *The Church, Marriage, and the Family*, Proceedings from the 27th Annual Convention of the Fellowship of Catholic Scholars, edited by Kenneth Whitehead. South Bend, Ind.: St. Augustine's Press, 2007: 363-377.

Schouppe, J.-P. "Convergences et differences entre le droit divin des canonites et le droit naturel des juristes." in *Ius Ecclesiae* 19 (2000): 29-67.

Schreiner, Susan E. "Calvin's Use of Natural Theology." in Michael Cromartie, ed., *Protestants, Catholics, and Natural Law* (Grand Rapids, MI: Eerdmans Publishing, 1997), 51-76.

Scola, Cardinal Angelo. "The Dignity and Mission of Women: The Anthropological and Theological Foundations." *Communio* 25 (Spring 1998), 46-47.

———. "The Nuptial Mystery at the Heart of the Church," *Communio* 25 (Winter 1998), 634-647.

Sebok, Anthony J. "Legal Positivism in American Jurisprudence," *in Cambridge Studies in Philosophy and Law*. Cambridge: Cambridge University Press, 1998.

Shaffer, Thomas L. "Jurisprudence in the Light of the Hebraic Faith." *Notre Dame Journal of Law, Ethics, and Public Policy* 85 (1984).

Sheehan J. *German History 1770-1866*. Oxford: Clarendon, 1989.

Simon, Yves. *The Tradition of Natural Law*. Bronx, N.Y.: Fordham University Press, 1965.

Singer, M. "Golden Rule," in *Encyclopedia of Philosophy*, 2nd ed., edited by D. Borchart. Detroit: Thomson-Gale, 2006: 4:144-47

Skinner, Q. *The Foundations of Modern Political Thought: vol. II: The Age of Reformation*. Cambridge: Cambridge University Press, 1978.

Shklar, Judith. *Legalism: Law, Morals, and Political Trials*. Cambridge, MA: Harvard University Press, 1986.

Smallwood, E. M. *Documents Illustrating the Principates of Gaius, Claudius and Nero*. Cambridge: Cambridge University Press, 1967.

Sokolowski, Robert. *The God of Faith & Reason, Foundations of Christian Theology*. Washington, D.C.: Catholic University of American Press, 1995 [1982].

———. "What is Natural Law?" in *The Thomist* 68/4 (October, 2004).

Solier, J. "Supernatural Order." in *The Catholic Encyclopedia*, edited by C. Herbermann et al. New York: Appleton, 1907-13) 14:336-39.

Song, Robert. *Christianity and Liberal Society*. Oxford: Oxford University Press, 1997.

Stork, Peter. *Human Rights in Crisis: A Cultural Critique*. Saarbrüken: Verlag Dr. Müller, 2007.

Strauss, Leo. *Natural Right and History*. Chicago: University of Chicago Press, 1953.

Suárez, Francisco. *Tractatus De Legibus ac Deo Legislatore* [1612] Volumes 5 and 6 in *Opera Omnia*. Paris: Ludovicus Vivès, 1856-1861.

Tanquerey, A. *Synopsis Theologiae Dogmaticae Fundamentalis*, 24th ed., edited by J.B. Bord. New York: Benziger, 1937.

The New World Dictionary-Concordance to the New American Bible. New York: World Bible Publishers, 1970.

Uccello, Sebastian, S.S.S. *Philosophia Scholastica ad Mentem Sancti Thomae*. Turin: Marietti, 1921.

Van Steenberghen, F. *Ontology*. Translated by M. Flynn. New York: Wagner, 1952.

Veatch, Henry. *Human Rights: Fact of Fancy?* Baton Rouge: Louisiana State University Press, 1986.

Vendemiati, A. *La legge naturale nella Summa theologiae di san Tommaso d'Aquino, Temi di morale fondamentale*. Roma: Edizioni Dehoniane, 1995.

Viladrich, Pedro Juan. *The Agony of Legal Marriage*. Navarra, Spain: University of Navarra, 1990.

Wassmer, T.A. and S.A. Long, "Natural Law," in *New Catholic Encyclopedia*, Second Edition. Vol. 10. Detroit: Thomson Gale, 2003.

Weinreb, Lloyd L. *Natural Law and Justice*. Cambridge, MA: Harvard University Press, 1987.

Whitehead, Kenneth. *The Church, Marriage, and the Family*, Proceedings from the 27th Annual Convention of the Fellowship of Catholic Scholars, edited by. South Bend, Ind.: St. Augustine's Press, 2007.

Williams, Wendy W. "Notes from a First Generation." *University of Chicago Legal Forum* (1989).

Williamson, Peter. *Ephesians*, *Catholic Commentary on Sacred Scripture*. Grand Rapids: Baker Academic, 2009.

Witte, John Jr. "A New Concordance of Discordant Canons: Harold Berman on Law and Religion." *Emory Law Journal* Vol. 42 (Spring 1993): 525.

Wolfe, C. ed. *Same-Sex Matters. The Challenge of Homosexuality*. Dallas: Spence: 2000.

Wolters, Albert. *Creation Regained*. Grand Rapids, MI: Eerdmans, 1985.

Contributors

The Editors

Jane F. Adolphe, LL.B/B.C.L, J.C.D. is Associate Professor of Law, Ave Maria School of Law, Naples, Florida. She began her legal career clerking for the Alberta Court of Appeal and Court of Queen's Bench. After practicing with the Bennett Jones law firm, she served as a prosecutor with the Alberta Crown Prosecutor's Office. She then worked as a legal consultant with the law firm of Capua, Varrenti e Associati in Italy. She has served the United Nations by participating in conferences on children's rights and the International Criminal Court, and most recently participated as a delegate of the Holy See. Professor Adolphe's course offerings include Family Law, Canon Law, International Law, and International Human Rights. She holds a Bachelor of Arts from the University of Calgary, as well as common-law and civil-law degrees from McGill University. She also earned a Licentiate in Canon Law and a Doctorate in Canon Law from the Pontificia Università della Santa Croce in Rome.

Robert Fastiggi, Ph.D. is Professor of Systematic Theology at Sacred Heart Major Seminary in Detroit, MI. From 1985-1999, he taught at St. Edward's University in Austin, Texas. He holds an A.B. from Dartmouth College, and a M.A. and Ph.D. in Theology from Fordham University. His publications include *The Natural Theology of Yves de Paris* (Scholars Press, 1991); *The Mystical Theology of the Catholic Reformation* [co-author, José Pereira] (University Press of America, 2006); *What the Church Teaches about Sex* (Our Sunday Visitor, 2009); *Called to Holiness and Communion: Vatican II on the Church* [co-editor] (University of Scranton Press, 2009); and *De Maria Numquam Satis: The Significance of the Catholic Doctrines on the Blessed Virgin Mary for All People* [co-editor] (University Press of America, 2009). He is the co-editor of the English edition of Denzinger-Hünermann (43rd edition) to be published by Ignatius Press, and the Executive Editor of the 2009, 2010 and 2011 supplements of the *New Catholic Encyclopedia*.

Michael Vacca, J.D., is a graduate of Hillsdale College, Hillsdale, MI and Ave Maria School of Law, Naples, Florida. He is a 2008 Blackstone Fellow with the

Alliance Defense Fund and a 2009 Edmund Burke Fellow with the Catholic Family and Human Rights Institute. As of October, 2010, Michael's work focuses on the defense of human life from conception to natural death and protecting the family founded on the exclusive union of one man and one woman. He is a member of the State Bar of Michigan.

Author of The Preface

Rev. John J. Coughlin, O.F.M., J.D., J.C.D. is Professor of Law and Concurrent Professor of Theology, University of Notre Dame, Notre Dame, Indiana. He holds and doctorate (J.C.D) and a license (J.C.L.) in canon law from the Pontifical Gregorian University in Rome, a law degree (J.D.) from Harvard University, a master's degree in theology (Th.M.) from Princeton Seminary, a master's degree in psychology (M.A.) from Columbia University, and an undergraduate degree in history (B.A.) from Niagara University. Fr. Coughlin was ordained a Roman Catholic priest in 1983. He is a Franciscan friar of the Order of Friars Minor of the Holy Name Province. A member of the New York bar, Fr. Coughlin clerked for the Honorable Francis X. Altimari on the United States Court of Appeals for the Second Circuit. He served as general counsel of St. Bonaventure University in Olean, New York, from 1990 to 1993. From 1993 to 1996, he served as legal and canonical counsel to the Holy Name Province of Franciscan Friars in New York. Upon appointment by John Cardinal O'Connor of New York, Fr. Coughlin served as Professor of Canon Law and Spiritual Director of St. Joseph's Seminary in New York from 1994 to 2001. He also served the Archdiocese of New York as a judge in the Appeals Tribunal, as vicar of canonical and legal aspects of health care, and as a member of the boards of several Catholic hospitals and educational institutions. During the summer of 1998, Father Coughlin was a member of the delegation of the Holy See to the United Nations treaty conference that established the International Criminal Court. From 1996 to 2003, he taught at St. John's University School of Law where he served as Professor of Law. During the Spring 2009, he served as Visiting Professor of Canon Law at the Pontifical Gregorian University in Rome. Fr. Coughlin's book, *Canon Law: A Comparative Study with Anglo-American Legal Theory* is forthcoming from Oxford University Press. Another book, Law, Person, and Community, is also under contract with Oxford University Press for publication in 2011.

Authors of the Chapters

Rev. Richard J. Cassidy, S.T.L., Ph.D. has been Professor of Sacred Scripture at Sacred Heart Major Seminary in Detroit since 2004. He holds a B.A. in Philosophy from Sacred Heart Seminary, Detroit; a M.A. in Economics from the University of Michigan; a S.T.L. from the Pontifical Gregorian University, Rome; and a

Ph.D. from the Graduate Theological Union, Berkeley, CA. He has taught at Fordham University, the Catholic University of America and Christ the King Seminary in East Aurora, N.Y. Fr. Cassidy is the author of six books, including *Paul in Chains: Roman Imprisonment and the Letters of Paul* (Crossroad, 2001) and *Four Times Peter: Portrayals of Peter in the Four Gospels and at Philippi* (Liturgical Press, 2007).

Robert Fastiggi (see above)

Rev. Earl Muller, S.J., Ph.D. is Professor of Systematic Theology and Bishop Kevin M. Britt Chair in Christology, at Sacred Heart Major Seminary in Detroit. He holds a B.S. from Spring Hill College, Mobile, Alabama, a M.Div., Regis College, Toronto; and a Ph.D. from Marquette University. He has taught at the Pontifical Gregorian University in Rome, Marquette University, Milwaukee, WI and Spring Hill College in Alabama. Among Fr. Muller's publications are: *Augustine: Presbyter factus sum, in Collectanea Augustiniana, vol. 2, Augustinian Historical Institute of Villanova University* (New York: Peter Lang, 1993), co-edited with Joseph Lienhard, S.J. and Roland Teske, S.J.; *Theological Education in the Catholic Tradition: Contemporary Challenges* (New York: Crossroad/A Crossroad Herder Book, 1997), co-edited with Patrick W. Carey; and *Trinity and Marriage in Paul: The Establishment of a Communitarian Analogy of the Trinity Grounded in the Theological Shape of Pauline Thought,* (New York: Peter Lang, 1990).

Eduardo Echeverria, S.T.L., Ph.D. is Professor of Philosophy, Sacred Heart Major Seminary, Detroit. He holds a B.A. from Trinity Christian College, Palos Heights, Illinois; a Ph.D. in Philosophy from the Free University, Amsterdam, The Netherlands; and a S.T.L., from the University of St. Thomas Aquinas, Rome, (Angelicum). He has taught at Molloy College in New York and Conception Seminary in Missouri. He is the author of *Slitting the Sycamore: Christ and Culture in the New Evangelization* (Acton Institute, 2008) and *Dialogue of Love: Confessions of an Evangelical Catholic Ecumenist* (Wipf and Stock, 2010).

Philip Blosser, Ph.D. is Professor of Philosophy, Sacred Heart Major Seminary in Detroit. He earned his B.A. from Sophia University (Tokyo, Japan), his M.A. in Philosophy from Villanova University, and his Ph.D. in Philosophy from Duquesne University. He has taught at Duquesne University, Harlaxton College (England), and Lenoir-Rhyne University in North Carolina. Among his publications are: *Seasons of a Priest: A Short Biography of Fr. Ed Sheridan on the Occasion of the 40th Anniversary of His Ordination* (Morganton, NC: Millennium, 2003); *Scheler's Critique of Kant's Ethics,* Series in Continental Thought, No. 22 (Athens: Ohio University Press, 1995); *Japanese and Western Phenomenology [co-editor]*

(Dordrecht: Kiuwer Academic Publishers, 1993), *Of Friendship: Philosophic Selections on a Perennial Concern* [co-editor] (1989; 2nd ed., Rowman & Littlefield Publishing Group, 2002), and numerous articles on moral philosophy. He is currently completing an English translation of H.G. Stoker's book on conscience, *Das Gewissen: Erscheinungsformen und Theorien.*

Mary Healy, S.T.D. is Associate Professor of Sacred Scripture, Sacred Heart Major Seminary, in Detroit. She has a B.A. from the University of Notre Dame; a M.A. in Theology from the Franciscan University of Steubenville; a M.A. in philosophy from the Catholic University of America; a S.T.L. from the International Theological Institute in Gaming, Austria; and a S.T.D. in biblical theology from the Pontifical Gregorian University in Rome. Among her publications is *Men & Women Are From Eden: A Study Guide to John Paul II's Theology of the Body* (St. Anthony Messenger Press, 2005). With Peter Williamson, she serves as series editor for the *Catholic Commentary on Sacred Scripture* (Baker Academic), and is author of its first volume, *The Gospel of Mark* (2008).

Rev. John M. McDermott, S.J., S.T.D. is Professor of Theology at Sacred Heart Major Seminary in Detroit. He completed his studies at Fordham College (A.B., 1967), Hochschule Sankt Georgen, Frankfurt (S.T.L., 1972), and the Pontifical Gregorian University, Rome (S.T.D., 1976). He subsequently taught at Fordham University (1976-87), the Pontifical Gregorian University (1987-99), and the Pontifical College Josephinum (1999-2006) before arriving at Sacred Heart Major Seminary. From 2003-2009, he served as a member of the International Theological Commission, and since 2008 as a consultant to the USCCB Committee on Doctrine. The author of numerous scholarly publications, his main interests are in Christology, Trinity, theological method, Vatican II, the Gospel of Mark, and the problem of suffering.

Authors of the Responses

Patrick Quirk, LL.M is Associate Dean of Academic Affairs and Associate Professor of Law at Ave Maria School of Law, Naples, Florida. He began his legal career clerking for a Deputy President in the tax division of the Australian Administrative Appeals Tribunal and later went on to practice in the commercial division of a major law firm in Sydney. He taught at Bond University Faculty of Law in Queensland, and at the Catholic University of America's Columbus School of Law, before joining the faculty at Ave Maria. Professor Quirk earned his Bachelor of Arts and Bachelor of Laws degrees from the University of Queensland and a Master of Laws from the Eberhard Karls University of Tübingen, Germany. He also received a graduate diploma in practical legal training from the Faculty of Law at the University of Technology, Sydney.

Brian Scarnecchia, J.D. is Associate Professor at Ave Maria School of Law, Naples, Florida. He also teaches at the Franciscan University of Steubenville, where from 2000-2009, he chaired Franciscan's Department of Humanities and Catholic Social Thought, and has directed the University's Human Life Studies and Legal Studies programs. Professor Scarnecchia lectures on human rights, natural law, bioethics, and cultural and political issues both nationally and internationally. He earned his Juris Doctor degree from the University of Akron, a Masters of Divinity from the Dominican School of Philosophy and Theology, and a Bachelor of Arts from Youngstown State University. He also has completed doctoral studies in Sacred Theology at the International Maria Research Institute at the University of Dayton.

Patrick Gillen, J.D., Ph.D. is Assistant Professor at Ave Maria School of Law, Naples, Florida. He practiced in the area of civil litigation for fifteen years, representing clients in both state and federal courts. Most recently, he served as litigation counsel for the Thomas More Law Center, where he worked on a wide variety of cases dealing with religious liberty, the sanctity of human life, and traditional family values. A former judicial clerk for Judge Robert D. Potter of the United States District Court for the Western District of North Carolina and Judge Daniel A. Manion of the United States Court of Appeals for the Seventh Circuit, Professor Gillen has expertise in Appellate Practice, Federal Courts, Civil Rights, Constitutional Law, and Religious Freedom. He received a Juris Doctor and Ph.D. from the University of Notre Dame, a Master of Arts in American History from Fordham University, and a Bachelor of Arts from Providence College.

Charles I. Lugosi, S.J.D. LL.M. LL.B. M.B.E. has been a visiting professor of law (2007-2009) at Ave Maria School of Law, Ann Arbor, Michigan and at the Duncan School of Law, Lincoln Memorial University, in Knoxville, Tennessee. Dr. Lugosi earned his doctorate and masters degrees from the University of Pennsylvania. His dissertation focused on the 14th Amendment and is the intellectual foundation to the Personhood Movement that seeks to protect the unborn in state constitutions. Dr. Lugosi is a noted criminal and constitutional attorney, where his work has influenced decisions in both the U.S. and Canadian Supreme Courts. He is a member of the British Columbia, Ontario and Michigan bars, the Eastern and Western District Courts of Michigan and the Sixth Circuit Court of Appeals. Professor Lugosi has published numerous articles and teaches constitutional law, criminal law, criminal procedure, jurisprudence, bioethics, torts, health care law, and property law. Professor Lugosi previously taught in the law schools at Michigan State University and St. Thomas University in Florida

Rev. Joseph Isanga, J.S.D. is Associate Professor, Ave Maria School of Law in Naples, Florida. He joined the Ave Maria faculty following his appointment as a postdoctoral research associate at the University of Notre Dame's Center for Civil and Human Rights. He is a widely published scholar on human rights in Africa and has expertise in international law, jurisprudence, and law, ethics, and public policy. Father Isanga is a priest from the Diocese of Jinja, Uganda. He received a Bachelor of Philosophy from Pontifical Urban University in Rome; a Bachelor of Divinity and a Bachelor of Laws from Makerere University in Kampala, Uganda; a Diploma in Legal Practice from Law Development Center in Kampala, Uganda; and a Master of Laws and a Juridical Sciences Doctorate from the University of Notre Dame.

Jane Adolphe (see above)

Artist for Front Cover Painting of St. Paul

Joseph Adolphe, B.F.A., M.F.A. is a Professor in the Department of Fine Arts at St. John's University, New York, His artwork is displayed in various private and corporate collections, and he currently exhibits with The Kehler Liddell Gallery in New Haven, CT. He received his B.F.A. from Alberta College of Art & Design in Canada and his M.F.A. from the School of Visual Arts in New York City. He lives with his wife and seven children in New Haven, CT, and he is the brother of Jane Adolphe, the co-editor of this volume.

Index

CPSIA information can be obtained at www.ICGtesting.com
Printed in the USA
BVOW071608060412

287088BV00001B/2/P

9 780739 168578